JERUSALEM SYNDROME

The Palestinian–Israeli Battle for the Holy City

To the memory of
Faisal Husseini,
a Jerusalem prince and faithful comrade in
the struggle to turn the City of Strife
into the City of Peace.

JERUSALEM SYNDROME

The Palestinian–Israeli Battle for the Holy City

MOSHE AMIRAV

sussex
ACADEMIC
PRESS

BRIGHTON • PORTLAND

2 4 6 8 10 9 7 5 3 1

First published 2009 in Great Britain by
SUSSEX ACADEMIC PRESS
PO Box 139
Eastbourne BN24 9BP

and in the United States of America by
SUSSEX ACADEMIC PRESS
920 NE 58th Ave   Suite 300
Portland, Oregon 97213–3786

British Library Cataloguing in Publication Data
A CIP catalogue record for this book is available from the British Library.

Library of Congress Cataloging-in-Publication Data
'Amirav, Mosheh.
[Sindrom Yerushalayim. English]
Jerusalem syndrome : the Palestinian–Israeli battle for the Holy City / [Moshe
  Amirav].
  p. cm.
Includes bibliographical references and index.
ISBN 978-1-84519-347-8 (h/c : alk. paper) —
ISBN 978-1-84519-348-5 (p/b : alk. paper)
1. Jerusalem—Politics and government—20th century. 2. Arab–Israeli conflict—
Jerusalem. 3. Israel—Politics and government. 4. Jerusalem—Ethnic relations.
I. Title.
DS109.94.A4513 2009
956.9405—dc22
                                                                    2009005824

The paper used in this book is certified by The Forest Stewardship Council (FSC),
a non-profit international organization established to promote the responsible
management of the world's forests. Products carrying the FSC label are
independently certified to assure consumers that they come from
forests that are managed to meet the social, economic and
ecological needs of present and future generations.

Typeset and designed by SAP, Brighton & Eastbourne.
Printed by TJ International, Padstow, Cornwall.
This book is printed on acid-free paper.

Contents

List of Illustrations		vi
Foreword by David Boyd		vii
Preface		ix
Maps		xii–xiii

CHAPTER ONE	Jerusalem Syndrome – Dreams and Failures	1
CHAPTER TWO	How Jerusalem Became Israel's Capita	35
CHAPTER THREE	The Struggle for East Jerusalem	59
CHAPTER FOUR	Why Israel is Losing the Jewish Majority in its Capital	82
CHAPTER FIVE	The Most Polarized City in the World	101
CHAPTER SIX	The Failed Attempts to Bring Peace	124
CHAPTER SEVEN	The Struggle Over the Holy Places	158
CHAPTER EIGHT	Epilogue – From City of the Dead to City of Peace	193

Notes		209
Bibliography – English		221
Bibliography – Hebrew		222
Index		226

List of Illustrations

1 Temple Mount in the Old City of Jerusalem (Israel Government Press Office, Photography Department).
2 A Christian pilgrim in Jerusalem (Israel Government Press Office, Photography Department).
3 Building the new neighborhoods in East Jerusalem, 1975 (Israel Government Press Office, Photography Department).
4 The Separation Fence in East Jerusalem, 2006 (author's personal archive).
5 Fragile co-existence in Jerusalem, 2001 (Ziv Koren).
6 The author as a wounded paratrooper near the Western Wall, June 7, 1967 (author's personal archive).
7 The author with Teddy Kollek, inaugurating the new bus station in Arab East Jerusalem, 1990 (author's personal archive).
8 The author with Faisal Husseini in the garden of Orient House, 1992 (author's personal archive).
9 The author with Crown Prince Hassan in Amman, 2001 (author's personal archive).
10 The author with former President Gorbachev, 2003 (author's personal archive).
11 The author with Prime Minister Ehud Barak, New York, 2000 (author's personal archive).
12 The author with President Clinton at Camp David, 2000 (author's personal archive).
13 The author with former President Wahid of Indonesia in New York, 2005 (author's personal archive).

Foreword by David Boyd

All my life I have dealt theologically and intellectually with the Holy City. Although I now live in Europe, my heart is still with her. I remember when I arrived in 1999. My heart skipped a beat as our bus crested Mount Scopus and I first laid eyes upon her. I stood there gazing over the city with its golden domed monument that reflected the sunlight casting shadows and glittering reflections. I wept.

I lived in Jerusalem for seven years, serving as President of a theological college in which we not only taught the Bible to Jewish, Arab and Christian students from all over the world, but tried to build bridges of peace and understanding between them. During these years I experienced the city's amazing cultural, religious, and interpersonal richness. These were the difficult times of the second intifada and the second Gulf War. We could feel tension and danger in the air. I underwent a metamorphosis wherein my attachment to "the heavenly Jerusalem" became rooted in the earthly Jerusalem.

I am now chairman of a charity operating in Jerusalem, "Beit Natanel," led by an incredible Jewish woman, Rahel Natanel, who hosts Christians, Arabs, and Jews in her home. Here, through discussions of the Bible, they open doors into each other's hearts. In this context, I met Moshe Amirav who, then as now, continues to build both bridges of concrete and bridges of understanding between Jerusalem's adversarial communities.

When he asked me to write a foreword to his book, I was quite surprised. I am not a famous politician, nor a scholar of political science. I am not Israeli or Palestinian. Why me? His answer was: "Both you and I build bridges in Jerusalem. We are the few." It is an honor for me to do so.

Amirav is a son of Jerusalem. His book is an expression of his love for her. He tells the sad story of his failure to build for her the bridges that would make her "Ir Shalom – The City of Peace" as she is called in the Bible. He draws back the veil and lets us see the heart of the conflict. In his honest way, he explains how the city and its leaders, Israelis and Palestinians, failed to reach a political agreement to end her suffering.

This book has prompted me to change some of my attitudes and to be more inclusive in my understanding of other people's love of the city – Christians, Arabs, and Jews. It has helped me understand the terrible paradox that is Jerusalem: how so much reverence and passion for her has led to the painful and seemingly intransigent conflict. Nonetheless, "Jerusalem Syndrome" ends on a note of optimism that one day the bridge that brings peace will finally be built.

David Boyd is a professor of theology and former president of the Israel College of the Bible in Jerusalem

Preface

Following the Six-Day War, one of Israel's chief aims was to consolidate its rule in its capital, Jerusalem. This endeavor was larger in scope than the entire settlement enterprise in the territories conquered by Israel in 1967. And yet, forty years of effort have yielded only disappointments and failures. The more Israel tried to unify its capital, reinforce its control and obtain international recognition for its sovereignty over Jerusalem, the more the delicate threads binding the city's two parts came unraveled – due to serious mistakes on the part of successive policy-makers.

This book originated with several articles I published in the 1990s, in various academic frameworks, on the subject of 'Israel's policy in Jerusalem.' This material later served as the basis of a master's level course in the Department of Public Policy at the Hebrew University in Jerusalem.

My students in the course kept asking me: "How could we have been so stupid?" In response, I suggested they read historian Barbara Tuchman's book "The March of Folly." After they did, they urged me to write a similar work about "the march of folly in Jerusalem." I promised them that one day I would write that book. And now, after five years of collecting and updating material, the promised book is here. I hope it will answer the question that was constantly posed to me: **"How could we have been so stupid?"**

This book is based on hundreds of research studies and official documents from the Jerusalem municipality and the Israeli government, as well as on numerous interviews that I personally conducted with dozens of policy-makers on both the municipal and national level.

The political struggle for Jerusalem has engaged me for many years, not only from the academic standpoint, as a researcher and lecturer on public policy, but also from the personal and public perspective, as someone who had close working relationships with the policy-makers on this issue. For twelve years, I served in various capacities under Jerusalem mayor Teddy Kollek; for many years I was intensively involved in an academic and public dialogue with the Palestinian leadership in Jerusalem; in 1987, while a member of the Likud central committee close to Prime Minister Yitzhak Shamir, I held a series of secret talks with Faisal Husseini, in an attempt to formulate agreements between the Palestinians and the Likud government regarding a political accord for Jerusalem;[1] in subsequent years I continued to maintain a dialogue with PLO leaders in Tunis and with Arab leaders in Jordan, Morocco and Egypt, with the aim of finding a political accord on Jerusalem. During the talks between Israel and the Palestinians at Camp David in 2000 and at Taba in 2001, which centered on the issue of Jerusalem, I served as Prime Minister Ehud Barak's advisor on Jerusalem affairs.

Because of my proximity to these important events, while writing the book I sometimes questioned my ability to describe policy decisions in an objective and academic manner. I worried that my closeness to the policy-makers and to the decision-making processes could in fact be a drawback. It was my colleagues in academia who encouraged me during the writing of this book to make use of my unique personal knowledge, citing the importance of my close familiarity with the policy-making process. I also bore in mind the words of the late European historian George Mosse: "It took me many years to understand that writing about historical problems that affected my life was no barrier to comprehending reality." My hesitance in this regard only made me more cautious in sketching my perceptions of the reality and my analyses of Israeli policy.

Following the Six-Day War, Israel's policy-makers set five 'national goals' for Jerusalem:[2]

- **The territorial goal** – An effort to settle more Jews in East Jerusalem in order to consolidate Israel's control there
- **The demographic goal** – Increasing the Jewish majority in order to prevent Jerusalem from becoming a bi-national city
- **The political goal** – Achieving 'Israelization' of, equality for and co-existence with the city's Arabs
- **The diplomatic goal** – Attaining peace and international legitimacy for Israel's sovereignty over the city
- **The inter-religious goal** – Separating the issue of the holy places from the political conflict over the city.

After forty years, not a single one of these goals has been achieved. This book aims to answer the glaring question: Why not?

As I conducted my research, there was another question, interesting in and of itself, which intrigued me: When it was already clear that a policy was yielding results that ran directly counter to Israel's interests, why did the country's policy-makers stick to it regardless? The answer lies, perhaps, in the title I have chosen for this book: 'Jerusalem Syndrome.' Jerusalem Syndrome is a well-documented pathological phenomenon whose schizophrenia-like symptoms include severe disassociation. It occurs exclusively in Jerusalem and affects visitors who come to the city in the grip of religious or historic delusions only to collide head-on with Jerusalem's harsh reality. Every year, about two hundred people afflicted with the syndrome are admitted to the mental hospital in the city's Givat Shaul neighborhood. Studies show that sufferers are seized by an "uncontrollable impulse" to bring about the "redemption of Jerusalem." The untenable contradiction between 'heavenly Jerusalem' and 'earthly Jerusalem' appears to disturb their mental balance. Having discovered in my studies of policy-making in Jerusalem that this illness seems also to have affected mayors, cabinet ministers and prime ministers, I almost thought it would be fitting to shift the research on this fascinating phenomenon from the Hadassah medical school to the Hebrew University's Department of Public Policy . . .

I chose to dedicate this book to Faisal Husseini, a friend and partner in the attempt to turn the 'city of strife' to a 'city of peace.' Husseini, a major Palestinian leader in Jerusalem, and ostensibly a rival, became my political partner and cherished friend. He is buried in the plot on the Temple Mount reserved for Palestinian luminaries, alongside his father, Abdel Qader Husseini, commander of the Palestinian militias in 1948, and his grandfather, Musa Qassem Husseini, mayor of Jerusalem under the British Mandate.

I owe him a great debt; Jerusalem owes him an even greater one.

The author gratefully acknowledges that publication of this book has been made possible by Beit Berl College School of Government (Israel).

MOSHE AMIRAV
Ein Kerem, Jerusalem

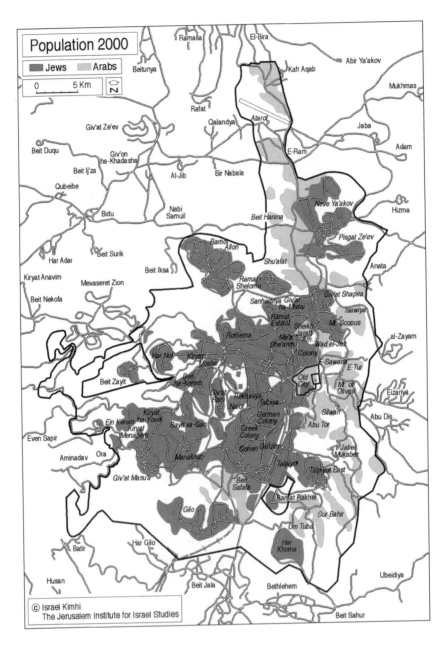

Since 1967, the Jewish population has spread to nine new neighborhoods, including Ramot, Neve Yaakov and Pisgat Ze'ev in the north, and Har Homa and Gilo in the south.

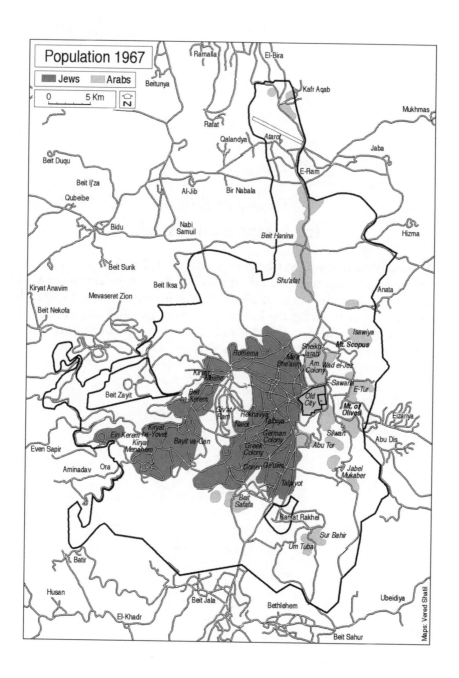

Population 1967

Jews   Arabs

0   5 Km

Ramalla   El-Bira
Beitunya   Kafr Aqab
                                                        Mukhmas
Rafat
        Qalandya   Jaba
                    Atarot
Beit Duqu   E-Ram
Beit Ij'za
Qubeibe   Al-Jib   Bir Nabala
Bidu   Nabi
              Samuil   Beit Hanina   Hizma
Beit Surik   Anata
Kiryat Anavim   Beit Iksa   Shu'afat
Mevaseret Zion
Beit Nekofa
                                              Isawiya
                                Sheikh   Mt. Scopus
                    Romema   Jarah
                                Me'a   Am. Wad el-Joz
Beit Zayit   Kiryat   She'arim Colony
                    Moshe   E-Sawana
            Beit   Old   E-Tur
            ha-Kerem   City
                    Giv'at Rekhavya Mt. of
                    Ram   Nayot Talbiya Olives
            Kiryat   German Eizariya
Ein Kerem ha-Yovel   Greek Colony Silwan   Abu Dis
        Kiryat   Bayit va-Gan   Colony Abu Tor
Even Sapir Menahem   Gonen Ge'ulim
Aminadav Ora   Jabel
                    Talpiyot Mukaber
                    Beit
                    Safafa
                    Ramat Rakhel
                              Sur Bahir
Batir   Um Tuba
Husan   Ubeidiya
        Beit Jala   Bethlehem
El-Khadr
                        Beit Sahur

Maps: Vered Shatil

To my children,
Iri, Natanel and Ariela

On the day each of you was born in Jerusalem, I seared the city's name in your name. Though the Bible calls it the City of Peace, no city in the world has known so many wars. Of all the battles in which I have fought, the battle for peace in Jerusalem has been the most glorious and difficult. In the story of Jerusalem, you will also find the story of your father. I pray that this city will truly be for you the City of Peace.

CHAPTER ONE

Jerusalem Syndrome

Dreams and Failures

A place of fire
A place of weeping
A place of madness –
                    (Zelda, 'Place of Fire')

1961 – Journey to the Divided City

Every Friday evening, I used to read to my children from Psalm 122 – verses describing the excitement felt by ancient pilgrims to Jerusalem:

A song of ascents, by David. I rejoiced when they said to me, "Let us go to the house of Hashem:
Our feet stood firm within your gates, O Jerusalem; the built-up Jerusalem is like a city that is united together . . .
Pray for the peace of Jerusalem; those who love you will be serene.
May there be peace within your wall, serenity within your palaces.
For the sake of my brethren and my comrades, I shall speak of peace in your midst . . .

I would draw their attention to the connection between the unification of Jerusalem, as a 'city united together,' and the importance the poet gives to **peace** in the city, repeating that word three times within the psalm. I also explained to them Professor Yehezkel Kaufman's interpretation of the phrase "those who love you will be serene." "The concept of Jerusalem as the city that is united together is not complete until one can say that there is peace in it. And peace also means peace for all those who are connected to it and love it."[8]

For all of my adult life, I have shared that feeling of the ancient pilgrims who journeyed to their cherished Jerusalem and prayed for the city to know peace. But the journey I undertake here was preceded by two other pivotal journeys in my youth: one to the divided city and one to that war which transformed Jerusalem into the city that is 'united together.'

Like Odysseus' journey home from the war in Troy, my journey from my boyhood home in Netanya to the war in Jerusalem took a full ten years. On Wednesday, June 7, 1967, at one in the afternoon, I reached the Western Wall as a wounded paratrooper, my head wrapped in a bloody bandage. This was the end of the journey! The journey began when I was a youth in Netanya in the late 1950s. At the time, dreams of forbidden journeys were reserved for the few who yearned to cross the Jordanian border to see the Red Rock of Petra. I, however, dreamt of crossing the border into the Old City of Jerusalem – to reach the Western Wall.

This dream was inspired by my two childhood heroes, who were considered madmen by most people. Both had infected me with their madness, and consciously or not, sent me on my journey to the Western Wall. The first, a Holocaust survivor and friend of my father from the 'Jerusalem of Lithuania' (i.e., Vilna), was Menachem-Mendel, and the second was the famed poet of Jerusalem, Uri Zvi Greenberg.

Menachem-Mendel was a regular visitor to our home and I'd known him since I was very young. He was a peculiar, scowling fellow. I never saw a smile on his face. My father told me that his whole life, Menachem-Mendel mourned "not for his family, but for Zion" and that he even belonged to a group called the Mourners of Zion, which met at his house. "What do they do?" – I asked, and my father's terse answer was: "They yearn for the Western Wall." At twelve years old, my curiosity was piqued, and I soon began attending the group's meetings.

At these meetings I learned that the name 'Mourners of Zion' originated in the period of the Babylonian exile, and that it referred to a Jewish sect whose adherents adopted signs of mourning, such as tearing their clothing, and abstaining from eating meat and drinking wine, as they awaited the redemption of Zion. I listened agape to Menachem-Mendel's stories about the 'Mourners of Zion' in every exile throughout the generations. He said that after the destruction of the Second Temple, important rabbis also joined the mysterious sect that engaged in mourning rituals. Some went so far as to abstain from marrying and having children. Concerned by the rapid spread of these customs and the sect's steady growth, the Sages decreed that there was no reason to afflict the soul and the body in this way, and that a symbolic and non-damaging act 'in commemoration of the destruction' would be sufficient. Thus, the Sages ruled that a person shall leave a *makom mu'at*, a small spot, of the wall of his house unplastered; leave a *davar mu'at*, a small thing, aside at his meal, and on a day of particular joy – a wedding – the celebrants shall commemorate the destruction of Jerusalem by breaking a glass. However, not everyone accepted the Sages' decree, and Mourners of Zion sects continued to exist. They went on singing and praying for Jerusalem, and tormenting themselves for its sake.

"Even in the Treblinka concentration camp we had a Mourners of Zion group," Menachem-Mendel told me. "One day a week we tormented ourselves by fasting." I could hardly believe my ears: Even in the death camp people fasted and mourned the destruction of the Temple?!

At other meetings of the Mourners of Zion group in Netanya, I learned about the history and geography of Jerusalem and of the Temple Mount. I was surprised to hear Menachem-Mendel say that the Western Wall was not a remnant of the Temple at all, but rather a supporting wall of the Temple Mount. "The sanctity of the Western Wall," he claimed, "developed relatively recently, in the Middle Ages. Up until then, Jews prayed on the Mount of Olives, across from the site of the Golden (Mercy) Gate."

That same year, Menachem-Mendel, who was a walking encyclopedia of Jerusalem affairs, taught me the history of the Western Wall and about all the legends surrounding it. He also knew the writings of the historian Josephus by heart, and often quoted his descriptions of the Temple in Jerusalem.

When I asked to join the Mourners of Zion group, he said to me: "It is written in Tractate Baba Batra: 'All who mourn for Jerusalem shall be privileged to see its joy.' Moshe, one day you will see its joy!" And so, in my teenage years, while my friends were focused on having fun, going out dancing and first crushes, I was making initial preparations for the journey that would lead me to the Western Wall.

As a group leader in the Betar youth movement, I read to my charges the poems of Uri Zvi Greenberg, the poet of Jerusalem who sang of the city that was in enemy captivity: "Encircle her with love/ Your hearts shall toll like bells for her alone . . . for she is eternal mother and bride."

Every other week I would travel to Tel Aviv for a political gathering of Lehi veterans headed by Dr. Yisrael Eldad (Scheib). Most of the members were daring former underground fighters, while I was the youngest participant. This group sought to translate the longing for Jerusalem into political action, and discussed in all seriousness the possibility of continuing the war for the liberation of Jerusalem by other means.

Scheib, a short fellow with glittering eyes and white, wind-tousled hair, was known for his fire-breathing speeches. He was also the editor of the bulletin *Sulam*, which was like a bible to me. In his speeches and writings, Scheib likened David Ben-Gurion and the Mapai government to the traitorous Petain government in France that had betrayed its country's legacy. Scheib's telling of the history of the War of Independence taught me that Ben-Gurion consciously chose not to liberate Jerusalem in 1948 – not for fear of 'what the non-Jews would say,' but for fear of 'what the Jews would say.' According to Scheib, the choice not to liberate Jerusalem was therefore linked to the State of Israel's complex regarding the way in which the Redemption was meant to occur. It's no coincidence, contended Scheib, who held a doctorate in history, that the touchstone work concerning Jewish emancipation is Moses Mendelsohn's *Jerusalem*, which treats the capital of Israel as an abstract, rather than a concrete or territorial concept. Ever since then, we have been afraid to conquer it lest Jewish emancipation become a national emancipation that demands a tangible capital rather than an abstract one.

As a teenager I was captivated by Scheib's fervor even if I didn't always fully comprehend all he said at those meetings. One thing was clear to me, though: a revolution was needed. And if it didn't culminate in a seizure of power, it would at least comprise symbolic, provocative acts that would demonstrate to Ben-Gurion once and for all that the nation truly yearned for the Old City of Jerusalem.

That same year, 1961, I made up my mind to act: I would cross the border and blow the shofar by the Western Wall at the end of Yom Kippur. I was joined in this scheme by Meir'ke Yeshurun, another Betar youth leader. Together we spent long hours at the home of Menachem-Mendel, who was our confidant in drawing up the plan to steal across the border in Jerusalem. Meir'ke and I believed that even if we were caught on the way (and all the more so if we were killed), our actions would shake the rafters and stir the people to rise up and liberate Jerusalem. We felt that we were reviving the honored Betar tradition – Betar members used to provoke the British authorities and the Arabs by blowing the shofar by the Western Wall as Yom Kippur ended. For this, they were sent to prison. "Let the Mapai-niks cross the border and get killed at the Red Rock in Petra," Meir'ke and I said. "We'll cross the border and die for the sanctification of the Western Wall."

Menachem-Mendel marked on a map for us the possible path of entry near Mount Zion, an area where there were no mines. Meir'ke and I put in our packs an Israeli flag, a shofar and a letter explaining our actions in the event that we were captured or killed.

Stage one of the plan called for us to arrive at Mount Zion on Yom Kippur morning and meet up there with our hero and prophet, poet Uri Zvi Greenberg. Every Yom Kippur he prayed there atop the roof of a building while gazing toward the captive city. According to the plan, he would bestow upon us the blessing for a successful journey. Then we would embark on stage two and head eastward from Mount Zion until we arrived at the Western Wall via the Dung Gate.

On that Yom Kippur, without a word to our families, we made our way to Mount Zion. Sure enough, Uri Zvi was standing there, wrapped in a white *tallit*, auburn hair whipping in the wind, eyes gleaming. We introduced ourselves and informed him of our plan. There was no doubt in our minds that he would eagerly offer his blessing. How astounded and disappointed we were at his reaction! Angrily raising his voice, he admonished us in no uncertain terms that it was sheer madness. "Go home right now!" he said. "Keep on teaching the Betar youths about the real Jerusalem, the one that's in enemy captivity. The end cannot be hastened, and there is no point in you dying. The day will come, and it is near, when Israeli soldiers will enter the city and liberate it." He fixed me with his gaze, firmly clutched my shoulder with his scrawny hand and said: "All who mourn for Jerusalem are privileged to see its joy, and the day of its joy must be near if you mourn for it so deeply."

When Yom Kippur ended, I returned to Netanya, to the Betar youth movement and to Menachem-Mendel's Mourners of Zion group. From then on, I waited impatiently for the glorious day which the poet had promised me would surely come.

1964 – Dialogue at Notre Dame

Three years later I had another illuminating encounter on the rooftop of one of Jerusalem's most striking buildings: the Notre Dame de France monastery situated on the hill across from the New Gate in the Old City walls, right on the boundary between the two sections of the divided city.

Built in the late 19th century, the massive Notre Dame de France monastery majestically overlooks its surroundings. On the eastern façade, two imposing turrets rise on either side of a large statue of the Virgin Mary.

The origins of the Notre Dame de France ("Our Lady of France") monastery lie in the rivalry that occurred among the European powers as they scrambled for influence in the crumbling Ottoman Empire. With unparalleled zeal, the French Consul, Charles Ladoux, set about acquiring land and building religious institutions. Helped by a young French nobleman, Comte Marie Paul Amedee de Piellat, a man of deep religious feeling and the scion of a family that traced its lineage back to the Crusaders, Ladoux launched the construction of Notre Dame in the 1880s.

In 1881, the young nobleman organized a "Crusade" of his own, a "journey of penitence" that drew the participation of nearly a thousand French pilgrims. The pilgrims pitched their tents on the hill where the monastery now stands. The young nobleman fervently preached to them about the importance of the site: It was from this very spot that Tancred the Crusader launched his assault upon the city a thousand years earlier, and this section of the wall had been known ever since as Tancred's Tower. "Right here," de Piellat promised them, "we shall restore France's glory and build a monument to our new empire." And in that one day, the pilgrims donated the entire sum needed to purchase the hill.

The pilgrims returned home, but Comte de Piellat remained in

Jerusalem to build the Notre Dame de France monastery. And when construction was finally completed, he did not rest there; he returned to France to organize expeditions of "penitent" pilgrims, who would reside at Notre Dame during their stay in Jerusalem. De Piellat also saw to it that equipment was installed to illuminate the monastery with electricity. Notre Dame was the first building in Jerusalem to be lit by electricity at a time when the rest of the city depended on kerosene lanterns for light.

The envy of the other Europeans and the Arabs in the city was only whetted further by the French's success – through diplomatic pressure and a good bit of bribery – in persuading the Turkish sultan to carve another opening in the Old City walls, opposite Notre Dame. The new opening was intended to create a substantial shortcut into the Christian Quarter of the Old City for the convenience of the pilgrims and monks in Notre Dame. Sultan Abdul Hamid consented on condition that the new gate be named for him – *Bab Abdul Hamid*, in the belief that this would ensure his place in history as junior partner to Sultan Suleiman "the Magnificent," who built the Old City walls in the early 16th century. But Abdul Hamid's name was soon forgotten and locals referred to the gate merely as *Bab al-Sultan*, "the Sultan's gate." Nowadays, it is called *Bab al-Jadid*, the New Gate.

In 1948 another king sought to conquer Jerusalem: King Abdullah of Jordan. Like the sultans and emperors before him, he attempted to conquer all of Jerusalem only to be halted here, at the foot of Notre Dame. That year, the Notre Dame monastery was the site of one of the war's most fateful battles, the battle that sealed Jerusalem's fate as a city torn in two, divided between Jordan and Israel. Just below the monastery, in the area that separates it from the New Gate, the battle for Jerusalem was decided. King Abdullah's attempt to penetrate the Western half of the city was a colossal failure. The Hebrew fighters had taken up positions on the roof of the monastery and hurled Molotov cocktails that incinerated the Jordanian armored vehicles that were heading for the western part of the city after conquering the Old City. The thwarting of the Jordanian offensive at Notre Dame meant the fight for Jerusalem was a draw, and it gave rise to what from then until 1967 was known as *hakav ha'ironi* ("the City Line") – the boundary dividing the city in two. The lofty location of the monastery provided a view over the Old City and became the Israel Defense Force's (IDF's) most important military post devoted to protecting the western section of city.

No other place in the world has witnessed the rise and fall of so many heroes, kings and kingdoms as has Jerusalem. Here by Notre Dame, all that is left to attest to the ephemeral glory of Crusader, Ottoman and French rule in Jerusalem are stone remnants: Tancred's tower, Suleiman's magnificent wall, de Piellat's monastery. And from 1948 to 1967, these were joined by the burned-out armored vehicles from King Abdullah's army.

In the summer of 1964, Paratroop Brigade 890, my unit, was given the assignment of guarding the city for five weeks – "to fortify the City Line," as the phrase went in those days. We troops thought of this assignment as a wonderful vacation, and I still remember it that way: A break from arduous training exercises, lodging in the well-appointed hospice right in the heart of the city, peaceful slumber in the pilgrims' beds, and plenty of time to read. I read a lot of books there on the roof of Notre Dame.

Every day we each had to do a six-hour shift in the outpost on the monastery's roof, which was protected by sandbags and concrete walls. From the outpost there was a marvelous view of the surroundings – the entire Old City lay spread out before us, and the sunrises and sunsets were breathtaking.

With our huge telescopic binoculars we could peer into the wide windows of the Jordanian Ambassador Hotel on top of Mount Scopus and observe female hotel guests undressing in their rooms, a pastime that was a source of much delight and excitement throughout the platoon. Reports of what could be glimpsed from atop Notre Dame frequently aroused the jealousy of soldiers stationed at the battalion's other posts at lower elevations along the City Line.

But no binoculars were needed in order to see the Jordanian Legion soldiers who were stationed just across from us over the New Gate. They sat right above the gate, in their outpost fortified with sandbags and concrete walls, their machine guns tilted slightly upwards, aimed at the top of the tall monastery.

In those days the "conflict" was still a distant, theoretical concept. The last war here had been in 1948, and since then the city had known relative quiet. In both parts of the divided city, there was a "ceasefire routine" which gave Jerusalemites, who would later live through the Six-Day War and two intifadas, a sense of security and calm. Nevertheless, our physical proximity to the Jordanian outpost was unsettling.

I'll never forget my first day doing guard duty at the outpost high atop the monastery. It was the first time I'd seen the enemy from so close up and I couldn't help feeling quite nervous and vulnerable. It would also mark my first confrontation with a paradox that would stay with me for many years to come: "the enemy as human being." On that day, from the outpost atop Notre Dame de France, I began a decades-long dialogue with the enemy. This dialogue always took place on two planes: the political and national plane on the one hand, and the personal, human one on the other.

On that summer day in 1964, Itzik Penso from Kibbutz Hulta and I went up onto the roof for our first stint of guard duty. Through our firing slits we clearly saw two Jordanian Legionnaires gazing at us through their firing slits. They were wearing red keffiyehs and dark green uniforms decorated with bronze medals that glinted in the sun. They looked a few years older than us. We knew from the briefing we'd received the day before that they were professional soldiers – Bedouin who served in the Legion's third division in Amman. Both of them had big and impressive black mustaches. Everything about their appearance projected the quiet strength of experienced military men. "Relax" – said Itzik, sensing my apprehension. "We're sitting here above them, in total control. If there's an order to open fire, we take them out with the first round . . . "

Suddenly, one of the Legionnaires stood up, waved hello to us and called: *Ahlan Wasahlan*! I stood up and craned my head over the top of the outpost to answer him with due courtesy, only to throw myself back down when I noticed him tossing some unidentified object at us. Itzik and I had instinctively placed our fingers on the triggers of our guns when a brown paper bag dropped into the outpost. Only after a few moments passed and nothing exploded did we dare peek inside the bag to examine its contents. We found three bars of fine English chocolate. The sound of the Legionnaires' laughter from across the way instantly dissolved the tension I'd felt. All of a sudden they were no longer an "enemy" but young men in uniform like us who wanted, even in this peculiar situation of non-war and non-peace, of not friends but not quite enemies, on either side of the boundary that rent the city in two – to build a human dialogue across no-man's land. Shortly afterward, the brown bag went sailing back to them. This time it held three packs of Ascot cigarettes which Itzik had received in the weekly care package his kibbutz sent to its troops.

In the days after that, the contents of the brown bag varied from chocolate and cigarettes to colorful Playboy magazines, photos of movie and soccer stars and even photographs of our girlfriends, who were far away back home – in Amman, Netanya or Kibbutz Hulta. The dialogue grew more personal when we learned their first names – Abdullah and Mohammed. They called us Ishaq and Musa. There were also hours of shared silence, during which I yearned for my Ziva back in Netanya while my counterpart dreamed of dark-eyed Aisha in Amman. This was at dusk, when darkness descended upon the divided city and all of us, on either side of the border, would gaze up at the stars scattered overhead, listen to the calls of the muezzins in the mosques and to the ringing bells of the nearby churches.

As the sun rose over Mount Scopus, the Old City appeared before us once again. The sun's rays burnished the golden dome of the Mosque of Omar, the 7th-century conqueror of Jerusalem. I saw Abdullah kneel inside his outpost, facing south toward Mecca in prayer, one hand resting on the machine gun pointed at Notre Dame. Like the sweetness of the

English chocolate, this image, too, has stayed with me for many years: They are my most potent memories from "the City Line," from the divided city, from my first dialogue with the other side.

The routine of the City Line was only rarely broken. Every other Wednesday the air around Notre Dame on the Israeli side and the Old City ramparts on the Jordanian side would crackle with the buzz of military two-way radios. Senior officers from the Legion and the IDF would arrive at our respective positions amid much hustle and bustle. The alert level on those Wednesdays was raised to Level C – combat readiness. It was time for the changing of the guard on Mount Scopus – a ceremony that had been taking place like clockwork every two weeks since the signing of the ceasefire agreement in 1949. Israeli soldiers dressed as policemen (according to the agreements, Israel could maintain an enclave on Mount Scopus manned solely by police personnel) would travel in a guarded convoy from the Mandelbaum Gate through Jordanian territory and ascend Mount Scopus in order to replace the other Israeli "policemen" there. The high level of alert was maintained until the convoy completed its safe return down the mountain.

During those hours there was no dialogue between us and our Legionnaire friends. Everyone wore a serious expression, as befitting a Level C alert, which meant that the potential for an outbreak of hostilities between Abdullah and me was at a peak. During this time Abdullah would remain crouched in his outpost in tense anticipation, with a flat steel helmet on his head and his finger on the machine-gun trigger. His eyes avoided meeting mine. At one in the afternoon, once the convoy had safely returned and the top brass from both armies had gone away and left us alone, the brown paper bag resumed its travels. More English chocolate crossed the international border into Israel. Within minutes, its delicious flavor filled my mouth as I listened to the laughter of Abdullah, the Legionnaire in the red keffiyeh who stood up straight atop the ramparts waving to me from "enemy territory," so close and yet so far.

And so the routine went for four weeks. In my last week there, as we were making final preparations for our pullback from the City Line, something happened that shook up the routine and which, for me, encapsulated the geopolitical reality of Jerusalem in that era. This event, which could certainly qualify as an "international incident," involved senior officers from the Jordanian Legion and the IDF, as well as representatives of Israel, Jordan, Cyprus, the UN and more.

This is what happened: One morning, the area around Notre Dame was suddenly abuzz again with the squawk of two-way radios. Within minutes, the alert was raised to Level C, and the senior officers showed up in a rush, their expressions stern. We were accustomed to seeing Israeli and Jordanian officers in such situations, but this time a whole bunch of people in civilian dress appeared, too – personnel from the Israeli foreign ministry, senior Jordanian bureaucrats and UN soldiers (blonde Swedes) in their blue berets. My curiosity was especially piqued by a group of monks, of apparently high standing in the Church, in black robes and priestly turbans. The excitement that gripped us soldiers also stemmed from the fact that not one of us had the slightest idea what all the fuss was about or what all these distinguished folks were waiting for.

It wasn't long before the mystery was solved: Some sort of valuable object had accidentally fallen from the ramparts into the no-man's land, and a request to retrieve it had been received. Fulfilling this request was no easy task: Not only might the area be strewn with mines, but entry to the no-man's land was permitted only to UN personnel; both the Israeli and Jordanian forces were under a standing order to open fire without warning at anyone else who ventured there. So, when a UN officer entered the area to conduct the search, the troops on both sides were instructed to lock their rifles and hold their fire.

We soon learned the identity of the mystery object that had stirred up this international commotion: As the mother superior of the convent next to the Old City wall was taking a stroll along the ramparts that morning, her dentures had somehow come loose and plunged into the no-man's land below. The false teeth could well have been abandoned to the same fate as the burned-out vehicles and other remnants of war that remained there, but the old nun insisted on getting them back. She had called the head of the Church, who called the Jordanian foreign minister who called the UN Middle East Coordinator stationed in Cyprus, who called the UN representative in Jerusalem at Armon Hanatziv, who called the IDF headquarters in Jerusalem. Soon all the disparate parties had rallied together for this crucial rescue operation. We stood there in a crowd of several hundred – Israeli paratroopers in red berets, Jordanian Legionnaires in green berets, UN soldiers in blue berets, senior officers from both armies, high-ranking officials in civilian dress and priests and nuns in their black garb – watching perhaps the most absurd spectacle to ever take place by the Old City ramparts, completely mesmerized by the scene before us: A tall Swedish UN soldier cautiously descended a rope ladder from the wall into the no-man's land, bent down and began searching along the bottom of the wall for the lost item. The dense shrubs that grew there amid the sooty hulks of the scorched vehicles made his task even harder and all the spectators expressed their disappointment each time he straightened up and shook his head to indicate 'no luck.' Suddenly, after long minutes of tense anticipation, the Swedish soldier stood up again and waved his hand up high, as if hoisting a world championship trophy, to show everyone what he had found. The whole crowd, on both sides of the border, cheered and went crazy. The exhilaration of this shared, international victory over the absurd reality, and the feeling of solidarity it sparked among Jews, Christians and Muslims – Israelis, Swedes and Jordanians who had managed to momentarily unite and return the nun's dentures to her – prompted all present to applaud wildly and whoop with joy. Sounds of rejoicing in Hebrew, English, Arabic and Swedish were borne aloft through the "mountain air clear as wine."

At that moment, Abdullah smiled at me and waved his red keffiyeh in the air, while I shouted with happiness and waved my red beret. I wanted to hug him but he was far away, in another land – on top of the wall. Instead, I hugged my friend Itzik Penso, who was still whistling as if he had just watched his team score a big goal.

A few days after this thrilling event, we bid farewell to our Legionnaire friends on the ramparts and to the Notre Dame monastery, which had been our home for five weeks. I didn't know then that I would be returning, to the Legionnaires and to Notre Dame, three years later. In June 1967, Itzik Penso and I encountered Jordanian Legionnaires under less amicable circumstances: On the night between June 5th and 6th, we fought in the paratroop brigade against the Legionnaires in the battle to liberate the Old City. The image of Abdullah with his big black mustache was in my mind during the fighting, in which we shot at the Legionnaires who were defending their city. A year later, in 1968, we took on the Legionnaires once again in a battle that took place in the Jordanian town of Karameh. My buddy Itzik Penso, who headed into this battle just before he was due to be married, did not return from it. He was killed by Jordanian Legion bullets, and instead of attending his wedding, I attended his funeral on Mount Herzl.

Some years later, I returned to Notre Dame, this time for a peace dialogue – for talks with the Palestinians about the future of the city. In the late 1980s, my friend Hanna Siniora and I convened a discussion group that met once a week at the Notre Dame monastery, a neutral location where the Palestinians were prepared to meet with Israelis. This was during the first intifada. Jerusalem was again effectively divided between east and west, and Notre Dame again marked the boundary.

The principles for peace and a political accord in Jerusalem that we formulated then in Notre Dame would later become the basis for talks between official representatives of the two sides. Some of those present at our meetings would later be part of the official delegations to the Camp David talks in 2000.

One day I walked around the monastery with Hanna Siniora. We went down into the spacious halls where impressive paintings brought here a century earlier by the French Comte de Piellat hung on the walls. The paintings depict the Crusader battles for the city. I told Hanna about the other dialogue I'd once had here with the enemy on the ramparts, and he replied: "Here, in a place where Christians, Muslims and Jews have battled over Jerusalem, we – Palestinians and Israelis – are trying to reach peace. Will we succeed, Moshe? Perhaps from here, from Notre Dame, the message will go forth – of one city that shall be two capitals – ours and yours."

As a Jerusalemite, I often find myself heading north through IDF Square and past the New Gate, where I gaze up at Notre Dame, at the statue of Mary holding the baby Jesus and smiling down upon the Old City. I smile, too, when I recall the sweet taste of the English chocolate that I ate there in her shadow. Somehow, it was in just those moments, as I guarded the dividing line, that I felt the real sweetness of hope, and had a vision of peace.

1967 – Journey to the Western Wall

On Monday, June 5, 1967, I arrived in West Jerusalem as a soldier in the paratroop brigade. The sound of explosions from the approaching battle echoed in the air. This time I wasn't carrying a shofar in my pack, but a camera. I had it all planned – When I reach the Western Wall, I'll have my picture taken there. On that day, my brigade commander, Motta Gur, was as yet unaware of something that I already knew for certain: We were on our way to liberate the Old City!

The Jordanian Legion shelled the city and that night we made our way from the Shmuel Hanavi district, through the mines strewn about the no-man's land, straight into the Sheikh Jarrah neighborhood. We spent the whole night advancing from house to house under heavy fire. The battalion was moving eastward, and I knew we were headed for the Old City, with the ultimate destination as obvious as could be – the Western Wall.

By the end of that night, which was the longest of my life, we reached the Rockefeller Museum. I climbed up onto the roof of an adjacent building, and at first light the Old City appeared before me, shrouded in smoke. Opposite me, on the northern ramparts, Legionnaires who had refused to surrender even in the face of our superior numbers and fire-power were still shooting. To the left, in the distance, I could make out the Mount of Olives covered with row upon row of white tombstones. "Those are the tombstones of the oldest Jewish cemetery in the world," I remarked to my buddy Itzik Penso, pointing to the east. "You're wrong," replied Itzik. "According to this aerial photo I have here, those are positions of a Jordanian mortar battalion that happens to be firing at us at this very moment, so I suggest that you take cover unless you want to end up in that cemetery sooner than you bargained on . . . "

Ofer the medic came up on the roof, too, and the three of us flattened ourselves there and fired at the Legionnaires atop the wall as we were being shelled by the Legionnaires on the mountain across the way. A formation of Israeli air force planes swooped over the Mount of Olives and dropped napalm bombs on the positions there.

"Where are we?" – Itzik asked me. "Where do we need to go from here?"

"We're at the northeastern corner of the wall," I explained. "It was from this exact spot that the Crusaders attacked the city a thousand years ago: Duke Gottfried of Bouillon and Tancred the Norman, and their 40,000 troops, including 1,500 knights on horseback."

"And how did they get past the wall?" – Itzik asked.

"They built a giant wooden bridge, charged the Muslims and Jews who were defending the wall and quickly breached the city," I answered, recounting what Menachem-Mendel had taught me. "The knight Raymond de Aguiliers reports in his eyewitness account that the Crusaders slaughtered all the city's inhabitants – about one hundred thousand men, women and children – and waded up to their knees in the blood that flowed through the city's alleyways."

For a few moments, the Jordanian bombardment ceased, and we also stopped firing.

"And what happened to the Jews?" – Ofer wanted to know.

"Tancred gathered up all the Jews, about six thousand people, herded them into the synagogue and set it on fire. Then he led his regiments up to the Temple Mount to plunder the gold and silver treasures in the Mosque of Omar," I told him.

At sunrise, the golden dome of the Mosque of Omar appeared before us in all its splendor. I could tell that we were close to the Lion's Gate, since I knew the map of the city and the way to the Western Wall by heart. It wouldn't be long now until I finally got there. I couldn't conceal my excitement. I was already picturing my first encounter with the Western Wall.

All at once, as if by some invisible signal, the battle resumed. The machine guns atop the ramparts fired at us, the mortars from the mountain bombarded us. An order came over the radio: "Forward! Take the Rockefeller Museum!" And I thought to myself: "Just don't let me get killed now, not when I'm this close . . . " Just one kilometer separated the outer wall of the Old City from the Western Wall, and now I was approaching the wall . . .

The time was exactly six a.m. I'd come down from the roof and positioned myself at a window, and was shooting at the Legionnaires and covering my comrades who had begun advancing toward the museum. Suddenly, a Jordanian shell exploded on a roof right across from the window where I was standing. The shock wave hurtled me through the air. I felt a shrapnel fragment rip into my face and seemingly blow my head apart. In a flash, blood was pouring down my cheeks and all I could hear were cries of "Medic! Medic!"

Ofer the medic quickly and skillfully applied a bandage to stop the bleeding.

"I can't see anything with my left eye and my whole face is burned!" I yelled.

Ofer tried to reassure me: "In a few minutes a jeep will come and evacuate you to the hospital. The wound doesn't look that serious. You might not be so handsome anymore, but you'll live."

In that instant I realized that the war was over for me.

"But I have to get to the Western Wall!," I cried.

Ofer looked at me as if I were out of my mind: "That's what you care about right now, the Western Wall?!"

A few hours later I was in Hadassah Hospital in Ein Kerem. The doctor assured me that my life was not in danger. But he also told me the X-ray showed that I had a piece of shrapnel in my head and that, in a day or two, once my condition had stabilized, they would operate and remove it. "In the meantime, just relax and enjoy the pretty female volunteers," he said as he headed off to tend to more seriously wounded patients.

In the bed next to mine lay Motti, who had been lightly wounded in the leg by a grenade fragment. We spent the night chatting with the volunteers. The gunfire from the Old City was audible in the distance. In the morning, we listened to Voice of Israel reporter Raphael Amir: "The time is 10:20 a.m., the seventh of June. At this moment, in a jeep with the deputy chief of staff and the commander of the forces, we are passing through the Lion's Gate. We are inside the Old City. The soldiers are sticking close to the walls and sounds of gunfire can be heard."

"In ten minutes he'll be at the Western Wall," I said to Motti. "At the first turn left he'll arrive at the Temple Mount plaza and then he'll turn at the Mughrabi Gate to the Western Wall."

"You've been there?" Motti asked. "How do you know the place?"

"Yes, I was almost there once," I spat in frustration, "and now, instead of being there I'm lounging in bed here . . . "

Over the radio, we heard the voice of Major General Uzi Narkiss, the commander: "Tell me, where is the Western Wall, how do we get there?"

"Go to the Temple Mount plaza!" I shouted at the radio, "and turn right at the end . . . "

A few minutes later we heard the reporter's voice: "At this moment I am descending the steps to the Western Wall, I am touching the stones of the Western Wall . . . " In the background were the sound of gunshots, cries of joy from the soldiers and the blowing of a shofar.

I couldn't stand to listen to the broadcast any longer. I got out of bed and told Motti: "I'm going to the Western Wall!"

"Me, too!," Motti replied.

We helped each other make the short leap from the ground floor window of the hospital. He limped along on his bandaged leg that was still full of grenade fragments, while I had a bandage wound round my head, one eye shut and a face that was swollen and painful. We raced toward the Old City in a military jeep. Less then half an hour after making our escape, the jeep driver let us off at the Lion's Gate.

It was now 12:30 in the afternoon. The sound of gunfire was all around. Motti and I picked up a pair of helmets and submachine guns from the jeep and hurried, limping and panting, toward the Temple Mount.

I will cherish that first encounter with the Temple Mount and the Western Wall until my dying day. In my wounded state, I kept on running together with a group of soldiers who were trying to find their way there, as the shooting and explosions never let up.

All at once we found ourselves in an enormous plaza, gaping at the beauty of this place that was adorned with cypress trees and marble pillars and, above all, the spectacular golden dome of the 7th-century mosque. All at once it hit me that the place where we stood was the site of the Temple, the place where our forefather Abraham had prepared to sacrifice his son Isaac, the site of the *even hashtiya* – the Foundation Stone upon which God created the world.

Someone clambered up to the top of the dome and waved the Israeli flag, to the boisterous cheers of the paratroopers. But I didn't stop at the Temple Mount. I had another destination in mind. Gasping for breath, one eye covered by the bandage, I kept on running toward the Western Wall. I knew that only there would my personal journey truly reach its end.

It makes me smile to recall how I ran there, to the Western Wall, clutching Motti's hand, barely able to see where I was going. On and on, past the Mughrabi Gate, jostled by the crowd, moving as fast as we could. All of a sudden we came to a stop, thunderstruck. There before our eyes stood the Western Wall; gray, massive, still. Only once before in my life did I ever feel the way I did at this moment – when I was a little boy and my father led me up to the Holy Ark in the synagogue, and I was overcome with tremendous awe . . .

Reverently, I approached the Western Wall, like the emissary of the congregation going up to the Holy Ark; as the emissary of my father Hershel-Zvi from the "Jerusalem of Lithuania," of my grandfather Moshe and his entire family who were massacred at Ponar; of my teacher and mentor, the Mourner of Zion Menachem-Mendel, and all his family who perished in Treblinka, of Uri Zvi Greenberg, whose poems, such as 'I'll

Tell it to a child,' 'A Zone of Defense and Address of the Son-of-Blood,' which I knew by heart, had sent me here.

Someone next to me recited the *shehehiyanu* blessing – "Blessed art Thou, O Lord our God, King of the universe, who has granted us life and sustenance and permitted us to reach this time." I was too overcome to respond "Amen." I just placed my hand on the stone, and the tears that flowed from my eyes became part of the sea of prayers, melodies and longings of Mourners of Zion throughout the ages. All around me was a great commotion. The singing of Hatikvah, the national anthem, blended with the *El Maleh Rahamim* prayer. I took my camera out of my pocket and asked Motti to take my picture. "One day, when I tell my children the story of my journey to the Western Wall, they won't believe me unless I have proof – a picture of me at the Western Wall that I helped to liberate," I explained.

On the note I stuck between the stones of the Western Wall that day, I'd written a single word: Peace. I was confident that the Divine Presence that had never left the site of the Temple would willingly receive my prayer.

Later on, as I headed back to the hospital, I stopped on the Temple Mount once more. It struck me that this place, while overwhelmingly beautiful, had not stirred in me the same wonder I'd felt when standing at the Western Wall. At the Western Wall, I was an Israeli bursting with pride and contentment. For me, being there symbolized the culmination of a life-long personal dream, a dream interwoven with the dreams of so many generations before me. As I stood on the Temple Mount plaza before the Mosque of Omar, my pride gave way to a deep feeling of reverence for the sanctity of the place.

Two paratroopers were standing atop the golden dome, taking down the Israeli flag. I watched them in surprise. From time immemorial, all the conquerors of Jerusalem had been quick to proclaim their victory from this very spot, on the Temple Mount, and now that Motta Gur, the commander of my brigade, had just announced, "The Temple Mount is in our hands" – I wondered – Why don't we fly our flag here, too, atop the Temple Mount?

"We received an order to take down the flag because this is a holy site," the soldiers explained to me. "A holy site for Muslims."

The sense of surprise was replaced by a new feeling – of magnanimity in victory: 'We're not like all the rest of Jerusalem's conquerors . . .'

For many years I carried with me this image of the two paratroopers removing the flag from the dome out of respect for the site's holiness. And eventually, this memory was joined by a deeper insight: To me, the removal of the flag, which has not flown there since, remains an expression of the fact that while the Temple Mount may be in our hands, it does not truly belong to us, to human beings . . . What we have in our hands is a place that belongs to God, and God has no need to fly a flag there . . .

When I was released from the hospital, my father drove me back home, to Netanya. On the way, he told me that word had already spread that the son of Hershel-Zvi had liberated the Western Wall and cheated death, and that there was much excitement in the city. Sure enough, it was hard to get near our house because of the crowd that thronged Smilansky Street. My father and I got out of the car and walked together up the street, to great cheers and applause. I brought my father much happiness that day.

Standing there next to the house, waiting for me, was Menachem-Mendel. For the first time in my life, I saw him smile. We embraced as he laughed and cried and then whispered confidentially in my ear: "All who mourn for Jerusalem are privileged to see its joy, but not all who mourn for it are also privileged to liberate it. This privilege will belong to you and to your children and grandchildren, forever . . . "

A few days later, when I received the paratroop brigade medal that was awarded to the liberators of Jerusalem, I sent it to Uri Zvi Greenberg in Ramat Gan, along with a short letter: "Because of your poems, I set out on my journey to the Western Wall. At one stage, perhaps you remember – on Mount Zion six years ago, you promised me that the day was near, and now it has come. I was wounded in battle, but I liberated Jerusalem and reached the end of the journey – the Western Wall. I wish for you, a great fighter for Jerusalem, to have this medal."

In his reply to my letter, he wrote: "To you, who were privileged to be among Jerusalem's freedom fighters, who carried your love for her in your heart and were ready to give your life, and were privileged to liberate her. May you be blessed. I remember well that Yom Kippur day on Mount Zion. Write and let me know how you are. In friendship, U.Z.G."

Some years later, Uri Zvi Greenberg was the *sandak* at the *brit milah* for my son Iri (the name means "my city"), whom I named for Jerusalem – Menachem-Mendel's Jerusalem, Uri Zvi's Jerusalem, my Jerusalem.

Odysseus finally completed his journey after ten years, but the odyssey that brought me to the Old City in Jerusalem did not end on June 7, 1967, when I inserted my prayer for peace between the stones of the Western Wall. It was only just beginning.

For forty years, ever since that day, the various paths of my life – personal, public, literary and academic – have been inextricably bound to the ideas of 'preserving the unity of Jerusalem' and 'bringing peace in Jerusalem.' In my personal and public odysseys, I have searched long and hard for a way to merge these two concepts, because the city that I liberated and in which I wished for peace very soon became a 'city of strife.'

This book is about a similar journey, one that the State of Israel has undertaken since 1967 in an effort to secure its control over the united capital. Israel has been trying to bind together and reconcile the objective of control in Jerusalem with the objective of peace. So far, it has failed to achieve this goal.

Big Decisions – Big Mistakes

In June 1967, immediately after the war, the Israeli government made two big decisions that had a greater impact on the city's future than anything that followed: The first was the annexation of the holy places and the Old City to Israel, and the second was the demarcation of new borders for the city. The new borders entailed a major expansion that brought more Arab territories, villages and inhabitants into the city. Essentially, all the decisions made in the forty years since were a direct consequence of the constraints imposed on the policy-makers by these two initial decisions.

The background and characteristics of these two big decisions are identical: Both were made amid the atmosphere of euphoria and excessive self-confidence that prevailed in wake of Israel's stupendous military victory, and both were based on an analogy to the situation in 1949, when Israel was able to secure and preserve the achievements of the War of Independence. Both were made under the pressure of the events and the time; in haste, and without adequate discussion. In the course of the decision-making process, there was a fierce debate in which opponents of these policies – experts and also government ministers – warned of the severe implications of these decisions.

Once these two decisions were made and became 'national' policy, there was no retreating from them, even when it was apparent in retrospect that they were 'big mistakes.' When within just a few years it became clear that their repercussions were quite negative and ran counter to Israel's interests, it was already difficult for the policy-makers to backtrack and seek alternatives. They preferred to go on clinging to the failed policy out of some mystical faith it would somehow eventually achieve its objectives.

The first of these two big decisions concerned the future of the Christian and Islamic holy sites. The question was whether or not to include them under Israeli rule. Now that Israel had conquered the Old City of Jerusalem, in a debate that took place at the cabinet meeting of June 16, 1967, two options were laid out.

The first option was not to impose Israeli sovereignty upon the Christian and Islamic holy places, but to accord them the status of 'functional internationalization.' This option was based on reasoning that said the annexation of these sites would prove a burden and not an asset to Israel. It was supported by seven government ministers and all of the experts, including some senior foreign ministry officials, whose professional opinion the government had sought. According to this option's advocates, not only would the inclusion of these sites within the framework of the annexation of the Old City undercut the objective of attaining international legitimacy for a united Jerusalem, it would provoke unneeded conflict with the Christian and Muslim world, and prevent peace with the Arab states. As Defense Minister Moshe Dayan famously put it, "What do we need all this Vatican for?"[1]

A position paper by three experts presented to the cabinet warned that control of the Muslim holy sites would "sow the seeds of trouble in the form of a future jihad."[2] In their view, Israeli control of Haram al-Sharif (the Temple Mount) was liable to shift the conflict over the city from the political to the religious sphere, and consequently arouse hostility not only from the Palestinians and the Arab states, but from the entire Muslim world. The experts also argued that Israeli control of the Temple Mount might encourage Israeli extremists to strike at the Muslim holy places.

The most outspoken proponent of this view was Education Minister Zalman Aran. He warned that holding onto the Christian and Islamic holy places could ultimately lead to a re-dividing of the city that involved Israel's withdrawal from the Old City, a scenario he termed a *hurban* (using the Hebrew word that connotes the destruction of the Jewish Temple). He sternly reminded everyone of Ben-Gurion's big mistake in the triumphant aftermath of Israel's 1956 military victory – when he declared that the Sinai Peninsula would forever remain in Israel's hands. Just days later, international pressure compelled the Israeli prime minister to order a withdrawal.

In the end, the government chose the second option – inclusion of the Christian and Islamic holy places holy within the framework of the city's unification, on the basic that the world would eventually come to accept this reality. The opinion of a majority of the ministers, headed by Prime Minister Levi Eshkol, was that this move would not hurt the chances for peace with the Arabs in the future. In the atmosphere of euphoria and self-confidence that pervaded the government at that meeting, about two hours of discussion was enough to alter the historic policy of the Zionist movement and the State of Israel, which hitherto was opposed to Jewish sovereignty over the Christian and Islamic holy places and favored functional internationalization.

This decision served as the basis for a policy that, in the years to come, would prove cumbersome and strewn with contradictions. The policymakers had naïvely presumed that the Muslim world would be satisfied with religious autonomy and not raise political demands concerning the holy places. In time, this premise was shown to be mistaken; over the years, Israeli control of the Temple Mount became a symbolic rallying point for the opposition of the entire Muslim world, and not just the Arabs, to the unification of Jerusalem. Just as the experts had predicted, the Temple Mount became a 'powder keg' in the Middle East conflict, and Israel's hold on it encouraged worldwide Muslim solidarity with the Palestinians' struggle for a state of their own.

At the Camp David summit in 2000, it became evident that this issue overshadowed all other issues in the conflict and was blocking a potential solution. As Israel's then Foreign Minister Shlomo Ben-Ami described it, the holy places had changed from an "asset" into a "burden."

The second of the two big decisions was made a few days after the first, on the twenty-fourth of June, 1967, and concerned the territorial issue of the city's borders.

Here, too, the government had two options: The first was proposed by municipal representatives and won the support of Defense Minister Moshe Dayan and Mayor Teddy Kollek; it spoke of applying the 'unification of Jerusalem' solely to the Jordanian city (seven square kilometers) and annexing that section to the western section of the city (thirty-seven square kilometers). The second option called for expanding the annexation to incorporate broad swaths of territory in the West Bank. Numerous experts and several government ministers warned that the addition of these twenty-eight villages and their Arab inhabitants would double the city's population and thus was clearly unwarranted. However, these warnings were rebuffed by a majority of the ministers, who put no stock in any gloomy predictions and even believed, in their boundless self-assurance, that the Jewish majority in the city would steadily increase until it hit 90 percent.

Hence, the government rejected the option of annexing only the Jordanian city which comprised a limited area, and elected to pursue the second option – territorial expansion. Thus the 'unification of the city' was applied to a broad area (sixty-four square kilometers) that unnecessarily tripled the size of the capital.

The tenfold increase of the annexed territory – from seven square kilometers to about seventy square kilometers – created a need to exert control over this large area. To this end, tens of thousands of housing units had to be built. And yet, paradoxically, it was the policy of extensive construction of new Jewish neighborhoods in these areas that gave rise to the rapid growth of the Arab minority in the city. This massive building effort required Arab manpower, and this in turn helped spawn the 'demographic problem' that in the years to follow would keep many a policy-maker awake at night. Within forty years, the proportion of Arabs in the city, which prior to the annexation of the territories stood at 18 percent (solely in the Jordanian city), had risen to 34 percent. With the present birthrates, within the next thirteen years, it could well reach 50 percent of the city's population. Moreover, the resources that were allocated to construction of the new Jewish neighborhoods came at the expense of strengthening the infrastructure for employment, industry and tourism, thus spurring the city's economic decline. From today's vantage point, the annexation of extensive territory in the West Bank to the city appears to have been the key constraint dictating the development of Jerusalem over the past forty years.

These two fateful decisions – applying Israeli sovereignty to the Christian and Islamic holy places, and expanding the city's boundaries from an area comprising thirty-seven square kilometers to seventy square kilometers – undermined Israel's ability to achieve the national goals that were intended to ensure the unity of Jerusalem.

Five National Goals – Five Failures

In answer to Shakespeare's question in *Romeo and Juliet*, "What's in a name?," the conquerors of Jerusalem throughout the ages might say: "A name is an expression of our custody of the place." The Roman emperor Hadrian changed the name of Jerusalem to Aelia Capitolina after he conquered the city at the end of the Second Temple period; the Muslim caliph Omar, who conquered Jerusalem in the 7th century CE changed its name to Al Quds ('The Holy'), and so it remained for the next thirteen hundred years. In 1948, Al Quds came under Jordanian rule, while the western part of the city, which was declared the capital of Israel, became known as Jerusalem (*Yerushalayim* in Hebrew, *Urshelim* in Arabic).

After conquering the eastern part of the city, Israel also took symbolic action to 'give expression to its custody of the place' by means of 'the name game': The names of streets and sites which had honored the city's previous conquerors were replaced by new names commemorating the new conquerors. Thus, Allenby Square, named for the British conqueror of Jerusalem, became Tzahal (IDF) Square, and one stretch of Sultan Suleiman Street, named for the 16th-century builder of the Old City walls, became Paratroopers Street.

The most significant change of this nature was in the designation of the city's official name. Now that the city was unified, the authorities wished to change its Arabic name in the hope that this would lead Arabic-speakers the world over to recognize the city's unity. A few days after the city's unification, the Israel Broadcast Authority was instructed to refer to the city in its Arabic broadcasts from now on as *Urshelim*. Most Israelis, who didn't listen to the Arabic broadcasts, were completely unaware of the change, but it aroused much anger throughout the Arab world. Some even mocked the Israeli attempt to give the city a 'fabricated' name that had never been used in Arabic. In wake of these reactions, the Jerusalem municipality proposed that Jerusalem continue to be called by its Arabic name – Al Quds – but state officials objected, maintaining that the name change was a vital step in the city's unification. This dispute led the cabinet to devote a special session to the question: What should be the Arabic name of the united city? In the end, a compromise was reached: Henceforth, the city would be known in Arabic as Urshelim – Al Quds, and referred to accordingly in all official documents and national radio and television broadcasts. The government was pleased that it had succeeded in 'uniting the city' with mere words, while Jerusalem's Arabs ridiculed the supposed achievement: 'See how we have managed to prevent the unification of the city – The proof is that from now on it has two names: Urshelim for the western part and Al Quds for the eastern part.'

The tale of the city's name only serves to illustrate the policy-makers' belief that legitimation for the city's unification could be obtained through mere semantics. This, too, derived from the pervasive euphoria and self-confidence that convinced the government ministers they need only set goals for the city unification policy and these would surely be achieved sooner or later. And so, in the days and months that followed, a series of utopian, unrealistic goals were proclaimed, all flowing from the same policy and all given the binding definition of 'national objectives.' The achievement of all, or at least a majority of, these objectives, was always portrayed as a prerequisite for the full unification of Jerusalem.

The first objective of Israeli policy in Jerusalem was territorial: **Consolidation of Israeli control of East Jerusalem by settling more Jews there.**

Government and municipal decisions outlined three components of Israeli territorial control of East Jerusalem, which were made manifest in working papers and master plans: building Jewish residential neighborhoods in most of the eastern portions of the city, loosening the grasp of the city's Arabs on these areas, and cutting off the Arab neighborhoods from the Arab population centers surrounding the city.

As noted, the cabinet decision of June 1967 led to a substantial expansion of the area of East Jerusalem under Israeli control from seven square kilometers (the area of the Jordanian city) to seventy square kilometers. From the start, the idea of settling this entire area was a utopian vision. And indeed, in the first three years the Eshkol government sufficed with promising 'control of the Old City' by means of the construction of a belt of 'inner neighborhoods' surrounding it. Thus, by 1970, control of the Old City was already assured. However, in the early 1970s, Golda Meir's government amended the objective from 'control of the Old City' (about one square kilometer) to 'control of all of East Jerusalem' (about seventy square kilometers).

This drastic shift in policy gave rise to the construction of a belt of 'outer neighborhoods.' The building plans drew unprecedented criticism of the government. And first and foremost among the critics was Jerusalem mayor Teddy Kollek. He believed that this construction was completely unwarranted politically and refused to sign off on the building plans for the new neighborhoods. Academics and urban planning experts also objected, and warned of the detrimental impact it would have on the city's character. Building planners and architects whom the Construction Ministry had asked to draw up the plans also refused to lend a hand to the scheme, arguing that it would bring an urban "disaster" upon the city. They even went so far as to resign from their posts in protest. However, the Golda Meir government was steadfast in its belief that control over most of the areas of East Jerusalem could be achieved, and it invested vast resources in the construction effort. In the end, not only did all the construction fail to secure the territorial objective, it also undermined the demographic objective, by increasing the proportion of Arabs in the city. The construction of the 'outer ring' neighborhoods did not achieve their purported aim of strengthening Israel's territorial grip on a majority of East Jerusalem: The Jewish neighborhoods there now occupy just a third of the area, while in the other two-thirds, the Arab neighborhoods have greatly expanded and are home to a majority of East Jerusalem's Arabs. In addition, the great territorial endeavor sparked an Arab counter-reaction – a wave of illegal construction which Israel has been unable to curb. In the 1980s and 1990s, approximately 20,000 housing units went up without building permits, turning East Jerusalem into a 'Wild West' and causing very serious urban damage. The attempt to territorially separate the Arabs of East Jerusalem from their brethren in the West Bank also failed: East Jerusalem joined with the West Bank and became its political and economic hub.

The second objective of Israel's policy in Jerusalem was demographic: **Increasing the Jewish majority in the city to 80–90 percent, in order to create a 'uni-national' city.**

The demographic data from 1967 indicate that had the Israeli government made do with the annexation of Jordanian Jerusalem, then the Jewish majority in the united city would now stand at 82 percent, versus an Arab minority of 18 percent. The decision to annex to Jerusalem broad areas of the West Bank, including 28 Arab villages, increased the number of Arab inhabitants from about 40,000 to about 68,000, and raised their percentage of the city's population to 24 percent.

The policy-makers, relying once again on a mistaken analogy, reckoned that the percentage of the Arab population in the city would decrease from year to year, based on the demographic trends during the years of Jordanian rule. This data showed that the number of Arab residents had decreased by almost half in the period from 1947–67. Ironically, it was the government's construction of the 'outer ring' neighborhoods in the 1970s that created employment opportunities for the city's Arabs. Israel's relatively liberal policy granted them more advanced health services and numerous social benefits from the National Insurance Institute. Jerusalem therefore became a magnet for the Arab population from the West Bank and the negative migration trend that had characterized Jordanian Jerusalem was reversed. The ratio of Arabs in the city's population steadily rose to 34 percent, while the Jewish majority fell to just 66 percent.

And if the misguided policy of the 1970s that promoted the growth of the Arab minority weren't enough, a much graver folly was soon to follow. In the 1980s, Israel's governments knowingly acted to lower the ratio of Jews in the capital! The Likud's rise to power in 1977 led to a clash between two national objectives: increasing the Jewish majority in the capital, and establishing settlements in Judea and Samaria in the areas surrounding Jerusalem. Both the Jerusalem municipality and outside experts advised that the settlement project around Jerusalem be halted, warning that it would detract from the potential to boost the city's Jewish majority, but the government refused to heed this counsel. Following the construction of Ma'aleh Adumim, Betar Illit, Givat Ze'ev, Efrat and other settlements throughout the area surrounding the capital, approximately 120,000 Jews abandoned Jerusalem during the 1980s and 1990s and moved to the outlying communities. As it turned out, the national objective of settling the territories undermined the national objective of increasing the Jewish majority in the capital.

Jerusalem gradually but consistently evolved into a bi-national city. The yearly Arab birthrate in the city is about 3.5 percent, while the Jewish birthrate stands at just 1.5 percent. Theoretically, if the city's Arabs, who now comprise about a third of the population, were to decide not to boycott municipal elections and to participate in them in 2013, they could establish a national party that, with enough organized support, could already win a majority of seats on the city council, perhaps even the mayor's office.

The third national objective was political: '**Israelization**' **of, equality for and co-existence with the city's Arabs.**

In his speech to the United Nations following Jerusalem's unification, Israeli foreign minister Abba Eban proclaimed to the world that Israel promised the city's Arab minority full equality in rights and services. The

Israeli government had a different attitude toward Jerusalem's Arabs than it did toward the Arabs of the territories. While the political future of the Arabs in the territories was uncertain (there was talk of either a Palestinian state or of autonomy in the territories), the policy in regard to Jerusalem's Arabs was clear: They were an inseparable part of the unified city.

On this issue, too, drawing on the same old analogy, the policy-makers were confident that within a few years the Arab residents would integrate into the life of the city the way Israeli Arabs integrated into the state after 1948. The government decided to allocate special resources to this agenda and also enacted liberal legislation regarding Arabs' status and rights. But it wasn't long before the resources that were needed to improve the level of services and infrastructure in East Jerusalem were being directed solely to strengthening and increasing the Jewish majority. The Israelization policy that touted "equality" for Jerusalem's Arabs was soon displaced by a new policy that imposed numerous hardships upon them, with the aim of spurring them to leave Jerusalem and thereby reduce their percentage of the city's population.

One of the main areas in which such measures were taken was construction. Planning policy in the city operated by two different standards: urban planning for Jews and political planning for Arabs, which substantially curtailed the latter's possibilities for building. And because of these measures, the city's Arabs reacted with growing hostility toward the government and the municipality. They circled the wagons and adopted a policy of *sumud* – of clinging steadfastly to the city from which the Jews sought to remove them. The first intifada expanded the gaping chasm between the city's two populations even further: Jerusalem Arabs joined in the demonstrations, rock-throwing and violence, and became a part of the uprising launched by Palestinians in the West Bank and Gaza. East Jerusalem's political, religious and financial elite, which was supposed to spearhead coexistence in the city, instead became the leadership of the intifada against Israel. The intifada years furthered the goals of the city's Arabs: The city was effectively divided between east and west in a 'geography of fear' and even Teddy Kollek, the avowed optimist and standard-bearer for coexistence for twenty years, admitted: "Coexistence is dead!"

Israel's original policy of 'Israelization' of the city's Arabs was thus supplanted by 'Palestinization'; the Palestinians in Jerusalem identified with the struggle for national liberation. They no longer sought equal rights or services and benefits. They sought to separate from Israel and to establish their capital in East Jerusalem!

That being the case, the political objective of coexistence and of integrating the city's Arab residents in the unified city was yet another failure.

The fourth and perhaps the most important goal was the diplomatic goal: **Obtaining international recognition for Israel's sovereignty in Jerusalem.**

UN Resolution 181, passed in 1947 and better known as the Partition Plan, contains a clause stipulating that an international administration be established in Jerusalem. However, the provision calling for the internationalization of the city was basically ignored from 1949 to 1967, when the city was divided between Jordan and Israel.

From the time of the state's inception, every government, without exception, has aspired to attain international legitimacy for Israeli sovereignty over Jerusalem as the capital city, and has done everything in its power to achieve this goal. In the 1950s, this diplomatic effort was somewhat successful, as 24 countries agreed to recognize Jerusalem as the capital of Israel and transferred their embassies there. However, the United States and the major European countries were not a part of this group. They refused to recognize Israeli sovereignty in Jerusalem, let alone consider the city the capital of Israel.

Following the conquest and reunification of the city in 1967, the Jerusalem issue was placed back on the UN's agenda. To Israel's dismay, the option of internationalization of the city was revived, as was the possibility of returning the city to Jordan. Yet, Israeli policy-makers, with misplaced optimism based on more faulty analogical thinking, believed that this time, too, UN Resolution 181 would fade away and that the international legitimacy Israel had begun to receive in the 1950s would continue to grow in the coming years and eventually apply to the Old City as well. This hope sprang, for one thing, from the Arab states' failure in July 1967 to get a Resolution passed in the UN defining Israel as the 'aggressor' that would have paved the way for sanctions against it. Israel's rosy outlook was also bolstered by the position of the United States, which as a member of the UN Security Council had consistently blocked any Resolutions aimed at imposing sanctions on Israel. The American position suited Israel, since it emphasized the need for a united city, even while calling for the city's future to be decided in negotiations between Israel and Jordan.

As noted, Israel's government believed it would be able to obtain legitimacy by means of a policy of 'establishing facts on the ground,' analogous to what the Ben-Gurion government did in the 1950s when it declared West Jerusalem to be the country's capital. For Israel, the time element was critical, since the premise of its policy was that time would only work in its favor on this issue; from here on, the goal was to gain time and in the meantime to consolidate its sovereignty in united Jerusalem.

The annexation of the Islamic and Christian holy sites in 1967, followed in 1980 by the enactment of the Basic Law: Jerusalem proclaiming that "Jerusalem, complete and united, is the capital of Israel," kindled the international community's wrath. The Basic Law: Jerusalem, initiated by MK (Member of Knesset) Geula Cohen with the support of Prime Minister Menachem Begin, did not contribute anything to the strengthening of Jerusalem. Just the opposite: Twenty-two of the twenty-four countries that had previously recognized Jerusalem as the capital of Israel moved their embassies out of the city. Only two embassies stayed put: those of Costa Rica and El Salvador. In the summer of 2006, these two countries also announced the adoption of a new policy whereby they would no longer recognize Israel's sovereignty in Jerusalem, and transferred their embassies out of the city. Even the United States, Israel's closest ally, made it clear that until there is an agreed-upon arrangement with the Palestinians, meaning a division of the city, it will not recognize Israeli sovereignty in Jerusalem or move its embassy there.

Forty years of diplomatic effort on this front have brought Israel nothing but disappointment and failure. The working assumption of the Eshkol government, that time was on Israel's side, was proven erroneous. Nor did the 'facts on the ground' created by Israel lead the international community to accept the city's unification. Israel's most important goal in Jerusalem – international recognition of the united city – has not been achieved.

The fifth goal of Israeli policy in Jerusalem after 1967 may be characterized as inter-religious: **Separating the issue of the holy places from the Israeli–Arab conflict.**

The issue of the holy places in the city has always been the most sensitive and difficult to resolve. The holy places are what repeatedly made Jerusalem a battle ground throughout its long history; from the 19th century on, they were the pretext for involvement by the colonial powers in the Middle East.

From the outset, the policy of the Zionist movement sought to separate this issue from the issue of the political conflict over the land. As Chaim Weizmann memorably remarked: "I would not accept the Old City even if they gave it to me for free." The 'Gordian knot' binding these places to the city was always a hindrance to Zionist policy, which wished to wash its hands of them. Even after 1948, the official policy of the governments of Israel supported 'functional internationalization' of the holy places as a substitute for the 'internationalization of the city' which the UN sought to impose on the entire city in 1947.

This is the place to point out that the 1948 conquest of the Old City by Jordan gave rise to the rarity of a common interest between Israel and the Arab states, which preferred 'functional internationalization' for the holy places over Jordanian control of them. In 1949, Ahmad Shukeiri, Syria's

UN Representative, called for "internationalization of the holy places that are under Jordanian rule." This unusual confluence of interests also endured briefly after the holy places fell into Israeli hands in the Six-Day War. In July 1967, the secretary-general of the World Muslim Congress (later known as the League of Islamic States) declared that "Seven hundred million Muslims will never consent to Israel's physical control of the places holy to them in Jerusalem. The only solution to the problem is functional internationalization of the occupied places, under UN sponsorship."[3] For the first time in the history of the Arab–Israeli conflict Israel had a chance to resolve the issue of the holy places in accord with the international community and the Muslim world. But as could have been expected, in the euphoric and self-assured atmosphere of the time, the proposals from ministers and experts at the June 1967 cabinet meetings saying that Israel should impose its sovereignty solely upon the Jewish Quarter of the Old City and the Western Wall and not on the Islamic and Christian holy sites were rejected. Thus did Israel miss a golden opportunity to internationalize the holy places and separate them from the issue of the Israeli–Arab conflict.

A series of historic missed opportunities clouded the attempts to reach a solution to the issue of the Temple Mount, such as the talks with Sadat in the 1970s and the secret talks with King Hussein in the 1980s regarding the possibility of internationalization or the Jordanian Option. By now, one can certainly say that Israel has failed to achieve the aim of consolidating its sovereignty and control over the Temple Mount. Since 1967, Israeli policy on this issue has been characterized by hesitation and confusion, and managed to consign Motta Gur's famous declaration – "The Temple Mount is in our hands" – to ancient history.

A most striking illustration of Israel's failure to separate the Temple Mount issue from the Israeli–Arab conflict is the significant weight given this issue in the 2000 Camp David summit talks. In essence, contrary to Israel's original policy goal, the holy places became the real core issue of the conflict.

The Division of Jerusalem: The Rueful Mayor

In the summer of 2000, the country was all stirred up over Prime Minister Ehud Barak's readiness, at the Camp David talks, to divide Jerusalem.

At the time, I was serving as the prime minister's advisor on Jerusalem affairs, and I put together a large team of experts that came up with a number of alternatives for a political accord in the city. This team of fourteen included some of the most eminent scholars in the various relevant fields: Professor Shlomo Hasson of the Hebrew University Department of

Geography; Professor Ruth Lapidoth, a world-renowned expert on international law; Professor Moshe Maʻoz, a Near East scholar and head of the Hebrew University's Truman Institute for the Advancement of Peace; Professor Elinoar Barzaki, head of the Department of Architecture at Tel Aviv University and the former city engineer for the Jerusalem municipality; Mr. Amir Cheshin, a former mayoral advisor on Arab affairs; attorney Shmuel Berkowitz, an expert on the holy places; Dr. Menachem Klein, a Near East scholar from Bar-Ilan University; Dr. Yeshai Sefarim, an economist from the Hebrew University; Major General Aryeh Amit, the former Jerusalem district police chief; and others.

The team's conclusion, that the city had to be divided, was unequivocal. This need derived, to a great extent, from the fact that in the thirty-three years of its rule in East Jerusalem, Israel had not attained any of its national goals in the city, on any level. It was this assessment which gave rise to the experts' consensus that a division of the city – i.e., that Israel part with Jerusalem's Arab neighborhoods, whose residents already comprised 32 percent of the city's population – was vital. The expectation was that a division of Jerusalem would strengthen the city economically and provide an opportunity to refocus on urban development and functioning, which since 1967 had been completely scuttled due to the political constraints. Another consensus was that there was an unbridgeable contradiction between a city united under Israeli sovereignty and peace with the Palestinians, let alone the entire Muslim world.[4]

In July 2000, the Prime Minister's Bureau conducted public opinion surveys regarding the division of Jerusalem. The findings indicated that the previous across-the-board support for a united city had begun to crumble in wake of the first intifada. The surveys found that a majority of the public (65–70 percent) already viewed Jerusalem as a divided city. A smaller majority (56 percent) was prepared to accept a division of the city within the framework of a comprehensive agreement with the Palestinians. In fact, the public's recognition of the failure of the unification policy in the city had been documented a year earlier: In a public opinion survey conducted in January 1999, 50 percent of the respondents agreed that, 'Effectively, Jerusalem is already divided into two cities: the eastern city and the western city.' The only issue on which these surveys did not find majority support for concessions was the status of the Temple Mount.[5]

The decades-long failure of the policy to unify the city, combined with the data from the public opinion surveys on this issue, was a significant factor in Prime Minister Barak's thinking as he formulated his position in favor of dividing the city.

In those days of discussion about the possibility of dividing the city, the prime minister was seeking public support for his positions on the matter.

Aware of my good relationship with former mayor Teddy Kollek, he asked me to meet with him to recruit his support for the idea of dividing Jerusalem. Such backing from a figure of Teddy Kollek's stature could have a major impact. Kollek was universally perceived as a symbol of Jerusalem's unification, and looked upon by the world as an eminent statesman. He had managed to soften the image of the Israeli occupation and to paint it, in Jerusalem at least, as "enlightened."

My relationship with Teddy Kollek had been through many ups and downs. It began in 1973 when I returned to Israel from New York after completing a master's degree in urban administration. That was when I first became involved in the public debate surrounding the construction of the 'outer ring' of new neighborhoods in East Jerusalem. At the time, I considered myself something of an 'expert on Jerusalem' and published a critical article in the *Yedioth Ahronoth* newspaper. I wrote that the 'Build as much as you can' credo spurring the construction craze throughout East Jerusalem had to stop; I warned about the folly of allotting resources to construction rather than to sources of employment, and about the unnecessary eastward spread at the expense of the city center; I noted that the latest studies in the field of urban planning, which I was familiar with from my studies in the United States, confirmed that a capital city was best off concentrating on the infrastructures of employment, administration, culture, education and government institutions, rather than on industry, trade and finance. I concluded my article with a call to 'demonstrate against the municipality and the government for their dereliction in the planning of Israel's capital, a situation that will only bring endless trouble." (Filed in my personal archive are dozens of articles that I have published in the press over the past thirty years, and all are essentially variations on what I wrote in that very first article about the pitfalls of politically motivated urban planning in the capital.)

To my surprise, the day after the article appeared, the mayor's office contacted me with an invitation to come meet with Teddy Kollek. I was overcome with excitement in anticipation of meeting, for the first time in my life, the man who for me and many others of that generation epitomized "the unification of Jerusalem" and was nothing short of a legend. His admirers called him "The Israeli Herod", while detractors derided him as "the Defender of Islam."

In the days before the meeting, I went over all the reasons in my arsenal for preferring a "smaller" Jerusalem to a "greater" Jerusalem. But when the time came and I at last entered the mayor's office, I was struck dumb by the sight of Teddy; there he sat behind his massive desk, and the wall behind him was covered with dozens of flags, medals, citations, artwork and pictures from all over the world. All were gifts to the man who, in the eyes of the entire universe, was the very embodiment of Jerusalem.

After I declined the Cuban cigar he offered me, he lit one for himself and launched into a monologue that lasted about fifteen minutes and began as follows:

"Young man, I was impressed by the article you wrote, and I agree with you one hundred percent. The problem is that it is really the government that runs Jerusalem, not I, and unfortunately the government and I are in disagreement about the way the city should develop. I think that they're making historic mistakes. All I can do is shout . . . "

He went on with his monologue, enumerating all the reasons why the government was going about it all wrong. His explanations were remarkably similar to the academic explanations I'd brought back from my urban administration studies in New York. The more Kollek talked, the more my astonishment grew: This was my first lesson on Israeli politics in Jerusalem; the vast difference of opinion between the mayor and the prime minister reflected the contrast between a rational vision of what was good for the city and the emotional vision of governments that subscribed completely to the myth of the 'unity of the city.'

When Kollek at last finished speaking, I sat there mutely in my seat. He looked at me with a cynical and slightly wicked smile (which, over the years, I learned to identify as the precursor to a punch line that would leave the listener stunned) and said: "Young man, your government – They're all drunk. One day they'll sober up, but it will be too late . . . "

He signaled with his hand that the meeting was over and went back to perusing the papers on his desk, enveloped in clouds of cigar smoke. I got up and left the room without even saying goodbye, and without having managed to utter a single word at our meeting.

Seven years after that unforgettable encounter, we began working together. In my job as head of the National Road Safety Authority I took part in numerous work meetings at which he was present – concerning transportation, roads and accident prevention, subjects that were dear to his heart. In 1989 he asked me to take on the engineering and transportation services portfolio as part of my duties as a member of the municipal administration. Thus, all in all, we worked together for twelve years, from 1981 to 1993.

Despite the admiration he displayed for my initiatives, such as the preparation of a new master plan for the city's roads, we also got into arguments and even bitter disputes concerning the treatment of the Arabs of East Jerusalem. As chairman of the Municipal Committee for the Equalization of Services in East Jerusalem, I argued that the portion of the municipal budget allocated to the Arabs should be increased from 4 percent to 10 percent, as they accounted for approximately 30 percent of the population. He did not accept my view that the responsibility for building infrastructure and equalizing the distribution of services to the city's Arabs lay with the municipality, and asserted that it was a task for the national government. In 1989, when I publicly proposed that the city's Arab residents be allowed to establish their own municipal authority, he viewed my stance as undermining 'the city's unity' and sent me a letter dismissing me from my job as a member of the administration. However, about a month later, when his anger had cooled, he called me in for a 'clarification talk.' As a condition for regaining my post, he asked me to make a public apology. When I refused to apologize, he said to me:

"Young man, Jerusalem will never be divided . . . We haven't yet succeeded in uniting it, but there must be no talk of dividing it into two municipalities as you proposed. We will never divide Jerusalem."

I answered him with a question: "Teddy, how many years have to pass before we're convinced of our historic mistake and change course? Or, on the contrary, until we at last succeed in uniting the city?"

He gave me that familiar cynical look and responded: "Like all politicians, you have no historic vision. You can't just leap to conclusions like yours and divide the city. You have no patience, young man. And I'll tell you the answer to your question: One hundred years, yes, it will take a hundred years to unify the city!"

Despite my refusal to make a public apology, he gave me my job back. As I said, our relationship was not always a bed of roses. Amidst all the flattery that was continually showered upon him by all his associates, he was quite taken aback on those occasions when I voiced some harsh and very specific criticism on various municipal matters, though I believe that he respected my independent views.

To me, Teddy Kollek was like a Don Quixote tilting at the windmills of the government's policy. But Teddy was also a true master at public relations; more than once he was forced to accept government decisions diametrically opposed to his own regarding the city's development, but after the fact he made sure to take credit for the successes. He, who was one of the most vehement opponents of building the new neighborhoods on the grounds that they would spell an 'urban disaster,' and who considered the accelerated development of the city a 'historic mistake,' boasted about the neighborhoods' construction twenty years later. This is what he said in 1988: "The tremendous momentum, the accelerated development of the city and the construction of the new neighborhoods that are like satellite cities to Jerusalem constitutes an achievement of international magnitude . . . [6] The job of mayor of Jerusalem, even if meaningless in terms of the fateful decisions affecting the city, still brought him historic greatness in the eyes of many. However, despite this lofty stature, his long-held desire to serve as Minister of Jerusalem Affairs in the government was never realized, as successive prime ministers declined to appoint him to this position.

In 1993, as the Jerusalem mayoral election neared, we became closer than ever before. Therefore, I allowed myself to speak to him very candidly and try to convince him that he was about to lose the election to Ehud Olmert. He found it difficult to believe that the Jerusalem public would choose Olmert over him. I explained to him that it wasn't the same public that had previously put its trust in him time after time, and that the Jerusalem public now consisted largely of the ultra-Orthodox and the Arabs. "The Arabs won't go to vote, and the ultra-Orthodox will vote for Olmert," I added.

A few months before the elections, I went to great lengths to try to get the city's Arabs to vote. Accompanied by my friend, city council member Sarah Kaminker, I set out for Tunis to hold a secret meeting with PLO chairman Yasser Arafat. We met with the PLO Executive Committee and attempted to persuade its members to call upon Jerusalem's Arabs not to boycott the elections this time, and to vote for Teddy Kollek for mayor and for an Arab-Jewish list for the city council. But our efforts came to naught.[7] When I returned from Tunis, disappointed by the failure of the mission, I advised Kollek to retire from the race while still at his peak. I also told him that he was certain to lose the election and that it would be best not to delude himself.

But all the sycophants around him, as well as his genuine admirers within the party and the municipality, advised the exact opposite: to run at any cost. He followed their advice – and lost. Bitter and angry, Kollek wondered why the Jerusalem public had betrayed him. For him, the loss was a tragedy from which he would take many years to recover. For me, it was a time of sadness: This was not how Teddy Kollek's glorious, nearly thirty-year career as mayor was supposed to end. That said, despite my admiration for him, I always felt, and still do, that he was a wily politician who chose not to confront the government head-on, who never entertained the idea of resigning even when he became well-aware of the 'march of folly' in his city. He always protested against it, but in the end, he was a party to it.

On July 23, 2000, the prime minister sent me to visit Kollek at the old age home where he lived in Jerusalem's Kiryat Yovel neighborhood, to ask for his support for the idea of dividing Jerusalem. I found myself sitting across from an old, tired and very embittered man. I explained to him how important it was to the prime minister that he publicly state his support for a division of the city. I didn't expect to be able to persuade him, but to my amazement, I hardly had to try. Before our meeting ended, he said to me: "Young man (I was already 55 at the time), we failed to unite the city. Tell Ehud Barak that I support dividing it."

When we parted, I warmly embraced him. Tears welled in my eyes. I remembered what he said to me back at our first meeting in 1973: "This government and I are in disagreement as to the way in which the city should develop. I think they're making historic mistakes. All I can do is shout . . . "

As I left the room, I felt a need to tell him that to me he was and would forever be a Knight of Jerusalem.

I had never been one of those people who were always praising him and showering him with compliments. I'd caused him plenty of irritation and very little pleasure, but for me Teddy remained a knight, albeit a tragic one. But then, weren't all of Jerusalem's knights tragic?

Jerusalem's dazzling light blinds all of its heroes and rulers. Memories of past glories and grandiose dreams for the future knock them off-balance. They liken themselves to the city's earlier conquerors and are confident they will succeed where all their predecessors have failed. Captive to the myth of the holy city, they crash against the rocks of Jerusalem's reality and are afflicted with 'Jerusalem Syndrome' . . .

On January 3, on the day of Teddy Kollek's funeral, the historian and journalist Tom Segev wrote:

> The occupation did not turn into unification, and as the fortieth anniversary of the Six-Day War approaches, Jerusalem is emerging as one of the greatest failures in the history of the Zionist movement. Historically speaking, the Kollek era in Jerusalem therefore deserves to be remembered more as a story of illusion than as a success story.[8]

CHAPTER TWO

How Jerusalem Became Israel's Capital

Our political fate and near future would have been fundamentally different had we understood and dared to divide Jerusalem. To our misfortune, patriotic rhetoric won out in Jerusalem, the hollow and foolish rhetoric of a fertile national enterprise.

(David Ben-Gurion, 1937)

A City of Strife

Jerusalem has long been imbued with unique importance due to its concentration of sites holy to the three major religions – Judaism, Christianity and Islam. Throughout the ages, the special attachment to the city felt by hundreds of millions of people all over the world has made it a 'city of strife.' Thirty-six times in its known history, the city has changed hands, nearly always in a bloody war. Conquerors from various nations and religions demolished and burned down structures sacred to other faiths and built their own holy sites in their stead.

In the 18th and 19th centuries, the European powers sought a political foothold in the city, which then had long been under the control of the Ottoman Empire. A key milestone in this period was the retreat of the Egyptian army under Ibrahim Pasha from Jerusalem in 1840, an event that could be considered the starting point of the crumbling of the Ottoman Empire. From then on, Jerusalem became an 'international city,' with the European powers' continuing to make legal and diplomatic gains that fortified their standing in the city. The fading empire's weakness allowed the foreign consuls – the foreign powers' representatives in Jerusalem – to obtain influence surpassing that of the Turkish pasha who officially governed the city. The 'capitulation regime' to which the Ottoman Empire acceded gave the foreign consuls and Church representatives autonomous status, and the agreements between the European powers and the Turks produced what came to be known as "the status quo," which defined areas of responsibility, patronage and autonomy for each of the powers in Jerusalem. A violation of this status quo was one of the pretexts for the outbreak of the Crimean War in 1854 between Imperial Russia and France.

In 1917 the British conquered Jerusalem and in 1922, after four hundred years of Ottoman rule in the city, Jerusalem's international status received a legal seal of approval. The League of Nations declared it part of the 'human historical heritage' and placed it in the temporary custody of its British conquerors. The League of Nations' decision to grant the Mandate for Palestine to the British thus brought to an end the rivalries among the European powers over the division of colonial rule in the Middle East.

During the Mandate period, it was clear to all that in any future political solution in Palestine, Jerusalem would retain its international status. This was evident, for one thing, in a fundamental commitment made by the British made upon accepting the Mandate: to safeguard the interests of the international community and the Churches in Jerusalem. As the Israeli–Palestinian conflict continued to heat up during the years of the British Mandate, the international community became all the more adamant on this point, insisting that the city could not come under exclusive Muslim or Jewish rule. The Vatican's extensive influence in the 1930s and 1940s was another decisive factor in consolidating broad agreement in the United Nations for internationalization of the Holy City.

In the 1940s, when it was clear that the British Mandate would eventually come to an end, the international community was leaning toward one of two options: internationalization of the city or Palestinian-Arab control of it. Founded in 1947, the United Nations Committee on Palestine (UNSCOP) submitted its majority recommendation that same year: The land shall be divided into two states – Arab and Jewish, with Jerusalem coming under an international regime. The Zionist leaders were ready to accept this solution, since the alternative advocated by the minority – the establishment of a bi-national federal state in Palestine with Jerusalem as its capital – was, in their estimation, incomparably worse.

On November 29, 1947 the UN adopted the committee's recommendation in Resolution 181, better known as the Partition Plan. It called for Jerusalem to remain under international rule for ten years, after which the UN would examine various possible solutions, taking the inhabitants' desires into consideration. The Resolution also listed the arrangements to be instituted in the city, which included demilitarization, the preservation of neutrality between the two states, the assurance of freedom of worship for all faiths in their holy places and the election of a municipal council to oversee joint administrative arrangements. It was the UN's optimistic belief in those days that within a decade Palestinians and Israelis would come to agreements that would dampen the hostility, end the nationalist conflict and make possible a consensual solution in Jerusalem. Resolution

181 emphasizes that after ten years, a national referendum shall be held in Palestine in which the inhabitants will be asked to decide on the city's future (though the results would not necessarily be binding upon the UN). The UN also reserved the right to extend the international regime in the city or to determine its permanent status.[1]

Shortly before the outbreak of the war in 1948, a broad international coalition supporting internationalization took shape: The Vatican wished to safeguard the standing of the Christians and churches in the city, and was among the major forces pushing for passage of the internationalization proposal; the Zionist movement wished to secure UN support for the establishment of a Jewish state and supported the internationalization proposal as 'the lesser evil'; and some in the Arab League and the Muslim world, which at the time held relatively little power in the UN, were also leaning toward supporting it. Only the Palestinians and Jordanians were opposed. The Palestinians wanted Jerusalem as the capital of their independent state, while King Abdullah of Jordan was not prepared to give up his control of the Islamic holy places.

The outcome of the 1948 war precluded any immediate chance for internationalization of Jerusalem, as the city was divided between Jordan and Israel along the ceasefire lines. However, in the view of the international community, Israeli and Jordanian control of Jerusalem was illegal. The UN called on both parties to withdraw from the city to facilitate the institution of an international regime.

The international community's position on Jerusalem was no different two decades later, when Israel conquered East Jerusalem and imposed Israeli law there. To this day, the city's status remains controversial: Israeli and Palestinian claims to the city notwithstanding, the international community still considers it an international city.

One of Israel's chief goals since 1967 has been to acquire international legitimacy for its rule over all of united Jerusalem. The experts are divided on the matter of Jerusalem's legal status and the justness of the claims of all the relevant parties.[2] Some maintain that Jerusalem's status is subject to a stipulation of UN Resolution 181 that calls for the establishment of a separate body – a *Corpus Separatum* – under international rule (internationalization). Others insist that the Palestinian people possess legal sovereignty over all of the former territory of Palestine as it was under the British Mandate. Then there are those who recognize Israel's right to sovereignty in Jerusalem by virtue of Israel having fought a defensive war against Jordanian aggression in 1967. But all the experts agree that Jerusalem's status will not be resolved by any legal polemic. Rather, only a political accord agreed to by the three parties – the international community, the Palestinians and Israel – will formalize Jerusalem's status and affirm the rights of each side. Until that day comes, Jerusalem will remain at the center of the regional and international conflict – a city of strife.

Zionist Policy on Jerusalem

From the 1880s, when the first Zionist pioneers arrived in Palestine, until 1949, when the western part of Jerusalem without the Old City was declared the capital of Israel, the Zionist movement ranked Jerusalem low on its scale of national priorities. This attitude regarding the historic capital of the Jewish people derived from a fear that control of the city could undermine Zionism's attempt to achieve its most important goal – the establishment of a Jewish homeland in Palestine.

Jerusalem's marginality was evident in four ways: its lack of political centrality in the Zionist movement in Palestine; the disdain expressed for it in the movement's culture and literature; the relatively meager resources allocated to the city and to settlement efforts there; and acceptance of the likelihood that it would fall outside the framework of the future Jewish state.[3]

As early as 1882, a debate arose among the early Zionist pioneers as to where the movement's political and administrative center ought to be located – in Jaffa or Jerusalem. Some preferred Jerusalem because of the proportion of its Jewish population (approximately 17,000 Jews, in addition to 24,000 Christians and Muslims), and because of its history as the Jewish capital. Opponents raised three cogent arguments: Jerusalem was far from the ports where the immigrants arrive, and far from the designated settlement areas along the coast and in the Galilee; the nature of the Jewish population there, which was composed mainly of the zealously ultra-Orthodox and 'parasites' who lived off charitable donations, was the antithesis of the secular, 'productive' Zionist outlook that sought to create a 'new Jew' who lived off his own labor; the city's ultra-Orthodox inhabitants were even more hostile to the Zionist movement and its ideas than were the Muslim and Christian residents. In the end, these arguments won out, or as Eliezer Ben-Yehuda said: "The power of the coastal city vanquished the holiness of the nation's ancient Mother-City",[4] and Jaffa was chosen as the center of Zionist activity in Palestine.

The Jews who are part of the First Aliya in the late 1800s tended to differentiate between 'heavenly Jerusalem' as a positive symbol and 'earthly Jerusalem,' which was viewed as a place of wretchedness and humiliation. The Zionist idea was 'to take one's bread from the land' and not to live off the contributions of world Jewry.

This estrangement from Jerusalem was also reflected in the Zionist literature and culture of those days. Quoting from Zechariah (12:2–3), the early Zionist leader M. L. Lilienblum wrote: "We have no need for the walls of Jerusalem, for the Temple or for Jerusalem itself, a city which is not central . . . We need Palestine and we need a genuine center, not a 'cup of poison' or a 'burdensome stone for all the peoples." We need boldness and action.[5]

Even Theodore Herzl, the great Zionist visionary, did not see ancient Jerusalem becoming part of the future Jewish state. In May 1896, during his meeting with the Vatican envoy Nuncio Agliardi, he answered yes when asked this important question: 'Are you prepared to leave out Jerusalem, Bethlehem and Nazareth and to establish your capital much further north?' He expressed a similar position on this question in discussions with the Turkish government, when he learned that the Sultan "will not consent to have Jerusalem taken out of his hands, for the Mosque of Omar must remain in the hands of Islam."[6] Herzl's disdain for the idea of including ancient Jerusalem within the borders of the state was also evident in his vision of the founding of a new city that would be completely detached from historic Jerusalem. According to this vision, the new Jerusalem would be "a metropolis by twentieth-century standards":[7] modern districts would be built, surrounded by woods and gardens, and be criss-crossed by a network of broad, tree-lined avenues; the city would be traversed by cars, trams and trains that would run mostly on electricity. This electricity would be produced by means of the waters of a canal to be built between the Mediterranean Sea and the Dead Sea, and from the power stations built along the Dead Sea, producing hydroelectric energy.

From the early 20th century on, Zionism's policy goals focused on building up the territorial, settlement, administrative and military infrastructure for an independent state. Hardly any efforts at Jewish settlement were directed toward Jerusalem and the surrounding areas. Jerusalem was not included in the planned settlement map of 'the state in the making,' and the Jewish settlement blocs that were established in that period were far from the city and cut off from it.

The Zionist policy-makers did not envision Jerusalem as the political capital or economic center of the future state, but rather as a 'spiritual center.' This could be seen in the 'Zionist program' – the plan for establishing the Jewish Yishuv in Palestine in the early part of the century. The main cultural project slated for Jerusalem was a teachers' seminary. The founding of the Hebrew University in the 1920s outside the Old City, on Mount Scopus far from the Christian, Muslim and Jewish ultra-Orthodox institutions, also reflected the Zionist movement's aspiration for 'a different Jerusalem' that was an primarily an intellectual center for the Jewish people. Another manifestation of the movement's disregard for the Old City was its efforts to get Jews to move to areas outside of it.

As for the structure of the Jerusalem municipality, the Zionist movement sought to implement one of two options: a division of the city into three separate municipalities – Christian, Jewish and Arab, as proposed by David Yellin in 1930; or a division of the city into two municipalities – Arab and Jewish, as proposed by Ben-Gurion and Arlosoroff in 1932.

To the Zionist leadership, control of the new city was more important than control of the Old City, and sovereignty over Mount Scopus was more important than sovereignty over the Temple Mount. Zionist symbols took precedence over the old Jewish symbols. As the movement was opposed to Jerusalem having international status, political partition was the only possible way to ensure that (west) Jerusalem would be part of the Jewish state. Such a partition was proposed in a plan submitted by the Zionist leadership to the Peel Commission in 1937. The aim was to preserve what was most crucial to the future state – the Jewish neighborhoods in the western part of the city and Mount Scopus, where Hadassah Hospital and the Hebrew University had already been built, and to be rid of the millstone around its neck – the Old City. However, this proposal was unanimously rejected by the Palestinians and the British. Mufti Hajj Amin al-Husseini would accept nothing less than all of Jerusalem united under Palestinian rule as the capital of an undivided Palestine. The British, meanwhile, had proposed another partition plan to the Peel Commission, whereby Jerusalem would not be attached to the future Jewish state to the west of it, but to Bethlehem and the other Arab parts of the land, so as to create an eastern corridor to the Dead Sea, as well as to the Emirate of Transjordan, which would soon become the Hashemite kingdom.

The Peel Commission's conclusions confirmed the fears of David Ben-Gurion, who had already in the early 1930s sought to divide the city in two – into a Jewish city and an Arab city. Ben-Gurion had harsh words for those in his movement who had opposed this throughout the years. Now, with the Peel Commission plan, they were liable to lose the whole city. In a letter to the Mapai central committee dated July 1, 1937, he wrote:

> Our situation now in Jerusalem is completely different, and perhaps our political fate and our near future would have been fundamentally different had we had foresight enough to dare to divide Jerusalem. Unfortunately, patriotic rhetoric got the upper hand in Jerusalem . . . A Jewish Jerusalem liberated from the . . . Arab effendi and the English bureaucrat, detached from the Old City that has no future other than as a cultural, spiritual and religious museum of all the faiths, and free of the Arab neighborhoods that are sapping our strength, would have the effect of furthering our creative talent, and concentrating our capital and vitality. But instead, idle rhetoric has won out.[8]

From 1937 until 1967, when Jerusalem was united at the conclusion of the Six-Day War, the pre-State and Israeli leadership continued to view the Old City, with its holy places and its Arab population as, in Lilienblum's words, a "cup of poison" and "burdensome stone for all the peoples."

In 1947, the Zionist leaders were ready to accept the internationalization of Jerusalem in order to avoid the possibility of the city coming under Arab rule. And they expected this position to help them garner international support for the establishment of an independent Jewish state in Palestine. To them, the potential loss of Jerusalem was not unthinkable as long as the overall goal of obtaining a state was achieved.

Despite the drawbacks, the vast majority of the Jewish Yishuv viewed the Partition Plan laid out in UN Resolution 181 as a great accomplishment. Ben-Gurion expressed this in a speech to the Histadrut Executive Committee three days after the vote on the Partition Plan:

> It seems to me that all those sitting here are united in appreciation of this day in which the nations of the world decided to establish a Jewish state in Palestine . . . Without question, in this Resolution our ambitions were somewhat curtailed . . . since the area of the Jewish people's land was reduced. And, in particular, we must note that Jerusalem was made an international city. That over thirty of our [settlement] points remained in Arab territory, that almost all the mountains were taken from us and generally the boundaries that were outlined for the Jewish state are very peculiar . . .

Ben-Gurion also spoke of Jerusalem's future:

> We must make Jerusalem the center for the Jewish people in the entire world. Jerusalem has not been made the capital of the Jewish state, but Jerusalem was, and must remain, the heart of the Jewish people. It must be a center not only of a large and growing Jewish community but also a center for all the general and national Jewish institutions, a center of the Zionist movement, a center of the Israeli parliament, that will encompass all the Jews of Palestine, as well as the Jews who are outside of the Jewish state.[9]

Under harsh criticism from the Revisionists for his concessions, Ben-Gurion asked those present "to refrain from any pointless talk about conquering all the land, or conquering Jerusalem and so on . . . " Faithful to his pragmatic outlook, he added: "It is not talk but actions that determine the political facts in Palestine," and went on to say: "Let us remember that just as the Jewish state will not arise solely by declaration and constitution, but with great and continuous projects of aliya and settlement that will come after the state's founding, "**so the state will not exist if we do not display the desire and ability to acquire the genuine friendship of the Arab people both in and out of Palestine**" (emphasis added – M.A.).[10] A man of far-reaching vision, he could not help but insert an extra glimmer of hope for the future, in terms of the boundaries of the state and of Jerusalem: "We know that there are no final arrangements in history, no eternal borders and no final political claims, and that there will be many more changes and exchanges in the world.[11]

From this point forward until mid-1949, the Zionist leadership expected that Jerusalem would not be within the borders of the State of Israel. But despite the intensive focus on preparations for the anticipated war, some were also pondering the question: Where will the country's capital be? The issue was largely a practical one: Where would the state institutions – the government and the Knesset – be located?

According to Ze'ev Sharef, former cabinet secretary, Ben-Gurion proposed at a December 1947 meeting that the government be situated in Kornov in the Negev (also known as Mamshit) near what is now Dimona. Sharef says Ben-Gurion's vision was for the Jewish state to look southward and settle the Negev "where he saw a territory primed for Jewish, agricultural and industrial settlement." This was also the farthest place from any border on the Partition map. The problem was that at his stage, the IDF had not yet conquered the southeastern Negev, and no Jewish localities had yet been established in the area. As Sharef recalls, this upset Ben-Gurion even more than the loss of Jerusalem: "He would sigh when mentioning his proposal since he understood that there was no chance of implementing it under the circumstances of the time."[12] Golda Meyerson (later Meir) wanted to make Haifa the capital. She claimed that Theodore Herzl had dreamt of this, too, though her main argument was that Haifa had the deepest land mass behind it, an area that contained kibbutzim, moshavim and a big industrial center. Two cities composed memos outlining their potential advantages as the future capital. Zichron Yaakov, located between Tel Aviv and Haifa on a high hilltop overlooking the sea, deemed itself most worthy, and its leaders offered to allocate the Ramat Hanadiv area surrounding the tomb of the Baron Rothschild for the construction of a government center. Herzliya also vied for the honor, touting the fact that it was named for the visionary of the Jewish state, and proposed to build the government center in a seaside location, where Herzliya Pituach stands today. Other places under consideration, says Sharef, were the British military camps near Netanya and the Sharona colony near Tel Aviv. The question was brought up for discussion in early February 1948, and the choice made was Sharona, a former German Templar settlement in the Tel Aviv area that the British had converted into a military compound (akin to the so-called "Bevingrad," or "Russian Compound" in Jerusalem), which housed the Hagana headquarters at the time.

Historian and former politician Meir Pa'il quotes from Ben-Gurion's remarks at a ministerial Defense Committee meeting held on April 4, 1948: "Jerusalem will be the center, the center not just of the Land of Israel but of the entire people. The government institutions will have to be in the state . . . Pa'il also notes: "Militarily, the primary concern of the political leadership at this stage was to ensure that the Jewish Yishuv in Jerusalem was not conquered by the Arab armed forces."[13]

For about two years, beginning in November 1947, Israel's policy-makers were convinced that Jerusalem could not be made the capital of the new state. It was only towards the end of the war, in wake of the outcome of the battles in Jerusalem, that the idea of proclaiming the city as the capital of Israel really began to take hold. Ben-Gurion delayed the decision for many months for fear of the harsh international response it would evoke, and did not declare Jerusalem Israel's capital until December 1949.

Western Jerusalem was officially declared Israel's capital on December 13, 1949, about a year and a half after the state's founding. The war and the ongoing debates in the UN over the city's future had kept Ben-Gurion from doing this earlier. Ben-Gurion and his foreign minister, Moshe Sharett, were well aware that a premature declaration of this sort could likely be perceived as a provocation of the UN and cause serious diplomatic damage, and so they chose to wait. Their hesitation brought sharp criticism from both the opposition Herut movement and the Mizrahi (*Merkaz Ruhani*) and Mapai parties within the coalition.

Not until the military lines in Jerusalem were more or less stabilized in 1948 did Ben-Gurion start to talk about the possibility of making Jerusalem the national capital. On June 24, 1948, during a lull in the fighting in Jerusalem, after the Jewish Quarter had fallen to the Jordanian Legion, Ben-Gurion said: "As to the question of whether Jerusalem is within the state or not . . . Jersualem is within the jurisdiction of the Jewish government (for now, unfortunately, without the Old City), just like Tel Aviv."[14] He added that it would stay this way until peace was made and the borders were set with international approval and consent between the parties. It appears that by mid-1948 Ben-Gurion had made up his mind to declare West Jerusalem the capital of Israel, as his biographer Michael Bar-Zohar writes:

During the War of Independence Ben-Gurion disclosed in a number of private talks his intention to establish the capital in Jerusalem, as in the days of King David, however he was not hasty in his actions because he was conscious of the outside world's sensitivity to the city's fate. He suffered with limited steps that established a practical basis for the annexation of the city to the Jewish state.[15]

With the signing of the ceasefire on April 3, 1949, the lines dividing the city were firmly established. The fact that the Old City and the holy places would hereafter be part of Jordan and not Israel, made it easier for Ben-Gurion to go ahead with what he had apparently already privately resolved. As indicated by what he wrote in his journal, his hesitation stemmed from the possibility that the UN would try to impose a worse situation upon Israel: the Resolution calling for the return of the refugees. The passage of the Australian proposal for internationalization of Jerusalem on December 9, 1949 spurred Ben-Gurion to stand up to the UN and to press, cautiously but resolutely, for the city to be the capital. The first step was to transfer the Knesset to Jerusalem. At this point, Ben-Gurion figured that the move would no longer pose any risk to Israel, since the UN lacked the ability to impose internationalization of the city on the parties: "I do not see how they can implement the Resolution. The primary power is the Vatican. The Vatican has no army, and the Catholic nations are not about to send an army here . . . "[16] He also expected that just as implementation of the internationalization Resolution was blocked, the same could happen with the implementation of Resolution 194 concerning the return of the refugees. However, Ben-Gurion still refrained from explicitly proclaiming Jerusalem the capital of Israel. On December 13, 1949 he announced "a continuation of the transfer of government institutions to Jerusalem" and left it at that.

Writing in his diary the next day, Ben-Gurion described this act of defiance as a calculated gamble. He believed that if it succeeded, it would be possible to also rebuff the UN Resolutions regarding borders and refugees:

> Then the matter of the refugees will come up. And if it is possible force on us that which is against our will [the reference is to the internationalization Resolution he mentioned earlier – M.A.], then there is nothing to prevent the return of the Arab refugees. As soon as a campaign is launched, and given a humanitarian background, not only the Catholics will join in, because the claim of the dispossessed refugees has an 'appeal.' The Vatican is interested in strengthening the Catholic and Christian communities, there are other holy places in the country – the Kinneret shore, Kfar Nahum . . . They'll request administrative oversight of all the religious buildings and places in the country. This would spell the ruin of the state, its humiliation, it is internal anarchy. To stand up to the dangers is only possible from the start, on the question of Jerusalem. If we thwart the UN Resolution here, the

question of borders will also be eliminated and we won't be pressed on the refugees. Our success on the question of Jerusalem solves all international problems surrounding the State of Israel. Will we succeed? It is quite possible."[17]

Thus, all in all, three major factors contributed to the inclusion of West Jerusalem within the bounds of the State of Israel and its assignment as the capital: the military draw in Jerusalem between the IDF and the Arab Legion, which left the western city in Israel's hands; the UN's inability to impose internationalization of the city upon Jordan and Israel; and the fact the Islamic and Jewish holy places remained outside Israel's borders.

Israel's UN representative at the time, Abba Eban, noted some years later that sovereignty in Jerusalem and its declaration as the capital were never a national goal of the State of Israel, and the prospect of the Old City being under Israeli rule was in many ways undesirable. In a 1965 interview, Eban said:

Had the United Nations recognized our deep emotional attachment to Jerusalem, that may have been sufficient, for many of our leaders saw Jerusalem as an educational and cultural center and not necessarily, **or even desirably, as a political capital** (emphasis added – M.A.). The UN's disparagement of that attachment and the UN's lack of consideration are what pushed us to act and to proclaim to all that Jerusalem is an inseparable part of the state and its capital."[18]

Ze'ev Sharef, who was cabinet secretary then, remarked: "I never met anyone who believed that Jerusalem would be the capital. Through all of 1948 and until the first months of 1949 the question was never brought up for serious discussion, to the best of my knowledge."[19]

Israel and Jordan Try to Strengthen their Hold on the Divided City

Between 1947 and 1950, some interesting contacts took place between Israel and the Hashemite kingdom concerning the possibility of dividing the city by agreement. But these attempts were beset by fears and trepidation from both sides. Though 'understandings' were ostensibly reached between Abdullah and the Yishuv leadership regarding a division of the city between Israel and Jordan, the situation in Jerusalem continued to deteriorate up to the start of the 1948 war. The debate among historians as to who caused this deterioration has yet to be settled.[20] During the war, the fear that the entire city could fall to Jordan grew. The Jewish leadership, which no longer trusted Abdullah, decided to take action and ensure by means of the force of arms that West Jerusalem would be part of the future state. Thus, Israel initiated the battles in the Arab neighborhoods in West Jerusalem, and at a later stage the attempt to breach the Old City with the aim of adding the Jewish Quarter to the western part of the city. The Israel Defense Forces entered the Jewish Quarter on May 18, 1949, but were forced to withdraw just a few hours later. Immediately afterwards, on May 19, 1949, the Legion entered the Old City and conquered the Jewish Quarter.

When the fighting subsided and the situation stabilized, the City Line dividing Jerusalem was set: Jordan had lost the Arab neighborhoods in the west of the city – Baka, Talbiyeh, Katamon and part of Abu Tor and Beit Safafa. Israel lost the Old City. The Israeli proposal to the UN that the internationalization regime in the city be replaced by functional internationalization of the holy places, which were now under Jordanian control, did not win international support.

In January 1949, negotiations began between Israel and Jordan for a territorial exchange within the framework of the division of the city. With the government's backing, Moshe Dayan, the military commander in Jerusalem, submitted a proposal to annex to Israel the Jewish Quarter and the cemetery on the Mount of Olives, and to create a sovereign corridor to Mount Scopus, which remained under Israeli control. In return, Israel would agree to give up the Arab neighborhoods in the west of the city, Kibbutz Ramat Rachel and two Jewish neighborhoods – Talpiyot and Mekor Haim. Such an arrangement would allow Jordan an Arab territorial continuum from the Old City to the southeast of the new city, and a geographic connection to Bethlehem. The aim of this generous proposal was clear: To reach an accord as soon as possible that would preclude the possibility of internationalization of the city, and that would leave Israel with control of the Western Wall and the Jewish Quarter. This proposal was yet another reflection of the Zionist movement's longheld priorities: Mount Scopus surpassed the Temple Mount in importance, and international legitimacy for West Jerusalem as the capital of Israel surpassed the Old City. The United States was ready to support Israel's proposal as long as Israel refrained from declaring the western part of the city as its capital, and on condition that the accord as a whole received UN approval and supplanted Resolution 181. However, the two sides were unable to come to an agreement. During the talks, both raised more demands, which led to a stiffening of positions and, ultimately, the failure of the negotiations.

In November 1949 the UN proposed once again that the internationalization plan be adopted. This led Israel and Jordan to try one last time to reach an accord on a territorial exchange. On December 13, 1949, a draft was formulated promising Israel sovereignty over the Jewish Quarter and the Western Wall and promising Jordan territorial continuity and sovereignty in the Arab neighborhoods in the south of the new city. The talks continued from December 1949 until February 1950, but ultimately yielded no agreement.

Historians of this period note that during the time that passed between January 1949 and February 1950, circumstances and internal constraints in both Jordan and Israel made it difficult for the parties to come to an agreement. Some say that the political reality in 1950 lessened Abdullah's willingness to make concessions in the Old City. Others counter that in the political reality of 1950, in which the internationalization threat appeared to have been lifted from the city, Ben-Gurion's readiness to give up territory in West Jerusalem faded. He may have thought that in the next military confrontation, the time would be right to win the Jewish Quarter. At any rate, there is no doubt that the two sides missed the opportunity to forge an agreement on Jerusalem, one that perhaps would have given Israel the Jewish Quarter and the Western Wall.

From 1949 to 1967, the city remained divided along the City Line – a hostile border strewn with mines and barbed wire that wound from north to south, bisecting some neighborhoods. Both sides maintained a high military alert due to wariness of the other, and submitted complaints to the UN about violations of the ceasefire accords: Israel complained that Jordan was not honoring its pledge to make possible the resumption of normal life at the Hebrew University and Hadassah Hospital on Mount Scopus, and that Jews were being blocked from praying at the Western Wall and in the synagogues of the Jewish Quarter, and from burying their dead in the cemetery on the Mount of Olives.

Jordan complained that Israel was violating the demilitarization agreements for Mount Scopus; and that despite its pledge to maintain only a police force it had turned this into a military base, at a most important strategic position that threatened the Old City.

Throughout all these years, Israel readied for the possibility of 'another round' in Jerusalem, and drew up military contingency plans in the event of a military coup in Jordan or the collapse of the monarchy. Ben-Gurion, remaining faithful to the Zionist policy that sought to detach itself from the Christian and Islamic holy places, gave the IDF the go-ahead to prepare for the joining of Mount Scopus, the Jewish Quarter and the Western Wall to Israel, but vetoed any and all plans to conquer the entire Old City.[21]

Following the military stalemate in Jerusalem, King Abdullah and Ben-Gurion each sought to quickly obtain legitimacy from the international community their countries' gains in the city. However, both were in for a disappointment: Abdullah's attempts to gain international, Muslim and Arab legitimacy for the annexation to Jordan of the West Bank and the

Old City failed. Ben-Gurion's hopes that the world would accept the annexation of West Jerusalem since it did not contain any of the holy places were also frustrated. On December 10, 1949, the UN General Assembly voted to re-adopt the Resolution on the internationalization of the entire city, and called on Israel and Jordan to allow the UN to carry this out. Both countries disregarded the decision and instead undertook a series of steps to strengthen their standing in their respective parts of the city: Jordan built a Jordanian municipality building in the Old City, granted Jordanian citizenship to the Palestinian residents and began efforts to assimilate them into Jordanian society. Israel announced that it would continue transferring its government institutions to Jerusalem, unambiguously designating Jerusalem as the capital of the new state. In January 1952, the UN General Assembly again voted for internationalization of the city and repeated its call to Jordan and Israel to facilitate this. When this attempt met with failure as well, the UN, which could not impose internationalization on the two sides, made do with a legal ruling, based on international law, saying that Jordan and Israel had no rights to the city and that all their actions in it were considered 'temporary.'

Over the years, experts on international law in Israel and elsewhere have tried to address the question: "Who has the right to the city?" And all have concluded that regardless of whether Jordan and Israel's hold on their parts of the city is defined as 'occupation,' 'annexation' or 'custody,' their sovereignty in the city was not recognized by the international community. Undaunted, Israel and Jordan continued their efforts to secure international legitimacy for their sovereignty in the city. And in this respect, Israel was much more successful than Jordan.

About ten countries agreed to recognize West Jerusalem as the capital of Israel, though they qualified this by calling it 'de facto sovereignty.' An example of such recognition was the British formula, as expressed by the British foreign secretary:

> His Majesty's Government cannot recognize Israel's sovereignty in the part of Jerusalem which is held by it. Even though this matter is subject to the decision concerning the final standing of Jerusalem, we recognize [Israel's] de facto sovereignty. By granting recognition at the same time to the Kingdom of Jordan regarding those parts of Palestine found under Jordan's rule and custody, His Majesty's Government applies those same restrictions to the part that is held and ruled by Jordan.[22]

In one legal case, the British House of Lords accepted the definition of 'de facto' recognition, describing it as follows: "The difference between 'de facto' recognition and 'de jure' recognition is akin to the difference between a temporary and a permanent decision."[23]

However, Israel was not satisfied with 'de facto' recognition and continued to pursue the goal of 'de jure' international recognition.

The two main rationales behind Israel's policy of seeking recognition for its sovereignty were its readiness to relinquish the holy places in the Old City, and the relatively negligible importance of West Jerusalem to the outside world compared with its vital importance to Israel. These arguments were at the center of Israel's diplomatic efforts from the time of the UN debates over the founding of the state and throughout the 1950s and 1960s. Willingness to accept 'functional internationalization' of the holy places became a significant component of Israel's case in its quest for international recognition of its sovereignty over the western part of the city.

As early as July 1947, David Ben-Gurion, in a brilliant move during his appearance before UNSCOP (the United Nations Special Committee on Palestine), was able to neutralize the opposition of the Vatican and many of the Catholic nations to the founding of a Jewish state by declaring that Israel would support the granting of international status to the holy places. In so doing, Ben-Gurion created a distinction between the Old City of Jerusalem and the new Jerusalem. This position was repeated more forcefully during the 1950s, and won Israel growing sympathy, especially in light of Jordan's vehement opposition to functional internationalization of the holy places. In 1949, Israeli foreign minister Moshe Sharett proposed functional internationalization of the holy places and territorial internationalization of the Old City. In February 1950, Abba Eban, Israel's UN representative, echoed this proposal, adding that Israel was prepared to establish in Jerusalem an international body that would have sovereign standing in regard to the holy places and not be subject to Israel or Jordan. In subsequent years, Israel again proposed that the part of Resolution 181 calling for internationalization of the entire city be replaced by a Resolution that would limit the internationalization to the holy places alone.

Between 1953 and 1967, Israel managed to remove the Jerusalem issue from the UN agenda. The confrontations that occurred in the 1960s between Jordan and the Christian churches in Jerusalem helped Israel shift the weight of international pressure on the Jerusalem issue from the western part of the city to the Old City that was under Jordanian control. By the mid-1960s, the number of countries that recognized Israel's 'de jure' sovereignty in Jerusalem had risen to twenty-three. Most of these were South American and African countries that were the recipients of international aid from Israel in those years, but the group also included one European country – Holland. All of these countries moved their embassies to Jerusalem. And ten more countries were ready to offer 'de facto' recognition of Israel's sovereignty in Jerusalem.[24]

The Unification of Jerusalem: From Mount Scopus to the Temple Mount

Israeli government policy on Jerusalem from 1949 to 1967 focused primarily on strengthening the city economically and on attempts to bolster its international standing as the capital. The Ben-Gurion government decided that as long as the Hashemite Kingdom remained in power, and as long as foreign armies did not enter Jordan, Israel would not initiate any assault on the West Bank or East Jerusalem.

Uzi Narkiss, the head of the Central Command in the 1960s, writes in his memoirs that the question of what Israel would do if "a radical Arab element like Syria or Ba'athist Iraq, or the Palestinians took control in Jordan" was discussed on numerous occasions by the IDF leadership and Prime Minister and Defense Minister David Ben-Gurion. While the military brass supported a quick conquest of the entire West Bank and the Old City in that event, the political echelon was much more cautious. Apprehension over the implications of annexing the West Bank and its large Palestinian population, or annexing the Old City with its Islamic and Christian holy places, made Ben-Gurion reluctant to support such a scheme. This concern led him to instruct the IDF that in the event of the fall of the Hashemite regime, Israel would deploy along new lines in the West Bank and Jerusalem, but for defensive purposes only and not with the aim of conquest: "I cannot justify the conquest of Jenin by saying that it is being done for our defense" – he responded angrily to the general staff's proposal to conquer the West Bank.[25]

Conquering the Old City was not something that was considered at all at that time. Ben-Gurion's main concern throughout the 1950s and 1960s was of a possible attack by the Arab Legion that would cut off the city from the coastal plain in the corridor area, and this is what the army focused its preparations on in those years. Ben-Gurion was also concerned about Mount Scopus, and therefore instructed the general staff to prepare a contingency plan for connecting it to the Israeli part of the city. Narkis notes that Ben-Gurion repeatedly stressed that he meant "Mount Scopus alone, and only because in this case we have a reasonable claim: We must protect the lives of the Israelis who are stationed on the mountain."[26]

This contingency plan also included the conquest of the Arab neighborhood of Abu Tor in the south of the city, part of which had been conquered by Israel in the War of Independence. So it seems that the optimal scenario in Ben-Gurion's view during those years was a border change that would guarantee Israel all that it sought to achieve in 1948 – control of the Jewish Quarter, the Western Wall and the Mount of Olives, and a physical connection to Mount Scopus, but no more than that.

On the eve of the Six-Day War, as the skies of the Middle East were darkening with clouds of war, everyone was confident that King Hussein would not join forces with Syria and Egypt. However, with the torrent of belligerent radio broadcasts out of Cairo and Damascus that spoke of 'the battle of honor for which all your Arab brethren are preparing' and issued harsh condemnations of 'the bloody and criminal regime in Amman' which refused to join the fight, Hussein came to feel increasingly isolated in the Arab world. And his failure to show support for Nasser's blocking of the Straits of Tiran turned up the domestic pressure on him as well. Senior Jordanian Legion officers vigorously demanded that he immediately enter a military alliance with Egypt and Syria. Some warned that if he refrained from entering the war, Israel would exploit the war with Egypt and Syria to attack Jordan and seize the Old City away from it. After much wavering, Hussein finally decided to form a military alliance with Egypt. He welcomed the Egyptian general Abdel-Moneim Riad to Amman and acknowledged him as commander of the eastern front. He also announced that he would permit Iraqi and Egyptian forces to enter Jordan in order to attack Israel from the east. In a book he wrote years later, Hussein attributed his decision to join the war to the realization that Jordan would end up being dragged into it no matter what, and thus was better off joining of its own accord.

The Six-Day War began on the morning of June 5, 1967 with an Israeli strike on Egypt and Syria. At 8:45 a.m., Foreign Minister Abba Eban relayed an urgent message to General Odd Bull the head of the UNTSO (the United Nations Truce Supervision Organization), saying "We are at the height of a defensive war on the Egyptian front. We shall not take any action against Jordan unless Jordan attacks us. If Jordan attacks Israel, we will turn against it with all our might."[27] The message did not reach Hussein until 11:00 a.m., about an hour after the Jordanian Legion, under orders from the commander of the joint Egyptian, Syrian and Jordanian forces, General Abdel Hakim Amer, launched an assault on Jerusalem. The Legion began shelling the western part of the city and tried to capture the Armon Hanatziv area in the south. Throughout the afternoon, Israel made further attempts to obtain a ceasefire with Jordan. UN officers tried to convey Israel's ceasefire request to the Jordanian military commanders, and to impress upon them the fact that the Egyptian air force had been wiped out, but it was no use. Colonel Mohammed Daoud, head of the Jordanian ceasefire committee, believed the boastful false reports from Radio Cairo, which were trumpeting "great Egyptian victories," and so he scornfully rejected the Israeli request, not crediting the report about the destruction of Egypt's air force. He went so far as to say: "Before long, we'll be in Tel Aviv."[28]

Uzi Narkiss gives a detailed account of the sequence of events: "The defense minister ordered [in response to the conquest of Armon Hanatziv by the Jordanians] an immediate counter-attack . . . Time is now the critical factor: At dawn we expect to see the enemy's armored units threatening Mount Scopus."[29]

Narkiss ordered the IDF to open a corridor to Mount Scopus, but to pull rightward toward the Rockefeller Museum so as to be ready to invade the Old City. He talks about "the yearnings that filled me since 1948 to complete the mission that wasn't completed then," about the "somewhat mystical faith that never left me in all those years that the day would come when the mission would be completed."[30] adding: "Had we not conquered significant parts of East Jerusalem on the night between the fifth and sixth of June, and had the Jordanians requested a ceasefire on the morning of June 6, no one could have said with certainty that Israel would not have complied."[31]

Once the corridor to Mount Scopus was established and the conquest of the Sheikh Jarrah area completed, the political echelon faced the big decision of whether to push on to conquer the Old City. During the first day and a half of the war, no one in the general staff or the government proposed conquering the Old City. Only late on the second day of the war, when the magnitude of the victory over the Arab armies and the extent of the military gains in the West Bank became apparent, and the IDF had reached Mount Scopus, did the government begin to consider the possibility of riding this wave of success into the Old City as well. Ministers Menachem Begin and Yigal Allon asked Prime Minister Eshkol to convene the cabinet for a special session to decide this issue. "Begin and I want Jerusalem," Allon told the prime minister.[32] Eshkol, throughout his many years in leadership positions, had always been of the view that Israel mustn't conquer the Christian and Islamic holy places. Hence, he instructed the defense minister to encircle the Old City but not to enter it. The government originally voted to adopt Dayan's position, i.e. that "it is better to wait until the Arab residents wave white flags," and prevented the IDF from entering the Old City. But then mounting public pressure and the enormity of the historic opportunity combined to change Eshkol's mind. As Uzi Benziman writes:

> Eshkol didn't want his name to be associated once more with hesitation and reluctance to act [qualities that had characterized his behavior in the lead-up to the war and spurred public pressure upon him to bring Moshe Dayan as defense minister and the Gahal party aboard in a national emergency government – M.A.]. He clearly understood the importance of the hour and the opportunity it afforded to advance a national interest of the first rank. 'Es iz a gadank!' (In Yiddish: 'Now there's a thought!') – he said to Allon, slapping his forehead.[33]

Most of the government ministers, including Moshe Dayan, saw no reason to rush to conquer the Old City, but Eshkol's change of heart made all the difference. More and more ministers began speaking enthusiastically about the prospect and throwing their support behind it. The government voted to allow the IDF to enter the Old City, and things happened quickly from that point on.

By the end of June 6, the Old City was surrounded. IDF commanders excitedly gazed down upon it from atop the Mount of Olives. At dawn on June 7, the paratroopers entered the Old City. At 10:00 a.m., Dayan informed cabinet ministers, who were assembled at the Kirya military headquarters in Tel Aviv, that the paratroopers had reached the Western Wall. The exhilaration was overwhelming. Some ministers wept, others embraced with great emotion. Shouts of joy filled the room. And Eshkol muttered, somewhat stunned: "*Kol hakavod, kol hakavod . . .* ("Well done, well done")"[34]

A few days later, on June 11, the cabinet met to discuss the fate of the Old City. The ministers approached the occasion with mixed feelings – the tremendous thrill of the moment was tempered by an acute awareness of the gravity of the choice before them: Here was the chance to annex East Jerusalem to the State of Israel – to accomplish an act of historic justice from the perspective of the Jewish people. But the ministers also knew that such a decision would likely block any prospect of peace with the Arab countries. The discussion reflected their uncertainty. Prime Minister Levi Eshkol, though, was unwavering. He insisted that "just as East Jerusalem was under Jordan's control, it will be under Israel's control, and the chances of peace are equal in both cases."[35] Four ministers opposed annexation, but by the end of the meeting, a majority supported the idea of unifying Jerusalem and annexing the Old City to Israel.

A United Capital Seeks Recognition

Following the cabinet decision of June 11, 1967, a ministerial committee was formed to prepare the appropriate legislation and determine the boundaries of the annexation. On June 27, the Knesset passed several pieces of legislation aimed at formalizing the city's unification: amendments to the Law and Administration Ordinance and the Municipal Cooperation Ordinance and the Protection of the Holy Places law.

In presenting these bills, the government deliberately avoided any explicit mention of the terms 'annexation' or 'application of Israeli sovereignty' in regard to East Jerusalem. Foreign Minister Abba Eban explained the significance of the legislation in his response to the UN Secretary General on July 10, 1967, after the UN General Assembly condemned

Israel for annexing East Jerusalem. Eban said, "The term 'annexation' which was used by supporters of the vote is not accurate. The steps that were taken [by Israel] relate to the integration of Jerusalem in administrative and municipal areas, and served as a legal basis for the protection of the holy places in Jerusalem."[36]

It bears emphasizing that, contrary to popular notion, neither 'annexation' nor 'application of sovereignty' actually occurred, legislatively speaking, just as the foreign minister claimed. Legal expert Professor Yehuda Zvi Blum asserts, and most other jurists agree, that "there is no basis for the use of the term 'annexation' to describe the steps connected to applying Israeli sovereignty over territories of Palestine, including Jerusalem."[37]

The government's omission of these terms in the Knesset legislation propelled three representatives of the Free Center Party, headed by jurist Shmuel Tamir, to abstain from the votes on them. MK Eliezer Shostak said with disdain that in purposely eschewing this terminology, the government was resorting to legal acrobatics out of fear of what the *goyim* will say. "Why is the government acting like a thief in the night here?," he asked angrily.[38]

Indeed, the issue of sovereignty had come up in the discussions of the ministerial committee that formulated the Knesset legislation. Certain committee members wanted it to be clearly stated that these laws were meant to impose Israeli sovereignty on the annexed territory, but their proposal was rebuffed. Opponents argued that, in terms of international law, Israel could not impose its sovereignty on a conquered territory, just as Jordan's attempt to do so in East Jerusalem failed in 1948. Experts on international law, including Blum, agree that "the Jordanian annexation of Judea and Samaria never acquired general international recognition," and that [Jordan's] rights in the territory that was supposed to be "under the UN's international sovereignty" were at most, the rights of an occupier.[39]

Numerous legal studies since 1967 have pointed out that, according to the UN Charter, to which both Jordan and Israel are signatories, no country may receive sovereign rights over a conquered territory, even if the conquest occurred in the course of self-defense and in response to aggression from another party. For the purposes of sovereignty, two conditions must obtain: obsolescence, i.e., a lengthy period of time must have passed in which the status of the conquest remained unchanged; and during that entire time, the occupying nation must have functioned as the administrator and sovereign power in the conquered territory. Another way to acquire sovereignty is by international agreement or by agreement with the party from which the territories have been conquered. Most jurists concur that neither the Jordanian conquest of 1948 nor the Israeli conquest of 1967 accorded the conquerors the status of sovereignty over the territory. Furthermore, Jerusalem's status under international law is that which was determined by the UN in 1947, unless supplanted by another status determined by international agreement.

Even Justice Minister Yaakov Shimshon Shapira, who brought the three pieces of 'administrative' legislation to the Knesset, admitted that "no such act of sovereignty may be made in the absence of a number of prior conditions." He was referring to the conditions mentioned above. This is why the legislature in 1967 preferred not to use the word 'sovereignty' in regard to the unification of the city. Instead, the Israeli government chose to 'apply the state's law, jurisdiction and administration.' Similar language had been used when territories that were not within the State of Israel according to UN Resolution 181 were annexed to Israel in 1948.

Amid all the excitement and euphoria of the time, only a single Jewish MK opposed the three bills when they were brought to a vote. Meir Wilner of the Communist list called the legislation "an exacerbation of the state of war." Even the representative of the opposition to the national unity government, MK Uri Avnery of the Ha'olam Hazeh faction, enthusiastically supported the legislation, saying: "The people want the unification of Jerusalem and I support the unification of Jerusalem. The unification of Jerusalem is part of the overall arrangement for a solution to the problems stemming from the war, part of the overall debate about the future of the territories."[40] To hurry things along, the coalition factions opted to forgo their right to speak on behalf of the bills. And out of concern over the potential international reaction, the prime minister and several other ministers refrained from taking part in the debate and the vote, to avoid imparting too festive an air to the occasion.

Two days later, the barriers and defensive walls that had separated the two parts of the divided city were torn down. The historic Mandelbaum Gate crossing-point, through which for the past nineteen years foreign tourists and diplomats had crossed between the two countries, was also removed. Now Israelis and Palestinians could move about the city freely. Before long, public transportation lines were operating between both parts of the city, Israeli currency was designated as legal tender in East Jerusalem, in addition to the Jordanian dinar, and all the Arab residents were issued Israeli ID cards. As far as Israel was concerned, the city was now united. Israel chose to ignore the international legal aspect, as well as the fact that almost every nation in the world refused to recognize the city as united.

The legal question didn't bother the decision-makers in the least. They vividly recalled how, just nineteen years before, the same thing was done when Israeli rule was applied to the territories that were annexed in wake of the 1948 war. Territories in the Galilee and the Negev, villages and towns populated by Arabs, had, upon the decision of the Israeli Knesset, become a part of the Jewish state. As time went by, the international community grew accustomed to the situation and showed signs of offering it legitimacy. "Why shouldn't what worked before work now?," the asked themselves. What they deduced from this analogy was that the government must now wait for its action in Jerusalem to acquire "obsolescence," and in the intervening years continue taking steps to bolster its sovereignty, or else pursue international legitimacy via peace agreements with the Arab states, chiefly Jordan.

The international response to the legislation concerning East Jerusalem was not long in coming. And it was much more harshly worded than the Resolutions regarding the occupied territories, where Israel was not imposing its rule of law. Though they'd anticipated a protest from the UN, the severity of the reaction took Israel's policy-makers by surprise. The condemnations from the UN were echoed in demonstrations throughout the Muslim and Arab world, and even in East Jerusalem itself, where Arab residents came out to protest. Many countries, including some of Israel's friends, denounced these moves, saying the annexation of East Jerusalem was a violation of international law. Even the United States pointed out that "these moves can have no bearing on the fate of the holy places or Jerusalem's status."

The passage of UN Resolution 242, which called for 'territories in exchange for peace' (or 'the territories' – the exact meaning is a matter of semantic dispute) gave Israel time to reach peace accords with the Arab countries. However, when it came to Jerusalem, the situation was different: Israel tried to shut the door to any possibility of compromise in Jerusalem, particularly on the sensitive issue of the Old City and the holy places. This provoked tremendous anger. The UN General Assembly and Security Council passed a series of unanimous decisions decrying Israel's actions aimed at uniting Jerusalem as patently illegal, and called for an immediate halt to them. To this day, international opposition to a united Jerusalem under Israeli control has not abated, as shown, for one thing, by declarations made year after year by various UN institutions and other international organizations.

As the years have gone by, it has become readily apparent that the application of Israeli law to the territories of East Jerusalem did not bring about a repeat of past triumphs. Israel's success in the 1950s in getting the issue of West Jerusalem removed from the international agenda, and its achievements in the legitimization process for its rule in the city were not repeated, as the policy-makers had hoped. The conquest of the Old City led to a confrontation with the international community, and whatever international legitimacy Israel had managed to gain for its capital between 1949 and 1967 was undermined.

Opposition to the imposition of Israeli law on East Jerusalem also came from Israel's friends in the UN, primarily the United States. One reason for this was that Israel's moves left no further possibility for the arrangement which it had previously supported – 'functional internationalization' of the holy places. This idea had many staunch backers in the UN, the US among them. As noted, Eshkol had in mind Ben-Gurion's success in preventing the imposition of UN sanctions following his declaration of Jerusalem as Israel's capital in 1949, and anticipated that something similar would occur now. However, Eshkol failed to take into consideration the key difference between the two situations: This time, unlike in 1949, control over the Christian and Islamic holy places was at stake.

To Eshkol's credit, he was soon ready to admit his mistake and also tried to correct it. Just a month after the unification of the city, he decided to go back to the UN with Ben-Gurion's original proposal for 'functional internationalization of the holy places.' At Eshkol's instructions, this position was conveyed to Foreign Minister Abba Eban in advance of the important UN General Assembly debate on the status of Jerusalem that was held on July 14, 1967. In his speech to the General Assembly, Eban announced that Israel was prepared to consider internationalization of the holy places, noting that "for the first time in human history" a country that conquered the holy places in Jerusalem was ready to relinquish them. Israel's foreign minister proposed that an agreement be reached whereby the holy places would be transferred from Israel's control to that of an international or religious – Muslim or Christian – body. As he said: "In the holy places, which give Jerusalem its universal significance, exclusive and unilateral supervision and control [by Israel – M.A.] would be supplanted by agreed-upon arrangements that will safeguard the universal nature of the holy places."[41]

However, Israel's new proposal came too late, was too vague and was perceived by many as nothing more than a public relations exercise. While its proposal was entered into the record, practically speaking, Israel did nothing to advance the functional internationalization initiative. Had the prime minister announced three weeks earlier from the Knesset podium exactly the same things that the foreign minister told the UN General Assembly, the international reaction may have been quite different. Perhaps such a direct appeal to the Islamic lands and the Vatican, and the passage of special legislation in the Knesset, which would have separated the holy places from the rest of the Jerusalem issue, would have changed the face of the whole 'unification of Jerusalem' question. Given how things were done, the attempt three weeks later to rectify the missed chance was doomed to failure.

Over the next two years, until Levi Eshkol's death in 1969, Israel still periodically raised the idea of functional internationalization of the holy places. But in the 1970s, this proposal faded from the government agenda and was never mentioned again by any high-ranking officials.

CHAPTER THREE

The Struggle for East Jerusalem

Any part of the city that is not settled with Jews is in danger of being detached from the territory of Israel and delivered to Arab rule, and therefore the administrative ruling regarding municipal jurisdiction must be translated into action by means of construction in every part of this territory, beginning at its farthest edges.

(From the 1978 master plan for Jerusalem)

In the course of the 20th century, even as Jerusalem expanded exponentially from a total area of just a few square kilometers to encompass a much broader swath of territory, the Old City always remained the city's political, religious and historic center. Covering an area of just one square kilometer, throughout the ages it was the battlefield in dozens of wars, and a platform for both tremendous destruction and magnificent construction.

The Old City spreads out below Mount Moriah, also known as the Temple Mount, and is flanked by two steep valleys – the Ben-Hinnom Valley and the Kidron Valley. Around it are four more hills – Mount Zion and the Mount of Offense (*Har Hamashkhit* in Hebrew) to the south, and the Mount of Olives and Mount Scopus to the east. Its circumference is plainly marked by the wall built around it by the Turkish sultan Suleiman the Magnificent between the years 1537–41. Constructed partially from hewn stones dating from earlier periods, the Old City wall runs about four kilometers in length, and rise to a height of eight to fourteen meters. Suleiman left eleven gates in the wall; today, seven are open and four have been sealed up. Two of the most impressive are the Damascus Gate, located atop the site of the city's ancient Roman gate on the western side, and the Mercy Gate, the sealed gate in the eastern wall in front of the Temple Mount, facing the Mount of Olives.

In the mid-19th century, the city began to expand outside of the Old City walls. For the most part, the initiatives for this expansion came from the Jewish settlement organizations and from the Christian churches. In 1855, the cornerstone was laid for the first Jewish neighborhood outside the walls – Mishkenot Sha'ananim – and five years later, the Pravoslavic Church purchased a large plot outside the walls, the area now known as the Russian Compound.

The British Mandatory government was the first to see a need to plan the city's development in accordance with a modern master plan, and for this purpose it commissioned the British architect and engineer Sir William McClean, who had done similar work in Alexandria, Egypt. McClean was the first to outline what form the developing city should take, and his ideas were later echoed in numerous British, Jordanian and Israeli plans. He maintained that a distinction must be upheld between the old and new sections of the city: the Old City and its immediate surroundings would acquire the status of a historic site whose beauty must be preserved, and the modern city would develop to the north and west of the Old City while retaining a compact nature.

British planners who formulated master building plans during the Mandate period, including Patrick Geddes and Henry Kendall, relied on the principles set down by McClean and were careful to preserve the city's modest scale, to ban high-rise construction and preserve its valleys and green areas. Above all, they adhered to British governor Ronald Storrs' instruction to build exclusively with Jerusalem stone.

The outcome of the 1948 war spelled an urban disaster and severely disrupted the development of the Israeli city, which from this point on was bound by three constraints: It was completely cut off from the Old City and all the historic and religious sites; it was bisected by a hostile border and effectively transformed into a frontline town that was bordered on three sides by Jordan; and the need to absorb the mass wave of immigration in the 1950s, which led to the establishment of densely packed neighborhoods of inferior quality. Despite these constraints, the master plans of the 1950s still managed, well before 1967, to impart a governmental character to the capital.[1]

The reunification of Jerusalem in 1967 presented the policy-makers and city planners with an almost unprecedented challenge: To redefine the united city's character while grappling with the planning issues that arose in wake of the radically changed situation. Few places in the world contain such a large concentration of sites holy to the three major faiths within such a small area, or such an extraordinary collection of historic structures: city walls, churches, mosques, synagogues and archeological sites of great importance.

From 1970 on, political pressures changed the face of urban planning in Jerusalem, essentially turning it into political planning that was focused on a single objective: tightening Israel's grip on the extensive areas that were annexed to the city from the West Bank. Starting that year, dozens (!) of master plans were drawn up to further this aim. Unlike the 1968 master plan, which put the urban interest at the forefront, these later plans were intended to advance the goal of political control as set out by the government of Golda Meir.[2]

The shift in city planning policy in the 1970s gave rise to a clash between the need for sensitivity and gradualness in the city's development and the political desire to speedily establish of "facts on the ground." In addition, the need to invest resources in settling the eastern part of the city collided head-on with a need to invest resources in the city center and in the infrastructure for economic growth and employment.

Architect David Kroyanker, an expert on the history of urban planning in Jerusalem, had this to say about the impact of the political planning in the city, i.e., the attempt to solidify Israel's control of East Jerusalem:

> The boundary of the municipal jurisdiction was determined in 1967 by military men and politicians, on the basis of strategic and demographic considerations, and not by city planners focusing on clear urban needs . . . In the past twenty years, planning and implementation efforts were chiefly dedicated to the construction of the 'new Jerusalem' around the central city. These efforts were fueled by the political concept that sovereignty over the area is assured by means of a physical presence. Adherence to this belief perpetually clashed with fundamental planning concepts concerning the size of the city, its role and character and the need to preserve the values of landscape and aesthetics . . .
>
> The key question concerning the political, territorial and physical context of planning of Jerusalem, which has to do with the institution of a singleminded and comprehensive system of construction beyond the 1967 lines, is: To what extent have the construction projects and physical development precluded the possibility of dividing the city in the future? This question can also be turned around: By building these outpost neighborhoods and satellite towns, haven't past governments and the present government tied their own hands and blocked themselves and future Israeli governments from being able to find a diplomatic-territorial solution in Jerusalem that will also be acceptable to the other side?"[3]

Since 1967, and to a much greater degree since 1970, the territorial goal of Israeli policy in Jerusalem has been to 'strengthen Israel's control in East Jerusalem.' 'Control' – meaning 'Jewish settlement.' Not a single member of Golda Meir's government questioned whether, for the sake of preserving the city's unity, Jewish settlement was actually necessary in every part of the extensive territory that was annexed to the city from the West Bank. No one wondered if there was any connection between the massive construction of new neighborhoods and the chances of retaining the one square kilometer of the Old City as an inseparable part of the capital. And no one asked whether it was really best to invest billions of dollars in resources in the construction of new neighborhoods (unneeded neighborhoods, in the municipality's view), rather than using these resources to help boost Jerusalem economically and demographically.

From 1970 on, 'strengthening Jerusalem' no longer meant strengthening the city's economic infrastructure, but rather strengthening its territorial grip on dozens of completely superfluous square kilometers surrounding it.

Setting the City Boundaries: A Recipe for Endless Trouble

In June 1967, soon after the end of the war, the government made two 'big' decisions that shaped Jerusalem's future for the next forty years. The first, which was effectively a political decision, was to include the Old City (one square kilometer) within the framework of the united city; the second was to expand the city to three times its former size – from an area of about thirty-seven square kilometers to an area of about 120 square kilometers. My focus here is on the latter decision, the setting of the city's boundaries. Ostensibly just a matter of urban planning, at heart it was really a political decision – and perhaps the Israeli government decision of most profound consequence since 1967.

On June 11, 1967, at the first cabinet meeting at which the city's future was discussed, the lion's share of the session was devoted to a debate over the 'political' decision of whether or not to include the Old City within the framework of the 'unification of Jerusalem,' and the political and international ramifications of doing so. The second, so-called 'urban' decision concerning the geographical expansion of the city was hardly discussed at all. The members of Levi Eshkol's government were apparently well aware of the dramatic and historic significance of the first decision, but oblivious to the import of the second. To them, it was a marginal issue, a purely municipal matter, and so they did not take adequate time to consider the wider political implications. It was one of those 'evolving' decisions which afterwards no one could recall exactly how it came to pass. This is especially curious in light of the fact that the government's basic stance during that discussion was completely at odds with the subsequent decision. In time, this decision would be the major factor that altered the character of Jerusalem, and somewhat ironically, the main obstacle in the attempt to 'unify the city.'

At that same cabinet meeting, after much deliberation, the government voted to include 'East Jerusalem' in the united city. The interior and justice ministers felt that the meaning of the term 'East Jerusalem' was understood and required no clarification. The records of that cabinet meeting show that all the ministers believed that the city's expansion would be accomplished by annexing the one square kilometer of the Old City to the western city, or at most, uniting East Jerusalem (the 'Jordanian city') with the western city. The ministers never imagined that the territorial expansion would exceed the seven square kilometers that was the total area of East Jerusalem. And certainly none of them thought of expanding the city with territories taken from the West Bank.[4] Justice Minister Yaakov Shimshon Shapira, relying on the premise cited above, sought to 'unite' the two municipalities – the Israeli and the Jordanian. He even proposed the formation of a joint city council. Minister Eliahu Sasson said: "The Old City should be connected to the new city so that both parts may be supplied with common services";[5] while Interior Minister Moshe Haim Shapira spoke of "annexing the Jordanian city by order of the Interior Ministry, as a municipal act which, once in effect, will expand Jerusalem's borders and unite the two separate city administrations into a single administration."[6] The basic spirit of that cabinet meeting was expressed by Justice Minister Yaakov Shimshon Shapira, who said: "A 'Law of the Municipality of Jerusalem' should be enacted that would proclaim the annexation of 'East Jerusalem' and at the same time safeguard the holy places."[7]

Further indication that the term 'annexation' was used by all in the government to refer to the addition of either the area of the Old City alone or the Jordanian city comes from Meron Benvenisti, who was the official in charge of the administration of East Jerusalem under Mayor Teddy Kollek: "Many people, myself included, thought that this one-time event [the unification of the city – M.A.] applied to the one square kilometer that is the area of the Old City within the walls."[8]

If so, the obvious question is: How did the government's decision to annex East Jerusalem (seven square kilometers at most) turn into a massive annexation of seventy square kilometers of the West Bank to the city, including twenty-eight villages with thousands of Arab inhabitants?

At the ministerial committee meeting, most of the time was devoted to three "more important" issues – the legal process by which the city would be united, the status of the city's Arab residents and the Protection of the Holy Places law. When it came time to discuss the fourth issue – the matter of the city's boundaries – not only had no clear proposal been formulated, but those present also had no information about the number of Arab residents in all the villages that were due to be annexed to the city. Nor were the ministers presented with any serious forecasts regarding the urban and economic impact of expanding the city beyond the boundaries of the Jordanian city. The annexation of 28 villages, in which the level of development was extremely low, necessitated the creation of an enormous urban infrastructure.

The ministers were not shown any maps, and therefore had only the faintest idea about the area to be annexed. For example, they were completely unaware that the "additional territory" was populated by approximately 30,000 Arabs in 28 villages, which would now be added to the approximately 40,000 Arab residents of East Jerusalem. They didn't know that this addition also included jurisdictional areas of Bethlehem and Ramallah. Nor were they aware that this annexation would also bring the Shuafat refugee camp, home to about 4,000 refugees supported by international aid organizations, under Jersualem's jurisdiction. These refugees had been removed from the Old City a year earlier at the order of King Hussein, who didn't want them to be part of his Jerusalem. Now Teddy Kollek was going to get them as part of a 'package deal.' The ministers were not cognizant of the economic implications of annexing these territories as far as the need "to provide conditions, services and infrastructure equal to that of urban Jerusalem"; from now on, the State of Israel would bear responsibility for services throughout the area and have to build water and sewage systems, electrical networks, roads and sidewalks in the annexed villages. It would also be obligated to compensate farmers for their losses in years of drought, and all this from the city and state coffers.[9]

Teddy Kollek, while stunned by the scope of the annexation, which he opposed, never imagined at the time that the addition of this territory from the West Bank would utterly change the face of his city. Before long, these territories would be sanctified in the Israeli consciousness as an integral part of united Jerusalem.

From 1967 to 1969, Teddy Kollek and Levi Eshkol tried, mostly in vain, to play down this major territorial expansion to areas that had never had any connection to Jerusalem. In fact, the first master plan, drawn up in 1968, designated these areas as 'green' rural spaces. However, before long, the fear of a 'division of the city' led, in the 1970s, to a decision to build Jewish neighborhoods throughout this territory as a way of asserting 'Israeli control.' The annexation of West Bank territory transformed Jerusalem from a city of thirty-seven square kilometers to a city of about 120 square kilometers, making it the largest city in Israel in terms of physical size – bigger than Tel Aviv and Haifa put together. In the 1970s, Israel invested a fortune in building Jewish neighborhoods in the annexed areas so that these would be 'united' with the city of Jerusalem. The settlement enterprise in these territories, which was unnecessary from the start, quickly became the largest such project in scope and budget, outstripping all the rest of the Israeli settlement effort in the West Bank.

1969: The Plan that Changed the Face of Jerusalem

In December 1969, the plan that would most radically alter the face of

Jerusalem was born. This was the Rogers Plan, the first peace plan for the Middle East ever put forward by the United States, named for the US Secretary of State, William Rogers. The plan's objective was to obtain peace between Egypt and Israel, based on the principle of 'territories in exchange for peace.' In regard to Jerusalem, the draft submitted to the Israeli government reflected a continuation of the American position that held **"the city must remain united."** However, the document also contained something new. This was the section that stated: **"We believe Jerusalem should be a unified city . . . and there should be roles for both Israel and Jordan in the civic, economic and religious life of the City."** It included made clear that the United States "cannot accept any unilateral actions by any party to decide the final status of the city" and that it continues to view East Jerusalem as 'occupied territory.'

The Rogers Plan, which hinted very clearly at the possibility of a division of sovereignty in the city, drew a swift reaction from the government of Golda Meir: Not only did the cabinet vehemently reject the plan, it also resolved to take action to point up its opposition to any territorial concessions in Jerusalem. To this end, Golda Meir, in her capacity as chairperson of the Ministerial Committee for Jerusalem Affairs, convened a special session in May 1970 to begin re-planning Jerusalem.

The new guiding principle was extensive settlement in areas of East Jerusalem combined with accelerated development and construction. On August 30, 1970, the Israeli government approved the inter-ministerial committee's recommendations that Israel move to strengthen its territorial grip on East Jerusalem.

The committee's recommendations were based on a number of political motives, all antithetical to the principles of sound urban planning: the construction of Jewish neighborhoods throughout the open green area designated as 'rural' in the 1968 master plan; the construction of Jewish neighborhoods in the northern part of Jerusalem, the region that in the 1968 master plan was designated for Arabs; and limiting the spread of Arab construction. The upshot of all this was a steep increase in government spending on construction at the expense of investment in industry and tourism; the abrupt cessation of the process of equalizing services and infrastructure for Arabs; and the suspension of the preparation of building plans for the Arab neighborhoods and the issuing of appropriation orders for 12,280 dunams of Arab lands in northern and southern Jerusalem (the areas that became the neighborhoods of Neve Yaakov, Ramot, East Talpiyot and Gilo).[10]

The final key objective in the new plan propounded by Golda Meir's government was to strengthen the city's Jewish character by doubling the rate of Jewish population growth in Jerusalem. Ministers vied to outdo one another with baseless promises to boost the Jewish population in

Jerusalem. Some spoke of doubling the number of new immigrants who would come to live in the city, while others promised to transfer the government offices located in Tel Aviv along with their thousands of employees to Jerusalem.[11]

The government's self-persuasion was so complete that Construction and Housing Minister Ze'ev Sharef vowed to build thousands of new housing units in East Jerusalem for the tens of thousands of Jews expected to flood into the capital. As noted, these new neighborhoods were slated to go up in areas previously designated for use by the Arab population. Not one member of the cabinet remembered that much of this land was never meant for residential use but rather as green areas. Nor did anyone remember that the addendum to the recommendations of the committee that dealt with the city's boundaries explicitly mentioned the possibility of converting these areas into a separate regional council. As a matter of fact, all the government needed to do at that point was to vote to grant these areas the status of a 'regional council,' and that would have been sufficient to block the dreaded possibility of a division of Jerusalem.

No one in the government asked where the enormous budgets required for building this massive amount of new housing would come from, and at the expense of what. No one thought of checking with the Jerusalem municipality to see whether there was actually any need for more housing units. Had they taken the trouble to look into it, they would have found out that the city already had thousands of empty housing units, as well as thousands of dunams available for construction.

The government's decision provoked an outcry in Israel. Public figures, politicians, intellectuals and ordinary citizens vociferously protested, the general argument being, as an editorial in one of the daily newspapers put it: "Neither this or that neighborhood or a highway here or there will affect the form of the political accord in the future. It will be determined by the balance of power in the region, by the international situation and by Israel's diplomatic ability."[12] Similarly, the author Amos Ayalon wrote:

> An air of franticness currently pervades Jerusalem. Its source lies in the panic aroused by the Rogers Plan. Our political leadership is suddenly frightened of an imposed accord . . . It's as if the rulers said to themselves: Better an ugly Jerusalem that is still ours. The planning caution that was a hallmark of the authorities [largely thanks to the alertness of Teddy Kollek] since the city's unification in 1967 has been tossed to the winds. Gone is the great aesthetic sensitivity of the early days . . . Our rulers, whose thinking was shaped in the 1920s and 1930s when every plowed dunam was a conquered dunam, are now convinced that a Jewish neighborhood atop the Nabi Samuel hill will propel Mr. Rogers to withdraw his objection to substantial territorial

changes . . . No neighborhood or road will help us hold onto areas that are beyond the Green Line . . . The aesthetic evil presently being cooked up in the Housing Ministry is immeasurably more malignant because of the panicky secrecy surrounding the various projects . . . The dictum that patriotism is the scoundrel's last refuge is apparently being applied as the ultimate justification of the lousy city planner who subjugates aesthetic sensitivity to what he accepts, without sufficient criticism, as 'a supreme national duty.'[13]

Much criticism was also heard from officials who were directly affected by the need to implement the decision, above all Teddy Kollek, with whom the government had not consulted at all. The mayor made it dramatically clear that the Jerusalem municipality was completely opposed to the changes in the development plans for the city, since new neighborhoods were not needed in order to strengthen it. He also warned that the government's hasty and shortsighted decision could cause serious urban damage and weaken the city economically and politically. Kollek, who also served as the chairman of the local planning and building committee, announced that no building plan in the city would be approved without his signature, and that he refused to sign any plans that called for expansion into the peripheral areas of East Jerusalem.

Prime Minister Golda Meir countered that planning in Jerusalem was a political, rather than a municipal, matter, and that his refusal to sign off on the plan would not alter the national policy in Jerusalem. The Construction and Housing Minister, Ze'ev Sharef, elaborated on this at a press conference, explaining that the international situation that put the Jerusalem issue on the table obligated Israel to take symbolic as well as concrete steps to prove to the world that it was determined to hold onto all the territories in East Jerusalem. In these extraordinary circumstances, explained Sharef, there was no cause to abide by the Planning and Construction Law – 1965, which required that detailed plans be submitted to the local committee for approval. Instead, it was the time "to act and not to talk."[14]

Within days, dozens of bulldozers were already priming the areas designated for the new neighborhoods. This activity was carried out in violation of the law, without the required permits. The Housing Ministry had no detailed plans whatsoever regarding the character of the neighborhoods, the anticipated scope of construction or the costs entailed.[15] The Justice Ministry, which was aware of the legal violation and wished to circumvent Kollek and the Jerusalem municipality's opposition to the construction, formulated 'emergency regulations' that abrogated all authority from the local planning and building committee and transferred it to the government.

Meron Benvenisti describes the parallel between this construction project in East Jerusalem which was dubbed 'Operation Fact,' and another historic project that was also aimed at establishing facts in the field – the pre-State policy of the Jewish Yishuv known as 'Operation Tower and Stockade':

> The new 'Operation Fact' began at a feverish pace. Within a few months, the skeletons of the buildings had sprung up. The outposts of the 1970s joined the outposts of the 'Tower and Stockade' settlements of the 1930s. Israel's leaders proved that an entire generation after the founding of the sovereign Jewish state, the policy of 'a dunam here and a dunam there' is alive and well.[16]

During the initial weeks of the development works the Construction and Housing Ministry enlisted a group of well-known architects to prepare detailed plans for the new neighborhoods. When the architects were given the guidelines regarding the desired location and size of the neighborhoods, they unanimously announced that, for reasons of conscience, they would not draw up the plans. They called on the government to backtrack at once from its intention to build in the green areas, and demanded that it adhere to the 1968 master plan. The architects' refusal also stemmed from their professional judgment – The 'Tower and Stockade' method, characterized by improvisation and a lack of planning, was now obsolete, and totally inappropriate for the capital city of a sovereign state.

This episode, popularly known as 'the architects' revolt,' caused a big stir in Israel. The government's response to the architects' charges, including the 'professional' argument, was not long in coming: "Yes, we are using the old policy. However, it proved its effectiveness. Thanks to it, we have come this far. What you preach has yet to be proven. We are not taking chances and are not prepared to experiment in relation to Jerusalem. Jerusalem is too important."[17]

The overwhelming public opposition took the government by surprise and had a sobering effect on some of its members. The construction and housing minister and the justice minister decided to delay the project and try to talk with the municipality about reducing the scope of the plan. For a moment, it even seemed that the government regretted its rash decision and was retreating from the idea of building the outer neighborhoods. But then renewed international interest in Jerusalem spurred Golda Meir's cabinet to re-embrace its original position all the more fiercely.

Granted, the Israeli government's negative stance effectively neutralized the Rogers initiative; however, the large-scale appropriation of Arab land put the Jerusalem issue squarely on the international agenda, and with greater urgency. At the meeting of the United Nations General

Assembly on February 16, 1971, the United States joined in the denunciation of Israel's moves in Jerusalem. State Department spokesman Robert McCloskey said that the United States condemns the land appropriations and calls upon Israel not to construct new neighborhoods in these areas, adding: "Until a custody arrangement for Jerusalem is found, which is essentially a part of the negotiation, it is our belief that any unilateral act that could be construed as altering the city's status is unacceptable."[18]

The Americans were confident that this firmly worded statement would be enough to block the plan. But then it didn't know the Golda Meir government all that well. The American condemnation sparked an uproar in the cabinet, which reacted by proclaiming that, in light of McCloskey's statements, it had no choice but to go ahead with its original decision, and that the construction projects would be carried out wherever the government saw fit, albeit on a slightly smaller scale.

Now the government went on the counterattack against critics of the plan, openly accusing them of "a lack of patriotism."[19] The frenzy of these allegations prompted opponents of the plan, most prominently Teddy Kollek, to hastily withdraw their objections. Kollek signed off on the plans, and by late February 1971, the plan that would change the face of Jerusalem was underway.

The project to massively expand Jerusalem was not conceived by a team of experts but by politicians who viewed it more as a 'symbol' than a 'plan.' The legend of the early Zionists conquering a dunam here and a dunam there merged with the legend of Jerusalem that had to be conquered anew. David Kroyanker aptly describes the difficulty faced by the policy-makers in Jerusalem when myth collided with reality in the city:

> One of the basic and most difficult problems that the city fathers and planners are facing today and will continue to face in the future is the problem of the gap between Jerusalem's picturesque image in the eyes of the world and the legend that has attached to it over the centuries, and the present reality. The shattering of this myth is often accompanied by 'Jerusalem Syndrome,' which is a psychological reaction to the mystical religious experience undergone by devout believers who come to the city . . . [20]

New Planning Guidelines:
Territorial Control and Demographic Hegemony

From the early 1970s to the present, Jerusalem has had no real master plan. While numerous city plans have been proposed over the years, none ever received formal approval or legal validity and thus could more accurately

be called 'conceptual plans.' In fact, the last plan for the city to be officially approved and which is still valid today is Master Plan no. 62 from
1959 (!).

The plethora of plans put forward since 1970 created much bewilder-
ment among the national and municipal officials charged with
implementing them. These plans were lacking most of the elements that
are a part of master plans in most cities in the world. Most glaringly absent
was a consideration of the balance between urban, economic, social and
architectural aspects and the residents' quality of life. And whenever these
topics were cited in some of the plans, it was only as a flimsy attempt to
make the plan look better.

Amnon Niv, who was the city engineer in the 1990s, described the
development process in the 'city without planning' as follows:

> Processes that in a regular city last for decades or centuries occurred in
> Jerusalem in less than a generation. Doing often took precedence over
> thorough planning and many problems remain unresolved. Ad hoc deci-
> sions of great significance were made, without any possibility of
> consolidating a clear and unequivocal outlook as to the city's structure
> and character. Planning was often guided by politicians who did not con-
> sider what kind of physical structure was desirable for the city . . . [21]

Ever since then, all the 'temporary' plans in Jerusalem have been subject
to two chief guiding principles: achieving territorial control over a
maximum of territory; and achieving demographic hegemony so as to
attain a 'uni-national' city.

In the various plans, the first principle – maximal territorial control –
was interpreted as the need to establish as many Jewish neighborhoods as
possible in the eastern part of the city. This objective is expressed quite
clearly in the master plan (which was not approved) from 1978:

> Any area in the city that is not settled with Jews is in danger of being
> detached from the territory of Israel and delivered to Arab rule, and
> therefore the administrative ruling regarding municipal jurisdiction
> must be translated into action by means of construction throughout
> every part of this territory, beginning at its farthest edges.[22]

According to this outlook, the city's unity would be guaranteed not by
military force or diplomatic legitimacy, but rather by means of massive
Jewish settlement in the eastern areas of Jerusalem. Architect David
Kroyanker called this "a perpetuation of the Zionist policy that for over
a century was based on the idea that Jewish control over territory may be
ensured solely by Jewish settlement."[23]

The aim of achieving demographic hegemony, which has been at the basis of every city plan since 1972, was understood by the policy-makers to mean preserving a constant 'demographic balance' between Jews and Arabs in the city. Yisrael Kimhi, who was director of the planning policy department in the Jerusalem municipality in the 1970s, viewed demographic hegemony as a prerequisite for obtaining the 'unity of the city':

> One of the cornerstones of the planning process in Jerusalem is the demographic question. The city's growth and the preservation of the demographic balance among the ethnic groups in it were the subject of a decision of the Israeli government [a decision of the Golda Meir government, see below – M.A.]. This decision regarding the city's growth rate is currently one criterion for the success of firmly establishing Jerusalem as the capital of Israel.[24]

This principle, too, like its predecessor, does not exist in any master plan for other cities in Israel or elsewhere, as it constitutes a policy of discrimination against minorities.

The experience of the past forty years has proven that city planning based on development that openly aims to increase the Jewish majority in Jerusalem is nothing but a 'vicious circle': An increase in the proportion of the Arab population stimulates an expanded target growth rate in the city, in the hopes of boosting the Jewish majority; this in turn spurs an acceleration in construction, in order to meet the needs of this anticipated growth; the construction boom requires cheap labor and hence encourages an increase in the city's Arab population, as Arabs flock to fill the jobs in the industry; and so on and so forth. Thus, the policy that derived from worry about an increase of the city's Arab minority yielded just the opposite of the intended results.

While, in the first years following the unification of the city, the Eshkol government focused primarily on establishing territorial facts that would prevent the possibility of the Old City (one square kilometer) being cut off from West Jerusalem, from 1970 onward, the Meir government sought to achieve territorial objectives that comprised the whole of East Jerusalem (sixty-three square kilometers), with the aim of preventing a re-division of the city.

Many questions should have been asked about the impact of this ambitious, practically utopian, policy of promoting extensive Jewish settlement in parts of East Jerusalem and of establishing an additional, outer ring of neighborhoods: At the expense of what other needs was funding directed at all this new construction and development? What effect would this massive expansion have on Israel's ability to achieve its primary objective of controlling the Old City? It wasn't until the late

1970s, when most of the new neighborhoods were almost completed, that the government prepared a master plan (1978) that retroactively 'explained' the need for them: "Every part of the city that is not settled with Jews is in danger of being cut off from Israel and delivered to Arab rule."[25] When Mayor Teddy Kollek, during a discussion of the plan by the city council, asked whether the expansion of territorial control wouldn't harm the character of the city, its uniqueness as a capital and both the Jewish and Arab residents, his deputy mayor, Likud member Yehoshua Matza, wrote in response: "The national political considera-tion must be the primary consideration, with the urban consideration only coming after it."[26] In this same spirit, the government responded to the economic experts who questioned whether the allocation of vast sums to the construction of these neighborhoods wouldn't adversely impact the city's economic growth, in terms of industry and tourism, especially. To those who wished to leave these areas as 'green spaces' – as parks and natural landscapes – the government's reply was that under the present circumstances, the national-political consideration had to trump any environmental concerns.

In the early 1970s, work on the construction of the outer ring of neigh-borhoods proceeded at a rapid pace. Within a few years, Jerusalem was utterly changed: From a compact city in which the distance between the northernmost and southernmost neighborhoods was just 7 kilometers, it became a sprawling metropolis with 16 kilometers separating its northern and southern tips. The new neighborhoods were attached to the city by long roads, giving the appearance, as one planner put it, "of balloons tied to it by a string."

The situation of the outer neighborhoods right at the edge of the munic-ipal territory left other areas further inside open to extensive Arab construction. Ironically, the construction of the Jewish neighborhoods, which was intended to create a Jewish territorial continuum, ended up creating an unwanted 'Arab territorial continuum,' which raised the threat of the eventual detachment of the outer ring neighborhoods from the city. The new neighborhoods became 'islands' of Jewish settlement surrounded by Arab settlement. At the end of the 1970s, Arab neighborhoods covered about 40 percent of the territory of East Jerusalem, while the area covered by the new Jewish neighborhoods did not exceed 20 percent. This situa-tion gave rise to the 'paradox of the Jerusalem ghetto' – Arabs felt surrounded on every side by Jewish neighborhoods that were closing in on them, while Jews in the new neighborhoods also felt surrounded on every side by Arab neighborhoods.

Today, more than 30 years after its launching, one can say that the project of building the outer ring neighborhoods throughout East Jerusalem did not achieve its stated objective of territorial control in the eastern parts of the city. Jewish settlement currently encompasses about a third of the area of East Jerusalem; Arab neighborhoods are spread out across the other two-thirds, and are home to approximately 240,000 residents, who comprise a 60 percent majority in the eastern part of the city. The objective of cutting the Arabs in the city off from the West Bank by means of surrounding them with Jewish neighborhoods was not achieved either. The city's Arabs continued to form every kind of attachment – political, cultural and economic – with the West Bank. Above all, this failed policy inflicted severe urban damage, having drained all the vibrancy from the city center, eliminated the capital's close-knit atmosphere and completely stymied economic growth due to the allocation of vast resources for – unmet – political aims.

The satirist and journalist B. Michael had this to say about what happened to Israel's capital as a result of this misguided policy:

> Even the biggest lovers of Israel will have to admit that twenty years of political construction have expanded the city to grotesque proportions, so that it now appears as if Schwarzenegger's torse was screwed onto the legs of Rumpelstiltskin. Like a weird hybrid of Cambridge and Philadelphia. On top of a city center that's about the size of a pea, and a shrunken urban infrastructure, there now lies an urban monster of half a million residents, with the distance between the city center and the outermost neighborhood about the same as the distance between Dizengoff Square and Herzliya Pituah.[27]

Reducing the Arab Hold on the Territory

The difficulty in achieving the ambitious territorial goals set forth by the Golda Meir government led policy-makers to conclude that the effort to enlarge areas of Jewish settlement was not sufficient, and that the scope of Arab settlement and Arab hold on areas of East Jerusalem had to be reduced as well. To this end, starting from the mid-1970s, Israel adopted a policy intended to shrink the Arabs' hold on the territory while simultaneously encouraging them to quit the city. In typically blunt style, Mayor Teddy Kollek remarked that the government's aim was "to make life difficult for the Arabs, not to permit them to build, so maybe they'll leave of their own accord."[28]

Kollek aptly described the government's policy towards the city's Arabs:

> Whatever the governments of Israel could do to make life difficult for the Arabs in East Jerusalem, they did; whatever they could do . . . to

prevent them from developing, from expanding, from building, from improving their quality of housing, they did.[29]

Amir Cheshin, the mayor's advisor on Arab affairs, acknowledged that "the planning and building laws in East Jerusalem are based on a policy of placing obstacles in the way of planning in the Arab sector."[30] Cheshin maintained that the reasoning behind this was that "if too many new houses are permitted to be built in the Arab neighborhoods, this will translate into there being 'too many' Arabs in the city." The idea was to populate East Jerusalem with as many Jews as possible and to get as many Arabs as possible to move out of the city.

Elinoar Barzaki, who headed the Jerusalem district in the Construction and Housing Ministry, and later became the Jerusalem city engineer, also noted that the way to reduce the proportion of Arabs in the city's population was by reducing the 'housing potential': "The government's wish to reduce the ratio of Arabs in the city (to just 30 percent, say), is apparent in the growth potential provided in the plans for construction and residential capacity for Arabs."[31]

Here the question must be asked: How could such a blatantly discriminatory policy have been implemented in the capital city of liberal and democratic Israel, which has freedom of speech, a solid court system and laws meant to ensure justice and equality? And the answer is: By means of governmental prerogatives used in such a way as to make the Israeli public, the courts and the media view these moves as 'legal.' The planning and development policy relied on a host of such tools: land appropriations; delays in the preparation of neighborhood master plans; reductions in the allotted percentages of building capacity; prevention of the construction of Arab neighborhoods; curtailing the granting of building permits; thwarting the development of infrastructure; and actively fighting illegal Arab construction.

The invocation of the governmental prerogative to appropriate is a most extraordinary step, and therefore severely restricted by law. The law says that such a step may be taken only when there exists a 'public need' that justifies it. But the law does not specify just what constitutes a 'public need,' given that the government has much leeway in defining this. For this reason, Israeli government decisions to appropriate land in Jerusalem have always been officially defined as 'appropriations to serve public needs,' and were backed by the courts, which accepted the argument that "the development and settlement of Jerusalem" qualifies as a "public interest,"[32] and that these appropriations were for the sake of "the public good."' However, the reality appears to be that in Jerusalem, the term 'public' refers exclusively to the Jewish majority and not to the Arab minority.

Thus it is no stretch to say that the appropriation of lands in East Jerusalem really derived from a 'political need' and not the 'public interest.' From the urban perspective, the Jewish neighborhoods that were to be built on these lands were completely unnecessary – Municipal records from the 1970s show that a shortage of housing was a problem for the city's Arab population alone; and Jews could build on lands that were abundantly available in the west of the city. Elinoar Barzaki openly admitted as much, acknowledging that the purpose of the appropriations was to establish control in Arab territory, and not an answer to a housing shortage.[33]

Israeli civil rights organizations and attorneys frequently protested against the land appropriations, citing the relevant sections of international law that prohibit the confiscation of private property in 'occupied territory' (apart from appropriations necessary for the needs of the occupying army) for 'political' purposes or for the sake of 'colonization' of the occupied territory.[34] However, the courts always accepted the position of the Israeli government, which said that East Jerusalem was not 'occupied territory,' and therefore decided not to intervene in what the municipality and the government termed 'public' and 'planning-related' interests.

Israel's governments always made sure that about 5 to 10 percent of each appropriation consisted of Jewish land. Then, when impelled to justify the move, they strenuously pointed out that the appropriated lands were not solely Arab, and that the move was intended to serve the interests of the city's population as a whole. However, not one of these land appropriations has ever served the Arab public; not a single neighborhood has been built for them in these areas. Of the approximately 40,000 housing units that were built on appropriated lands, not a single apartment was designated for Arabs.

The second tool used by successive governments to promote the policy of weakening the Arabs' grip on Jerusalem was footdragging in the preparation and approval of development plans for Arab areas in East Jerusalem.

In 1967, the government annulled all of the Jordanian building plans on the basis of which permits had been issued to residents of Jerusalem and the surrounding countryside, with the promise that within a short time it would prepare a new master plan for East Jerusalem. In the meantime, East Jerusalem was left without any planning framework. In such a situation, it was impossible to develop road, sewage and water infrastructure in the Arab neighborhoods, or to issue building permits to their residents. The only option available to residents of the Arab neighborhoods who wished to submit requests for building permits was to invoke section 78 of the Planning and Construction Law – 1965, which stipulated that requests for private construction could be submitted in a locality where there was no master plan, with approval being subject to the authorities' judgment. Ostensibly, Jerusalem's Arab residents should not have had any trouble, therefore, applying for and receiving building permits. But the reality was another story entirely. The vast majority of requests were turned down: Out of over 30,000 requests for building permits submitted by Arab residents of East Jerusalem from 1967 to 2001, only about 3,100 (10 percent) were approved.[35] And the few requests that were approved were first subjected to a bureaucratic runaround lasting several years on average. In this untenable situation, with a quarter of Jerusalem's residents unable to build their homes legally, the Arab areas became a veritable 'Wild West' of illegal construction, to an extent that could preclude any prospect of proper development there in the future. Ill-equipped to combat all the illegal construction, the Jerusalem municipality has repeatedly asked the government over the years to facilitate the drafting of master plans for East Jerusalem, only to be disappointed each time.

Discriminatory Planning

The Israeli government never officially acknowledged the political motives behind its planning policy in Jerusalem. Instead, three justifications were offered: The two populations have 'different needs'; each population prefers a different type of construction; and the discrepancy in the level of development is the 'fault' of the Jordanian authorities who neglected East Jerusalem. However, a close examination of the facts shows that all three arguments are baseless, as 'rational' as they may sound to the general Israeli public which is not acquainted with the details, identifies with the idea of the 'unity of the city' and, understandably, perceives the Arab minority as an element that seeks to divide the city.

The first argument presupposes differential growth rates in each population, and is based on the 'population growth forecast for the city' as determined by the government. But it was the government that 'decided' that the Arab population cannot exceed a certain percentage of the overall population, and this figure was used to calculate their housing needs from then on.

The second justification for the discriminatory policy relies on the assumption that the Jewish population prefers "high-saturation" construction, while the Arab population prefers rural-style construction. This contention is also without foundation. True, before 1967, Jerusalem's Arab neighborhoods still had a rural ambience, but after the unification of the city, they became thoroughly urban neighborhoods, since they bordered on Jewish neighborhoods with an 'urban' character. In time, each of the 'villages' that were annexed to Jerusalem subsequently attained the size of an average Jewish neighborhood in Jerusalem (from 10,000–30,000 residents).

The third argument cited by Israeli governments in order to explain its failure to provide equal services and infrastructure development in East Jerusalem is mismanagement by the previous Jordanian government. Jordan, they say, did not conduct a proper registration of the lands there and turned a blind eye to the deterioration of infrastructure throughout the years of its rule in East Jerusalem. The Israeli assertion that the Jordanian government or the Arab residents themselves were remiss in not systematically parceling and registering the land is completely untrue: The Jordanian government acted at the time as would be expected of an enlightened government, and carried out a 'revolution' in the matter of land registration, overturning centuries-old arrangements: A concerted effort was made to divide the area into plots and subplots on the basis of Mandatory data so residents could prove ownership and obtain building permits. In 1967, Israel voided the detailed Jordanian land registration system in East Jerusalem and has declined ever since to institute a new system there, thus enabling it to retain oversight during the planning process while also preventing the registration of Palestinian land owner-ship. Those who complain about neglected infrastructure conveniently forget that Jordanian rule in Jerusalem lasted just nineteen years, while Israel has now ruled that part of the city for 40 years – sufficient time to develop infrastructure and services as would be expected of a modern nation.

The Israeli governments' chief concern in East Jerusalem hasn't been how to enable Jerusalem's Arabs to build, but rather how to prevent them from building – legally, and especially, illegally. To illustrate what sort of ordeal individuals who seek building permits are subjected to, I present the following account of a story I've been following for a few years now. It was first brought to my attention by a Palestinian acquaintance.

Fatima (she asked that her real name not be used), an elderly Arab woman from East Jerusalem, has been living for decades, since the period of Jordanian rule, in a lovely two-story house with a garden at the foot of Mount Scopus. Her home, like the few other houses nearby, sits in an area that now resembles a tiny Arab enclave hemmed in by the Hebrew University, the French Hill neighborhood and the Hyatt Hotel.

In 1967, shortly after she was issued a blue Israeli identity card, Fatima, then a young woman, wanted to add a third floor to her house and so she submitted a request for a building permit. Knowing that under Jordanian rule there was no problem in obtaining building permits in areas outside the Old City, she expected to receive the permit within a short time. However, the Jerusalem municipal officials to whom she addressed her request explained to her that the Jordanian plans for the area had now been canceled, but they promised her that soon, when a new plan for the area where her house was situated was completed, she would be able to get the permits.

A few years went by and Fatima waited patiently for this pledge to be kept, but the promised new plans were not forthcoming. So Fatima went to the municipality to inquire about the reason for the delay. The clerk she spoke to explained to her that since the Jordanian building plan was canceled, and an alternative Israeli plan was still not ready, the plan currently in effect was the 1959 Master Plan (no. 59). In this plan, the area where she lived was defined as 'rural residential area no. 5,' and according to the Planning and Construction Law – 1965, construction in an area so designated could not exceed two stories. Therefore, the municipality representative informed Fatima, her plot and those of her Arab neighbors in this enclave, was supposed to remain rural in character, i.e., with sparse and low construction. Fatima wanted to know how it was possible, now that her home had been annexed to the city, that its status had not changed from rural to urban. To which the clerk replied: "It won't be much longer. Just be patient."

A few years later, Fatima noticed that just north of her house, no more than several dozen meters away, Jews were building three and even four-story buildings. Now she found herself living right next door to a new Jewish neighborhood – Givat Shapira (better known as French Hill). One year passed, and then another, and Fatima saw that to the east of her house, just a few dozen meters away, the buildings of the Hebrew University were rising to a height of five or six stories. A few more years passed, and right near her home, the eight-story Hyatt Hotel was built. And whenever Fatima asked someone at the municipality the meaning of this discrimination, she was given the same explanation: The university, the hotel and the Jewish neighborhood surrounding her house on every side came under a different classification – 'urban' – and could therefore build as high as eight stories.

During all this time, some of Fatima's Arab neighbors took matters into their own hands and built without waiting for building permits. Fatima, a law-abiding citizen, refused to be tempted into building illegally. She also repeatedly turned down offers from representatives of the Hebrew University and from other Israeli entrepreneurs and prospective buyers who continually tried to purchase the land on which she lives. "Where would I go? I'm staying in Jerusalem and will stay here until the day I die," she told them. Even now, every couple of years Fatima checks with the municipality to see whether the new plan for the area upon which her house is built is ready, and each time she comes back disappointed.

Meanwhile, Fatima has grown older. She's now in her seventies and the additional floor she wished to build 40 years ago for her offspring has yet to materialize. Her children and grandchildren have left the house to live in the A-Ram neighborhood outside of Jerusalem, though they continue to register their home address in Jerusalem. Fatima chose not to break the law, and she's still waiting for that permit.

How East Jerusalem became the Wild West

Successive Israeli governments employed a policy of restricting the scope of Arab construction in East Jerusalem so as to prod as many Arabs as possible to leave the city, and thereby reduce their numbers. However, as noted above, not only did this policy fail to achieve its goal, it often brought about results that were completely at odds with the national interest and with Jerusalem's best interest in the urban context; the policy aimed at limiting Arab population growth in the city ended up encouraging the city's Arabs to remain and to cling all the more strongly to their lands.

From 1967 to 1970, under the Levi Eshkol government, a large number of Arabs abandoned the city, continuing a trend that had gained steam during the period of Jordanian rule. However, this trend was reversed in the 1970s, in wake of the implementation of Israel's territorial expansion policy in the eastern part of the city. This shift may be attributed to a host of causes, chief among them the economic factor – the massive Israeli construction activity in East Jerusalem created abundant sources of livelihood for the city's Arabs and thus prompted them to remain in the city. Another explanation, though, has to do with the political dynamic: Once Israel made construction in Jerusalem a 'political' issue, employing it as a governmental tool to push out the Arabs, the Palestinians also made the issue a 'political' one. As a counter-move to the Israeli policy, they proclaimed a policy of *sumud* – of clinging steadfastly to their land.

Faisal Husseini once described the struggle in Jerusalem as 'mirror-image *sumud*': "You are the strong, ruling side," he once said to me. "Generosity on your part would be met with generosity on our part; readiness on your part to cede part of Jerusalem would be met with readiness on our part to cede part of Jerusalem. Your attempts to remove us from the city by means of 'establishing facts on the ground' are met with the 'establishment of facts on the ground' by us as well." When I asked him how the Arabs went about establishing these so-called facts, he replied:

"We are the facts in the field. We have more children than you do. We build just as many houses as you, illegally of course, since we do not recognize your law. You want to expel us from the city, and therefore

we cling to the land and do not abandon the city. Sumud, clinging to
the land, is our answer to your 'establishment of facts'!"[36]

Indeed, Israel has built approximately 40,000 housing units in East
Jerusalem, with the encouragement and aid of the government, and practically doubled the number of Jewish housing units in the city since 1967.
At the same time, the Palestinians have illegally built – under much poorer
conditions and without public aid – approximately 15,000–20,000
housing units, and doubled the number of Arab housing units since 1967.[37]
And thus East Jerusalem became a Wild West in which each man is a law
unto himself and does as he pleases while completely ignoring Israeli law.
The designation of land as public space, industrial zones or residential
areas, which is usually left to planners, experts and government authorities, is determined here by residents on the basis of personal convenience,
with total disregard for the negative urban consequences of the construction.

In retrospect, one can say that in the battle over construction in East
Jerusalem, there are no winners, but only losers – both Jews and Arabs.
But the biggest loser of all is the city of Jerusalem. The Israeli policy of
territorial control caused great damage to Jerusalem's character. However,
this damage dwarfs in comparison to the irreversible environmental
damage caused to East Jerusalem by the illegal Arab construction; this
construction has changed the face of this part of the city and could easily
undermine any future chance for rational planning in these areas.

The Interior Ministry and the Jerusalem municipality are taking
numerous steps to try to halt the illegal construction in East Jerusalem:
Large budgets have been allocated to the issue (In 2004, the inspection and
demolition budget amounted to approximately $1.25 million) and dozens
of inspectors, police officers, lawyers, city officials and even helicopters
are engaged in enforcement efforts. But all to little avail.

The gravity of the situation and the cumulative urban damage has led
the Israeli authorities to impose a series of sanctions on violators, from
monetary fines to prison sentences to the demolition of illegally
constructed buildings. But none of these sanctions appears to be impeding
the Palestinians from continuing to build as they choose. On the contrary,
they only seem to further encourage illegal construction. The Palestinians,
just like the pre-State Jewish settlers, continue to vow that 'for every house
that is demolished, we'll build another in its place; for every olive tree that
is uprooted, we'll plant ten more trees.' Foundations have been established
for just this purpose that pay 'damages' to anyone whose house was razed
by the 'occupation forces.' House demolitions play into the Palestinians'
hands politically, too: Images of bulldozers wrecking the houses are shown
on television all over the world. Pictures of families sitting atop their

heaped possessions and lamenting their demolished houses have become the symbol of the Palestinian *sumud*. And more than anything else, this has helped to fix in the world's consciousness the notion that East Jerusalem is 'occupied territory' where the government is using aggressive tactics against the Arab residents.

CHAPTER FOUR

Why Israel is Losing the Jewish Majority in its Capital

In a few more years Jerusalem might, God forbid, no longer be the capital of the Jewish state and of the Jewish people, but have an Arab majority.

(Uri Lupolianski, Mayor of Jerusalem, 2003)

United Jerusalem's Finest Years

The sharp increase in the united city's Arab population brought about by the decision to annex 28 villages to Jerusalem did not worry the Eshkol government very much. Its complacency was aptly described by interministerial committee head General Rehavam Ze'evi, the 'moving spirit' behind the expansion of the capital's boundaries: "The government didn't know and didn't care how many Arabs were annexed to the capital, and it didn't matter, either".[1] The number of Arabs in the city and their ratio of the population seemingly had no bearing whatsoever on the political discourse concerning Jerusalem's future; even after the annexation of the villages, the ratio of Jews in the city reached its highest level in recent memory – 74.2 percent.

The policy-makers' approach to the demographic issue in the united city relied on two assumptions: The first was that the number of Jews and their percentage of the population would rise in the coming years due to an influx of newcomers from all over the country combined with immigrants from abroad, and primarily because of economic growth and prosperity. The fact that in the past Israel had managed to double the city's Jewish population within twenty years pointed to good odds of doing so again, possibly within an even shorter span of time. In discussions at the time, the experts and the policy-makers both predicted that the within a few years, the ratio of Jews in the population would reach 80–90 percent.[2] No one in the government had the slightest doubt that within a few years Jerusalem would be 'uni-national' in character, and this demographic dominance would bolster Israel's claim to sovereignty in the city.

At the same time, the policy-makers presumed, in their analogical thinking, that the ratio of Arabs in the city's population would continue to decline. This premise arose from the expectation that the encounter between East Jerusalem's Arabs and the more advanced Israeli society would promote sociological processes identical to those that occurred among Israeli Arabs in the state's first two decades when, in wake of the urbanization and industrialization of their communities, the previously high birth rate in that sector began to shrink steadily. On top of that, the policy-makers also expected the demographic trends that had characterized Jordanian Jerusalem from 1948 to 1967 to continue unchanged after its annexation to the Jewish city.

Both of these assumptions were extremely optimistic, and their fulfillment depended to a very large extent on government policy, particularly in the field of economics. Meanwhile, not a single official document predicted an increase in the city's Arab minority or viewed this as a potential threat to the Jewish majority. In the minds of the policy-makers, the 'threat' to Jerusalem's unity wasn't 'internal' but 'external': Above all, they feared an international attempt to impose a withdrawal on Israel.

The 1968 master plan for the city was formulated on the basis of these assumptions. It saw no need to boost the city's population or to accelerate Jerusalem's development. In fact, this plan warned that rapid development of Jerusalem could potentially upset the balance between Jews and Arabs, and even tip it in favor of the latter.

In the first few years following the city's unification, the policy-makers did not foresee any problem in attaining the objective of a uni-national city in which Jews comprised 90 percent of the population. For this reason, the Jerusalem municipality made co-existence with East Jerusalem's Arabs a top priority, and each year the various municipal departments went to great lengths to promote a wide range of activity in the Arab sector.[3]

In these years, the municipal development budget for East Jerusalem matched the percentage of Arabs in the city's population – 24 percent – and the aim was to close the gaps in infrastructure and in city services.[4]

In the first years after the 1967 war, Israel contributed to a significant improvement in the economic situation of East Jerusalem Arabs. From the start of the occupation, Israel allowed the Hashemite government to inject more funds into the city than ever before. At the same time, the city's Arabs also benefited from large budgets from the Israeli government and the Jerusalem municipality. The positive economic momentum that took hold in Jerusalem, combined with the social and medical services, and National Insurance Institute allowances from the government, all gave rise to an economic prosperity the likes of which Jerusalem's Arabs had never known before.

Jerusalem's public institutions and hospitals, and the Jerusalem municipality, employed hundreds of Arab employees. The Israel Police also absorbed all the Jordanian police officers to work in the Jerusalem district. The Arab officers were given Hebrew lessons and special policing courses, and served alongside Jewish police officers in various kinds of police work.

The municipality also introduced a host of programs that brought together Jewish and Arab youths. While the Arab minority still did not have any political representation on the city council, Arab youth were represented on the city youth council (5 out of 31 seats); the municipal youth soccer league included eight Arab soccer teams; Jewish and Arab schools held get-togethers and went on field trips around the country together; and dozens of Arab youths participated in the city-sponsored dance companies and traveled abroad with their Jewish colleagues to represent Jerusalem at international festivals.[5] Israelis and Arabs both were pleasantly surprised by the positive atmosphere engendered by these encounters.

Mayor Teddy Kollek was not worried about the existence of an Arab minority in the city, no matter how sizeable. It only went to prove his theory of the religious and ethnic mosaic of the "multi-cultural" city. Summing up the first four years of the city's unification, Kollek took particular pride in the achievements of Jewish–Arab co-existence, which were an outgrowth of the success of the city unification policy: "**These were Jerusalem's finest and most beautiful years.**"[6]

The 1970s: How Israel Created the Demographic Demon

Unfortunately, this idyll would be quite short-lived. Soon, there came a dramatic change in government policy. In 1970, amid growing apprehension over 'peace initiatives' that might call for a division of Jerusalem, the Golda Meir government resolved to strengthen Israeli control of the city by means of the construction of new Jewish neighborhoods throughout the territories annexed to Jerusalem in 1967 and by significantly boosting the city's Jewish population. These aims were diametrically opposed to the views of the experts and of the Jerusalem municipality, who warned that a wide-scale increase in construction would instead generate an increase in the city's Arab population – as the construction industry was a major source of employment for Arab factories and laborers, and accelerated development of this sort would bring more economic prosperity to Jerusalem's Arabs, and consequently draw more Arabs to the city from the surrounding areas.

But these arguments fell on deaf ears. Golda Meir's cabinet was not persuaded and disregarded Teddy Kollek's objections. The more criticism that was leveled at it, the more tenaciously the government clung to its position, certain that only the reinforcement of demographic hegemony in the city would prevent the division of Jerusalem.

The cabinet members did not deem the annual growth rate of Jerusalem's Jewish population, which had stood at 3 percent from 1967–70, adequate to achieve the target of a Jewish majority of 80 or even 90 percent. Carried away with this vision, the ministers made all sorts of fanciful proclamations about the number of housing units that had to be built, and the number of Jews that had to come to the city in order for demographic hegemony to be firmly established. Some talked about attaining an incredible annual growth rate of as much as 7–10 percent! Comments from some participants in the cabinet meetings to the effect that a growth rate of this magnitude would adversely affect other objectives did not faze Golda Meir in the least. She was absolutely determined to strengthen the capital in the face of perceived international threats.

Asked where all these hordes of people who were due to flock to the capital were going to come from, Absorption Minister Shimon Peres replied that, from now on, he would direct 50 percent of all new immigrants to Israel to Jerusalem. Other ministers initiated a special project to transfer 3,000 government employees from Tel Aviv to Jerusalem within one year.[7]

And what would happen if the masses of immigrants envisioned by Shimon Peres did not come to Jerusalem? Or if not enough veteran Israelis chose to move to Jerusalem? What would happen if the government was unable to transfer thousands of state workers to Jerusalem from Tel Aviv? The Golda Meir government was not prepared to contemplate any such scenarios. It firmly believed that its demographic objectives would be achieved without difficulty in just a few years. And how much should the realization of the demographic objective of a 90 percent Jewish majority cost? That question was of no concern, either.

In anticipation of the cabinet meeting that took place at the end of 1970, at which the demographic objectives were discussed, a detailed report was prepared by the Economic Planning and Consulting Corporation headed by economist Yigal Cohen-Orgad, who would later become finance minister in the Likud government. The report contained this explicit warning:

An accelerated rate of development will triple the demand for Arab workers. These workers will flock to Jerusalem from Judea and Samaria and give rise to political problems, and therefore, those who seek rapid development must be cognizant of this and guarantee that there is also an accelerated (double) increase in the migration of Jews to the city. An ordinary rate of development in the coming years would preserve the same ratio that currently exists between Jews and Arabs, i.e., 73.9 percent versus 26.1 percent.[8]

In June 1971, Teddy Kollek warned the government that "we will come to regret this pace [of development]. Quantity mustn't come at the expense of quality."[9] The government dismissed the mayor's admonition with typical scorn. Cabinet ministers continued to tout slogans about 'strengthening Jerusalem' and to pour vast sums into the construction of new housing units at an unprecedented rate of about 8,000 housing units per year. In 1971–1972, the government invested over two billion Israeli pounds in the construction of the new neighborhoods.

By the end of 1972, the government saw that none of its predictions had come true: The promised immigrants never arrived in Jerusalem; nor did Israelis rush to make the city their home; negotiations with government employees in Tel Aviv led nowhere, and the plan to transfer these offices and their personnel to the capital was an abject failure. A large portion of the new housing units remained vacant. Meanwhile, the experts' warnings about an increase in the Arab minority proved accurate. Not only did the construction boom in the city in these years halt the trend of negative migration among Jerusalem's Arabs, it also prompted thousands of Arabs to flood into the city from the West Bank. As early as 1972, a sharp upward spike was evident in the growth rate of the city's Arab minority, which now stood at 26.6 percent of the total city population, while the Jewish majority dropped to 73.4 percent.

In light of this situation, at the end of 1972 Golda Meir convened a meeting of the Ministerial Committee for Jerusalem, which she headed, for a discussion of the 'new' problem that had arisen in Jerusalem – 'the demographic problem.' The Economic Planning and Consulting Corporation was asked by the ministerial committee to prepare another report with new recommendations as to how to 'strengthen Jerusalem demographically.'

The company's second report indicates that the 'angry prophecy' of the earlier report had come to pass with a vengeance. According to the new report:

> The acceleration in Jerusalem's growth rate expanded the employment possibilities for the non-Jewish sector, and promoted the immigration of non-Jews. Thus, the growth rate of the Arab sector exceeded that which would come from their natural reproduction. Consequently, the goal of the decision to rapidly increase the population of Jerusalem, while maintaining the relative proportion of the Jewish population, was not achieved.[10]

Because of the rapid growth of the Arab minority in Jersualem, which resulted directly from the construction boom brought on by the new neighborhoods, the 'external' threat to the city's unity, i.e., peace agreements that would require its division, was supplanted by a 'threat from within' – the demographic threat. Golda Meir's government was 'surprised' by the wholly undesired demographic changes and appointed a inter-ministerial committee of experts, led by the budget director at the Finance Ministry, Arnon Gafni, to re-examine the policy and propose to the government ways of strengthening the capital 'demographically.'

Instead of courageously recommending a change in government policy, the Gafni Committee suggested a 'more of the same thing' approach, despite its proven failure. But beyond that, for the first time since the city's unification, the Gafni Committee also proposed that a ceiling be imposed on the growth of the Arab minority, and cited a 'desired ratio' of 26.6 percent – which was the figure that year.

The government adopted the Gafni Committee's recommendations regarding the demographic balance, and these became a matter of policy from then on. Starting in 1972, all national and municipal forecasts addressed the 'demographic threat' and made it the foundation of every development plan for the capital. In the ensuing decades, demographic objectives in Jerusalem have been determined not on the basis of urban or economic considerations, but on the sole basis of 'preserving the balance between Jews and Arabs in the city.' And all the working plans of the government and the municipality in the 1970s and 1980s ascribed supreme national importance to the sacred objective of 72 percent versus 28 percent.[11] Yisrael Kimhi, director of the policy-planning department in the Jerusalem municipality, admitted in 1976 that "the government decision that said the relative balance of Jews and Arabs must be maintained as it was in 1975 became the guideline for all the government ministries, for the Jerusalem municipality and for all the city planners."[12] Kimhi also said: "One cornerstone of the planning process in Jerusalem is the demographic question. The growth of the city and the preservation of the demographic balance between the ethnic groups in it were the subject of an Israeli government decision, which serves today as one of the criteria for success in the process of firmly establishing Jerusalem as Israel's capital."[13] And thus a reduction of the Arab population in the city became a national goal.

By the 1980s, even Teddy Kollek was worried about the 'demographic problem': "I'm concerned about the balance of power and the Arab increase within Jerusalem," he remarked.[14]

The 1980s: Settlements Grow as the Capital's Jewish Majority Shrinks

At the end of the 1970s, the Likud government headed by Menachem Begin set itself the goal of populating Judea and Samaria (the Israeli name for the West Bank) with Jews by means of building settlements. The area surrounding Jerusalem then became the central target of this policy. However, it soon became apparent that the settlement objective in Judea and Samaria would only be achieved at the expense of the demographic objective in the capital. As the government accelerated the pace of settlement construction around Jerusalem in the 1980s, the rate of people leaving the city for these places rose commensurately.

A typical example of the problems inherent in building new communities right near Jerusalem is the Ma'aleh Adumim settlement to the east of the city. Its rapid development was a direct outgrowth of the aim to turn it into the largest city in the territories of Judea and Samaria. Ma'aleh Adumim is connected to the capital by a modern highway, and benefits and incentives were offered to entice new residents. These conditions drew thousands of people to the brand-new community, almost all of them from Jerusalem. Concerned about the migration from the city to Ma'aleh Adumim, the Jerusalem municipality warned the government that the more that Ma'aleh Adumim grew, the harder it would be to achieve the demographic objective – namely, the addition of 100,000 Jews to the capital within ten years. But Begin rejected this argument. Suffused with the euphoria and enthusiasm that surrounded the settlement enterprise in the late 1970s, the Begin government was confident it could simultaneously achieve its demographic goals in both Judea and Samaria and in Jerusalem. And even once it became clear in the early 1980s that the majority of people moving to the settlements near the capital were leaving Jerusalem to do so, the government refused to scale back the development plans for Ma'aleh Adumim, Givat Ze'ev and Efrat, all in close proximity to Jerusalem. Construction continued apace and all three later siphoned off more of Jerusalem's Jewish population.

In 1983, Yitzhak Shamir's government announced a new policy meant to take this idea even further – 'strengthening Jerusalem with surrounding satellite communities.' The 'Greater Jerusalem' plan, as it was known, was based on a series of settlements around Jerusalem. The idea was that they would eventually be annexed to Israel and constitute an additional protective ring around the capital. This Likud plan was severely criticized by the Jerusalem municipality, which repeatedly warned that it would be to Jerusalem's detriment. But like the Begin government before it, the Shamir government gave priority to the demographic objective in Judea and Samaria over the demographic objective in Jerusalem.

From the early 1980s onward, Jerusalemites were abandoning the city for Ma'aleh Adumim and the other nearby settlements at a rate of 3,000–5,000 a year. The current mayor, Uri Lupolianski, had harsh criticism for the government as he presented data on the number of people who have left the city: Between 1990 and 2003, approximately 200,000 Jews left Jerusalem, with about half moving to the surrounding settlements. Lupolianski asserts that government actions encouraged Jewish residents to leave the capital, noting that most of the communities that are spurring this exodus are located just a ten-minute drive away from the city – a temptation that's hard to resist.

In recent years, the negative migration of Jews from Jerusalem has had a greater impact on the demographic balance than the growth of the Arab population. The fear is that if this trend continues unabated, then, as Lupolianski puts it, "In a few more years, Jerusalem might , God forbid, no longer be the capital of the Jewish state and of the Jewish people, but a city with an Arab majority."[15]

A Desperate Effort to Prevent a Bi-National City

By the end of the 1990s, the utter failure of the policy intended to achieve the demographic objectives in Jerusalem was plain to see, and Israel's capital was well on track to becoming a bi-national city. Only then did Israel's government begin to take dramatic steps to reverse the demographic trends. Reluctance to accept the obvious political conclusion – the need to part with the Arab neighborhoods – led the national government and the city government to undertake two moves that could more aptly be termed 'desperate measures' rather than 'policies.' However, it wasn't long before the irrationality of these steps became apparent. And when they, too, appeared to be achieving the opposite of the intended result, the government backtracked from them.

The first step taken was an attempt by the government to annul the residency status of thousands of the city's Arabs, in the hope that this would curtail the growth rate in that sector. In 1996, Interior Minister Eli Yishai and Mayor Ehud Olmert launched a wide-ranging 'operation' to identify Arab residents who had left the city limits due to the building restrictions placed on them by Israel but continued to register their home address in Jerusalem. The government planned to erase them from the city census rolls and to annul their residency status, reasoning that this would diminish the Arabs' numbers in the city. Interior Ministry and municipality estimates placed the number of people affected at between 50,000 and 80,000.[16]

Temple Mount in the Old City of Jerusalem (Israel Government Press Office, Photography Department).

A Christian pilgrim in Jerusalem (Israel Government Press Office, Photography Department).

Building the new neighborhoods in East Jerusalem, 1975 (Israel Government Press Office, Photography Department).

The Separation Fence in East Jerusalem, 2006 (author's personal archive).

Fragile co-existence in Jerusalem, 2001 (Ziv Koren).

The author as a wounded
paratrooper near the
Western Wall, June 7, 1967
(author's personal archive).

The author with Teddy Kollek, inaugurating the new bus station in Arab East
Jerusalem, 1990 (author's personal archive).

The author with Faisal Husseini in the garden of Orient House, 1992 (author's personal archive).

The author with Crown Prince Hassan in Amman, 2001 (author's personal archive).

The author with former President Gorbachev, 2003 (author's personal archive).

The author with Prime Minister Ehud Barak, New York, 2000 (author's personal archive).

The author with President Clinton at Camp David, 2000 (author's personal archive).

The author with former President Wahid of Indonesia in New York, 2005 (author's personal archive).

The operation was only partially successful at best; in its first six months, the Interior Ministry annulled the city residency of approximately 400 Arabs.[17] Then, in November 1996, the operation shifted into higher gear with the imposition of additional requirements for East Jerusalem residents. The birth of an Arab baby could only be recorded in the municipal registry if the mother proved that she or her parents had been living in the city continuously since 1967;[18] Arabs living abroad who wished to renew their visas were required to provide proof that their stay abroad was temporary. The same rules were applied to the thousands of Arab residents who hold an additional citizenship besides Jordanian citizenship. The Interior Ministry refused to register their children as Jerusalem residents and required them to give up the foreign passport in order to maintain their residency status in the city.[19] Contrary to past practice, the Interior Ministry now declined to approve requests for family unification by Arab permanent residents with spouses outside of Jerusalem. The Jerusalem municipality and the National Insurance Institute showed no mercy to the thousands of residents who had difficulty supplying all the numerous pieces of documentation they were suddenly obliged to present – many of these documents had been issued thirty or forty years before . . .

This 'harassment campaign,' as it was referred to by the media both in Israel and elsewhere, elicited a big public outcry. The State Comptroller who examined the issue also joined the chorus of critics, and declared that the Interior Ministry did not have the proper tools with which to investigate the residency status of Jerusalem's Arabs and that the decisions made in this regard were tainted by arbitrariness.[20]

Even these drastic measures did not bring about the results desired by the Israeli government. According to the Palestinians, by May 1997 Israel had only managed to annul the residency status of about 4,000 people in total.[21] The government and the municipality finally saw that the perpetuation of this policy would not yield a significant reduction in the ratio of Arabs in the city, and that annulling the residency of a few thousand people would not alter the demographic balance in any meaningful way.

As a matter of fact, like other misguided efforts before it, this strategy seemed to have backfired. After the new rules went into effect, thousands of Arabs who lived outside Jerusalem in neighborhoods like A-Ram, as well as many who had lived abroad for several years, began streaming back to the city. Many who may have considered moving to other cities in the West Bank, in Jordan or abroad stayed put out of fear of losing the benefits that city residency afforded them. By mid-1997, the government had decided to desist from its efforts to divest Jerusalem Arabs of residency status. Faisal Husseini, for one, was quite pleased with the results of the government policy, for it was effective in reinforcing the bond between thousands of Arabs who had left the city and their capital, Jerusalem, and joked: "When we have a state, we'll grant Interior Minister Eli Yishai the title of *Yakir al-Quds* ["Worthy Citizen of Al Quds] in appreciation of his important contribution to the strengthening of our *sumud.*"[22] Once again, Israel's government found to its dismay that draconian measures and strictures placed on the Arabs did not produce the desired result.

The second step taken by the government and the municipality in the late 1990s was the drafting of a new master plan for the city ('The Strategic Master Plan for the Year 2020'), which, according to its authors, was supposed to provide a fitting answer to the demographic threat. The paramount purpose of the plan was to bring to Jerusalem the Jewish residents it lacked, and thus halt the shrinking of the city's Jewish majority.

Mayor Ehud Olmert thought he had hit on the solution to the 'demographic problem': Expanding the city westward and building thousands of housing units in the last green spaces Jerusalem had left. The plan called for 47,000 housing units to be built in the far west of the city, which would bring in an additional 135,000 Jewish residents. As in the past, these figures were based more on wishful thinking rather than on any sober analysis of the actual urban processes taking place in Jerusalem. Nor could Olmert say just where all these thousands of new residents would come from.

Many experts warned over and over again about the anticipated economic and urban damage and about the destruction of the green landscape west of the city, but they could not persuade Olmert or the national government to halt the approval process for the plan. But this time would be different. Unlike in the past, public opposition this time included dozens of Knesset members, thousands of ordinary citizens and the top experts in the country – and in the end it was effective. In February 2007, after almost seven years in which the plan had made its way through all the administrative and legal hoops, the new mayor, Uri Lupolianski, announced its cancellation.

The Policy Fails: A Bi-National City Emerges

On May 24, 2006, as the Jerusalem Day celebrations were underway, data was made public that left no doubt as to the failure of the demographic policy:

The goal of attaining a Jewish majority in the eastern part of the city by means of the massive construction of Jewish neighborhoods was not achieved; the Arabs still maintained a 56–44 percent advantage in East Jerusalem. The goal of attaining a uni-national city with a Jewish majority of 80–90 percent had also failed to materialize; in 2006, the Jewish majority stood at just 66 percent, down from 73.5 percent in 1967. And the annual Jewish growth rate in the city, which was 3 percent in the early 1970s, had steadily plummeted to 2.3 percent in the 1980s, to 2.1 percent in the 1990s and to just 1.1 percent from 2000–2005.

Since the start of the Golda Meir government's policy for strengthening Israeli control in East Jerusalem, back in the 1970s, the trend of Jewish migration to the city gradually reversed to the point that the city is losing about 7,000 Jewish residents per year. All in all, Jerusalem has lost approximately 150,000 Jews since the 1970s.

If the current growth rates of the two populations hold steady, then by the year 2020 Jerusalem will essentially be a bi-national city: Out of a total population of close to one million, 59 percent will be Jews and 41 percent will be Arabs.

Professor Sergio Della Pergola, a pre-eminent expert on demography in Jerusalem, was a member of the team that drew up the 'Strategic Master Plan for the Year 2020' for the government and the Jerusalem municipality. He informed policy-makers that there were two distinct options: a bi-national city or 'disengagement' from the Arab neighborhoods in Jerusalem. In an article he published ahead of Jerusalem Day 2007, he called on policy-makers to muster the courage to make a painful decision that would entail a division of Jerusalem. As Israel marked the 40th anniversary of Jerusalem's unification, Della Pergola argued that "parts of the city that are populated mainly by Palestinians should be conceded."[23] The renowned scholar said his conclusions were based on the demographic circumstances and on the fear that the Jewish majority will continue to shrink, perhaps at an even faster rate, in the coming years.

In addition to the international implications of a bi-national city, the practical implications for political control in the Jerusalem municipality must also be considered. The ultra-Orthodox parties have already shown that a concerted effort to get out the vote in the mayoral election can lead a well-organized minority to gain a majority on the city council, and even the mayor's office itself. The ultra-Orthodox may make up no more than 20 percent of the city's population, but this did not stop them from becoming a dominant force in the city council after the last elections. Efficient organization and a resolute ideology pushed the ultra-Orthodox voting rate in the Jerusalem municipal elections to tremendous heights (95 percent, versus a 35 percent turnout among secular voters). The result was a surprising electoral victory. The ultra-Orthodox won about half of the 31 city council seats, and for the first time in the Jerusalem's history, crowned an ultra-Orthodox mayor – Uri Lupolianski.

Local Arabs followed the ultra-Orthodox campaign to 'conquer the capital' with much interest. And they must have been asking themselves: If 20 percent of the capital's residents can 'conquer city hall,' then why can't the Arab residents, who make up 34 percent of the population, do the same? Jerusalem's Arab residents have the right to vote in the municipal elections, but for political reasons they refrain from exercising this right; voting in the municipal elections is akin to giving legitimacy to Israeli rule in the city. Yet, this tradition of boycotting the elections could change if Jerusalem's Arabs ever calculate that the political benefit would outweigh the drawbacks of extending such recognition.

Were the Arabs to exercise their right to vote in the next municipal elections, they could, if properly organized, attain a voter turnout comparable to that of the ultra-Orthodox, and that would put incredible political achievements within reach; theoretically, they could obtain a majority on the city council and even crown an Arab mayor in Israel's capital.

In sum, the failure of Israel's demographic policy in Jerusalem derived from the same factors that undermined its attempts to achieve all the other objectives: a reliance on wishful thinking rather than on rational planning; mistaken analogies and, above all – conflicting goals. Thus, for example, the decision to build the new neighborhoods contradicted the aim of reducing the city's Arab population; and the policy of establishing and promoting the growth of settlements in the area surrounding Jerusalem contradicted the aim of increasing the city's Jewish population. Government after government chose to ignore the experts' warnings, and even when the harm caused by their policies became undeniable, for the most part they stubbornly refused to stop and reconsider their strategy, thus compounding the damage. In the grip of an unshakeable faith in the redemption of Jerusalem, they proceeded blithely on their march of folly.

CHAPTER FIVE

The Most Polarized City in the World

We said again and again that we would make the Arabs' rights equal to those of the Jews in the city. This was empty talk . . .

Whatever Israel's governments could do to make life harder for the Arabs in Jerusalem, they did. Whatever Israel's governments could do to prevent them from developing, expanding, building, improving their quality of housing, they did.

(Teddy Kollek, former mayor of Jerusalem, 1994)

A Policy of Domination in a Polarized City: A Comparative View

Jerusalem is one of a small group of 'divided' or 'polarized' cities in which two national groups live alongside one another. Researchers have delineated the characteristics of such cities and the ways in which the cultural, ethnic and national conflicts that occur in them are managed. In polarized cities such as Nicosia, Belfast, Montreal, Algiers, Sarajevo, Brussels, Beirut and New Delhi, the policy adopted by the ruling majority is based on one of two approaches, both of which aim to preserve stability: accommodation or domination.[1]

The difference between the two is substantial, and the choice of approach generally derives from the type of relations that have developed between the majority group and the minority group. When a minority challenges the legitimacy of the governing authority, this induces the majority to adopt a policy of domination, which leads to increased polarization. A minority that accepts the governing authority's legitimacy while requesting certain rights is likely to cause the majority to adopt a policy of accommodation.

Montreal, Beirut and Brussels are examples of cities characterized by a policy of accommodation. In these places, the authorities have managed to maintain stability by making concessions to the minority and offering it extensive autonomy. In contrast, in Jerusalem, Nicosia and until recently, Belfast, a policy of domination prevails, and stability is not easily maintained. Jerusalem is considered an even more extreme case than Nicosia, which is divided by a physical barrier.[2]

We must ask ourselves: Is the exacerbation of the conflict the cause for the policy, or its consequence? To what degree do these policy approaches affect the manageability of the conflict and the degree of stability?

One attempt to answer this question comes from the social sciences and the study of conflict resolution. Here, the policy itself is seen as the factor that shapes the political reality from the top down. According to this approach, deepening segregation patterns in a city, or a heightening of the conflict that takes the form of violent incidents or the exacerbation of socioeconomic gaps between the groups, are a direct result of the selection and implementation of a particular policy. A conflict that reaches the point of violent confrontation, segregation and a questioning of the government's legitimacy indicates a policy failure.

The struggle of a national minority fits into one of three categories: a struggle for equality, for autonomy or, in the most extreme case, a struggle for independence and secession from the majority. Different minorities in the world have fought for equality or autonomy and, having obtained their goal, and subsequently enabled the majority to preserve control, stability and legitimacy. In these cases, the ruling majority allowed the minority an equal share in the rights and duties of all the state's citizens. But in instances where the accommodation policy failed, conflicts have slid into violent confrontation, de-legitimation of the authorities and the aspiration for independence.

Israeli policy since 1948 towards the Arab minority living within the state's borders has been a policy of accommodation in which the state aspired to obtain legitimation from the Arabs in return for granting them equality. Israel has always been opposed to granting national autonomy to the Arab minority. Many scholars believe that this policy succeeded, for the most part, in achieving its national aim; the Arab minority in Israel is protected by a legislative system that guards its individual rights, and has integrated into the economic and political life of the state. This minority does not challenge the ruling majority, but it does insist on receiving full equality, which, it argues, can only be achieved when the State of Israel becomes 'a state of all its citizens.'

The relations between the Arab minority and the Jewish majority in Israel are characterized by fierce debates and disagreements, but this takes place within the legitimate framework of the democratic regime, and only rarely devolves into violent confrontation, into a civil rebellion or intifada of the kind Israel has experienced in the territories. The policy-makers in Israel viewed the Israeli–Arab model as successful and so, in 1967, they began applying it to the Arabs of Jerusalem as well. Jerusalem was the only place out of all the territories of Judea and Samaria to which Israeli law was applied.

In this chapter we shall attempt to answer the question of why Israel did not succeed in imposing a policy of accommodation (whose primary aims were co-existence and Israelization) on Jerusalem's Arabs in keeping with the Israeli–Arab model, and why is it that, even though the objectives of the policy in Jerusalem were identical to those of the policy towards Israeli Arabs since 1948, the results were just the opposite.

The answer lies in two prominent features of the policy towards Jerusalem's Arabs: One is the confusion and hesitation that led to frequent changes in policy, and the other is the inappropriate policy tools that were chosen. Over the years, the Israeli policy changed several times – from Israelization to autonomy, then later to Jordanization and finally to Palestinization. The accommodation policy adopted in 1967 was replaced in the 1970s by a policy of domination. In the end, the failure of this policy was made strikingly clear by the collapse of co-existence in the city and by Jerusalem's Arabs joining in the national Palestinian struggle for independence. The broad, almost unprecedented autonomy that Jerusalem's Arabs were given did not keep them from tying their fate, for better or worse, to that of their brethren in the West Bank who are not seeking 'equal rights' or 'autonomy,' but 'independence.' As the Israeli government set about establishing 'facts in the field,' Jerusalem's Arabs established facts of their own – an autonomous institutional infrastructure coupled with ever-expanding illegal construction. Faced with Israeli attempts to reduce the ratio of Arabs in the city population and to push them out, they countered with a policy of *sumud* – of clinging steadfastly to the land.

Starting with the outbreak of the first intifada in 1987, a process of polarization began, concurrent with a collapse of coexistence between the Jewish majority and the Arab minority in Jerusalem. Before long, the internal conflict in the city had turned into a violent representation of the national conflict between the two peoples. Jerusalem became the very core of the conflict: a city of strife.

1967: Israelization, Equality and Co-Existence

Already at the first cabinet meeting following the Six-Day War, on June 11, 1967, at which Jerusalem's future was discussed, it was evident that ministers considered the Arab minority in the city a marginal issue. The bulk of the discussion was devoted to the potential international reaction to the annexation of the Old City and to the issue of the holy places, while the question of the status of the city's Arabs received relatively scant attention.[3]

A number of options were proposed: The first was to grant Jerusalem's Arabs similar status to that of the Arabs in the territories, despite the annexation to Israel; the second was to transfer all the Arab residents of the city to the West Bank and consider them 'absentee,' as occurred in 1948 with the Arabs in the west of the city.[4] The government rejected these two courses of action in favor of a third option with which it was previously acquainted: granting Israeli citizenship and resident status to the city's Arabs, with the aim of bringing about a process of 'Israelization,' as occurred with the Israeli Arabs after 1948.

The decision to grant Israeli citizenship to Jerusalem's Arabs was an outgrowth of an analogical approach in which the ministers viewed the situation of the city's Arabs in 1967 as equivalent to that of the Israeli Arabs in 1948. The chief proponent of the Israelization approach was Prime Minister Levi Eshkol, who considered the annexation of the city's Arab population to Israel the obvious move. Just days after the conquest of the city, Eshkol convened in his office a team of senior officials, including Moshe Sasson and Shaul Ben-Haim of the Foreign Ministry, Haim Herzog – the West Bank governor – and Shmuel Toledano, the prime minister's adviser on Arab affairs, to outline the Israelization policy for Jerusalem's Arabs. This policy was supposed to be based upon the formula used earlier in regard to the Israeli Arabs. The justice minister and interior minister were also in agreement. Both thought it self-evident that Jerusalem's Arabs should have the right to political representation and citizenship, similar to the Israeli Arabs. There was no question that they should be democratically represented on the Jerusalem city council relative to their electoral power. They considered proposing the addition of six members of the Arab city council to the Jerusalem city council in time for the upcoming municipal elections. Since Teddy Kollek was of the same mind on this matter, the ministers and municipality representatives began looking into the Jordanian city council members' readiness to be integrated into a united city council. However, in the end, it was Teddy Kollek who had second thoughts about this move and thwarted it at the last minute (more about that below).

Once the decision was made to grant citizenship to East Jerusalem's Arabs, the various authorities began preparing for the new situation. The Jerusalem municipality readied to take on Arab municipal employees, and the Justice Ministry made all the legal preparations for recognition of their rights and for their transfer from the Jordanian to the Israeli municipality.

Another aspect of the Israelization policy was the government's decision to recruit all the Arab police officers who served in the Jordanian police force in Jerusalem. By the end of June 1967, a police command team had begun recruiting and training approximately 100 Arab police officers for the Israel Police. The policemen were given courses in Hebrew, citizenship and Israeli law, as well as professional police training, and were soon working in East Jerusalem as part of the capital's police force.[5] Major General Turjeman, who oversaw this process for the Jerusalem police, said: "The Arab officers integrated well and became an inseparable part of the police landscape in the capital, so much so that you can hardly tell the difference between them and the Jewish police officers."[6]

Another issue related to the Israelization policy that came up in those days concerned the level of services and infrastructure in East Jerusalem, which was greatly inferior to the situation in the west of the city. Teddy Kollek declared: "Equalizing the level of services and infrastructure between east and west will exemplify Jerusalem's unity. The municipality must maintain services at a uniform level and in accordance with set standards. The level of services provided by the Jordanians does not match what is to be expected from us from the moment we took upon ourselves responsibility for united Jerusalem."[7] On July 16, 1967, Levi Eshkol brought the matter up for discussion by the cabinet, which resolved: "Services shall be provided on a scope and level equal to those in Israel. The relevant ministries shall make an effort to equalize as soon as possible the provision of legally mandated services."[8]

And indeed, in the second half of the budget year 1967, the government increased its budgets for Jerusalem considerably. Development in East Jerusalem took off, with infrastructure for sewage, water, electricity, roads, education, welfare and public health put in place. A substantial portion of the funds was designated for the installation of completely new infrastructure where none had existed before during Jordanian rule, particularly in the 28 Arab villages that were annexed to the city. A particularly large budget was allocated for the school system in East Jerusalem – for the construction of schools and kindergartens and to fund things that hadn't existed previously, such as libraries, and cultural, athletic and youth activities, as well as to a lending fund for Arab business projects.[9]

The principle of equality in the Eshkol government's Israelization policy was also applied in the area of housing: On January 8, 1968, upon the appropriation of 3,830 dunams of land for the purpose of building the inner ring of neighborhoods – Givat Shapira, Givat Hamivtar and Ramat Eshkol – the prime minister announced that, in addition, residential neighborhoods would also be built for Arabs on these appropriated lands. The government allocated two million Israeli pounds (approx. $600,000) to this task, and Teddy Kollek announced: "From now on, 250 new housing units will be provided to the Arab sector each year."[10] In 1968, with the municipality's encouragement, the Wadi al-Joz housing project, which included 100 units, was begun. East Jerusalem's Arab residents were surprised that "the government was building houses for them"; they weren't accustomed to government housing aid under Jordanian rule. That same year, the municipality also signed agreements with Arab contractors to build a new Arab neighborhood in Beit Hanina, and the government reached agreements with Israeli banks to offer mortgages to Arab residents.

The new Jerusalem master plan (1968) designated the north of the city – Shuafat and Beit Hanina – as having "residential development potential for the Arabs in the city"[11] and the municipality announced that it was preparing a detailed plan for this area that would include the construction of approximately 18,000 housing units.

The policy-makers on both the state and municipal level saw the equality policy as reinforcing the unity of Jerusalem and as the best way to ensure the Israelization of the city's Arabs.

The integration processes that came out of the Israelization effort were the hallmarks of the Eshkol government's policy in Jerusalem and continued until the early 1970s. Jerusalem's Arabs were not considered an 'enemy,' but rather a minority entitled to the same privileges as the majority. They were considered Israeli citizens, even if they preferred to maintain their Jordanian citizenship and to receive Israeli IDs as permanent residents in the city. When asked at the time about the possibility of Arabs settling in the west of the city, as Jews were settling in the east of the city, Teddy Kollek welcomed the idea: "Of course, the aim has to be free, two-way movement among the neighborhoods."[12] In September 1967, shortly after the census was taken, and it became apparent that 3,000 or so Arab residents of Jerusalem who had fled the city during the battles or were abroad at the time wanted to return to the city, Levi Eshkol did not hesitate to approve this.

In the first years following the city's unification, there really was an atmosphere of 'one city' in which all the residents were equal and shared in its prosperity. Under the watchful eyes of millions around the world, Jerusalem projected an image of a united city where the 'occupation' was beneficial to Jew and Arab alike; never before had the world seen such an 'enlightened occupation.' Nor did the Arabs' collective boycott of the Jerusalem municipal elections in a gesture of refusal to grant legitimacy to the government affect their day-to-day cooperation with the Israeli authorities.

The policy of Israelization, which hinged on co-existence, integration and equality, appears to have been successful. These were "Jerusalem's finest years," as Teddy Kollek described it. But they wouldn't last long. The first cracks in the united city's idyll were already forming. Just a few years later, Israel dropped the Israelization policy and turned in a wholly different direction.

The First Cracks Appear

Levi Eshkol's view of Jerusalem's Arabs as a minority entitled to full equal rights was not shared by all of his ministers, nor even by Mayor Teddy Kollek. Some questioned the validity of the premise that the city's Arabs, like the Arabs in 1948, would 'come to terms with the facts' and integrate into the life of the country and the capital. They warned that the distinction the government wished to make between the status of Jerusalem's Arabs and that of the Arabs in the territories might not hold up over time.

Opponents of the government's stand, led by Defense Minister Moshe Dayan and Mayor Teddy Kollek, considered the connection between the Arabs of Jerusalem and those of the territories to be natural and even desirable. In their view, the solution for the political standing of both groups was not Israelization, but rather autonomy, under either Israeli rule or joint Israeli–Jordanian rule once there was peace with Jordan. And Minister Menachem Begin, who felt that the territories should come eventually come under Israeli sovereignty, also preferred autonomy over Israelization for East Jerusalem Arabs, and for the Arabs of the territories.

This disagreement, which would fester for several years, came up right away in a June 1967 cabinet meeting. A majority supported Levi Eshkol's position, which meant differential treatment for the Arabs of Jerusalem and the rest of the West Bank territories, while a minority vehemently protested such an arrangement, arguing that, in any case, all of the territories would have to remain in Israel's hands, and so the future of all the residents should be the same – citizens with equal rights, like those of the Israeli Arabs, or, as Begin and Dayan would have it, residents of an autonomous region.

The majority wanted to grant Jerusalem's Arabs automatic citizenship and equal rights to those of the city's Israeli citizens. Minister Bentov insisted that, with Israel being a democracy, this was the only possible path, and that the unification of the city under Israeli sovereignty required the granting of citizenship to its Arab population.

Menachem Begin, who opposed the majority view, wished to amend the proposal to say that 'only one who requests it' shall receive citizenship. While Begin's argument may appear to represent a liberal attitude – giving Jerusalem's Arabs the freedom of choice between retaining their Jordanian citizenship or obtaining Israeli citizenship – in truth, it was in line with his position that the territory should be annexed and the residents left with a standing in which they did not have Israeli citizenship. Begin's amendment was adopted, and thus a new possibility arose of 'non-citizen Arab residents'; they could enjoy full residency rights, including the right to vote in municipal elections, but without being 'citizens.'

In time, it became clear that Jerusalem's Arabs were not streaming en masse to request Israeli citizenship, since they could already obtain practically the same benefits with resident status. At present, four decades later, less than 6,000 Jerusalem Arabs have requested (and received) Israeli citizenship. Begin, of course, understood that, given the choice, the Arabs would not opt for Israeli citizenship, which is exactly why he made his proposal . . .

Another issue that led some to oppose the Israelization policy was the matter of the Arabs' political representation in the city council. At the cabinet meeting, the question was asked whether it was in Israel's interest to promote an Arab municipal administration in East Jerusalem.[13] A majority of the ministers supported this, and in the end, the government decided that the city's Arabs should have representation in the municipality. The ministerial committee headed by the justice minister was given the task of drawing up the legal formulation by which approximately a quarter of the city's population would be able to have their interests represented in the municipality. The government was at pains to portray this as a municipal and not a political act, so as not to put off the members of the Jordanian council.

In the days following the war, it became apparent that the administration of the Jordanian municipality, headed by Mayor Ruhi al-Khatib, was actually eager to cooperate with the military authorities and to help them restore order in East Jerusalem. It saw itself as a representative body of the local residents rather than as a representative of the Jordanian government, and therefore was ready to do its utmost to assist in getting the Arabs residents' lives back to normal. Mayor Al-Khatib convened the city council and passed an official decision to cooperate with Israel for the benefit of the residents. Municipal secretary Jarallah remarked later that "the joining [with the Israeli municipality] of the employees and elected officials' arose from a vision of their role as public servants. We serve the city. That it was we have always done and what we will continue to do."[14]

The interior minister met with members of the Jordanian city council with the aim of persuading them to join the Israeli municipality. He believed that this was truly feasible. He explained to them that the unification of the city would be officially executed by an order of the interior minister, by virtue of his responsibility for the municipalities, and that there was no political aspect involved: "The order will unite the city's two separate administrations into a single administration."[15] The government, which discussed the matter and decided that such an order should be issued, also noted that, in accordance with the amendment to the law, "the interior minister may appoint additional members to the city council from among the residents of the area."[16]

As all these discussions were going on, Mayor Teddy Kollek suddenly

informed the interior minister of his objection to this move. His explanation: "They'll get in my way . . . the Arab city council members will say
all kinds of things and cause political provocations."[17] The government
knew that without Kollek's support, the move would be impossible to
implement, and the idea was shelved.

The Jordanian mayor, Ruhi al-Khatib, expressed deep disappointment
over Kollek's stand. Just a few days earlier, the two had met and Kollek
had embraced him and said to him: "Cities don't wage war. We'll work
together . . . " He was astonished that Israel, as a democratic country, was
beginning its rule in the united city by preventing a quarter of the residents
from having political representation, and added: "Without equality and
representation for the Arab residents, Israel will not achieve unity of the
city."[18]

Al-Khatib would later say that the opposition to representation for East
Jerusalem Arabs was an administrative and political mistake on the part
of the Israeli authorities. Aharon Layish, who supported the move, also
considered its cancellation a grave error: "Their non-inclusion stood in
incredible disproportion to the degree of cooperation offered by them and
by Ruhi al-Khatib. It was a terrible mistake that a way was not found to
include them in the municipality."[19] Years afterward, Teddy Kollek would
also admit that "we made a mistake on this matter"[20] and various Israeli
governments would seek to turn back the clock with various proposals as
to how Arab representatives could represent their voters. So important did
this become to Kollek, that in every one of his election campaigns he was
prepared to reserve spots on his One Jerusalem list for Arab representatives from East Jerusalem. But what was done could not be undone; and
all of these later proposals met with rejection.

At the final meeting of the Jordanian city council, Yaakov Salman officially proclaimed its disbanding. The Israelis who were present in the hall
described the brief ceremony as 'awkward.' Salman's words of thanks for
their cooperation could not dispel the bad feelings in the air.

A few months later, members of the Jordanian administration and Ruhi
al-Khatib became leaders of the struggle against the Israeli occupation. Al-
Khatib was subsequently charged with 'subversive activity' and exiled to
Amman.

The two decisions made in June 1967, not to apply automatic Israeli
citizenship to the city's Arabs and to prevent them from having political
representation on the city council, turned out to have been misguided.
They constituted the first cracks in the Israelization policy.

From Israelization to Jordanization

As time went on, opposition to the Israelization policy continued to grow. The policy's two chief opponents, Defense Minister Moshe Dayan and Mayor Teddy Kollek, advocated a different policy – 'Jordanization' – in which Jerusalem's Arabs were to be perceived as a 'separate entity' to be given administrative, economic and educational autonomy without Israel getting involved in their affairs or imposing the symbols of Israelization upon them. The rationale behind the Jordanization approach was that it would be better for Israel if the processes of the disintegration of Palestinian society that began after 1948 were to lead to the Palestinians' eventual integration in the Hashemite Kingdom. The defense minister and mayor adamantly maintained that it was 'better to leave the Arabs alone' and not compel them to accept the symbols of the state, and its duties and privileges, and this line of argument ultimately led the Israelization policy to be replaced with the Jordanization policy.

Although they were in fast agreement on this point, Kollek and Dayan's motives were completely different: Dayan viewed the city's Arabs as Jordanian citizens who would one day receive administrative, municipal and perhaps also political autonomy. Kollek, on the other hand, had always considered himself their 'patron' in the colonial sense, and defined his rule as an 'enlightened occupation.' This philosophy of his was evident, for one thing, in his effort to protect 'his residents' from the restrictions that were later imposed upon them by Golda Meir's government. Kollek viewed them as an Arab Muslim community entitled to the trappings of cultural autonomy but not necessarily to rights equal to those of the Jews in his city. His fight to give the Arab minority special treatment ran counter to the Eshkol government's intended policy of equality.

The cooperation between Dayan and Kollek was boosted by their years-long acquaintance as key members of Mapai under Ben-Gurion. Both held a dim view of politicians who were big on rhetoric and slogans, preferring a 'practical' approach that focused on establishing facts in the field, even it that sometimes meant disregard for proper procedure, previous decisions and teamwork. Both had enormous self-confidence, openly sought to burnish their public images via the media, and during the first decade of Jerusalem's unification effectively spearheaded the shift in policy from Israelization to Jordanization.

Moshe Dayan, relying heavily on his broad public popularity in addition to his position as administrator of the territories, independently pushed the autonomy policy in East Jerusalem, which ran counter to the government's positions. Prime Minister Eshkol furiously rebuked him for this on a number of occasions.

A typical example of Dayan's maverick conduct was his meeting with members of the Muslim Waqf on the Temple Mount on June 7, 1967, just hours after the fighting ended. At this meeting, without consulting with Levi Eshkol and without the benefit of any government decision, Dayan set down the distinction between the Temple Mount (or Haram al-Sharif) as the holy site for Muslims and the Western Wall as the holy site for Jews. He informed the Waqf people that from now on he would permit them to run all the religious and administrative affairs on the Temple Mount, and that they would hold the key to the gates. The prime minister, along with the rest of the nation, heard on the radio the defense minister's surprising announcement regarding the transfer of administrative authority over this place to the Muslim Waqf. The government had not discussed the matter at all, and if it had, it may well have decided to apply an arrangement similar to the one used for the Cave of the Patriarchs in Hebron, with separate times for prayers and joint oversight of the place for Jews and Muslims.

Though Teddy Kollek lacked the political clout of the defense minister, his public standing still enabled him to take certain measures to promote autonomy for the city's Arabs. His advocacy of 'affirmative action' for Jerusalem's Arabs often roused the government's ire. Such was the case when he asserted that the unification of Jerusalem meant that the city would be 'multicultural,' or when he objected to making the anniversary of Jerusalem's liberation a municipal holiday, arguing that it was not a holiday for the Arab minority in the city. Kollek wasn't the least bit fazed when detractors derided him as the 'defender of Islam,' for he considered the city's Arab residents to be under his 'patronage' and as an 'enlightened occupier,' wished to make the occupation less oppressive for them. He saw no contradiction between his political stance that the unification of Jerusalem was 'a historic necessity' and his 'liberal' policy toward the Arab residents. In his mind, the latter were 'natives' who owed a debt of gratitude to those who brought them European progress – and having spent his childhood in Hapsburg Vienna, he counted himself in this group. In the first years of the city's unification, Kollek was one of the people most responsible for extending administrative, economic and educational autonomy to the Arab population. Years later, he came to realize that his 'liberal and enlightened' policy was a key factor behind the segregation of the Arab minority from the Jewish majority. The Arabs chose the Jordanian option and preferred autonomy to equality.

Israel Shirks Governmental Responsibility
in East Jerusalem

The debate among policy-makers in those early years of unification appears to have been clearly demarcated between advocates of Israelization (i.e. applying Israeli law and order and government to Jerusalem's Arabs), and advocates of autonomy (i.e. liberalization and 'enlightened occupation') giving the city's Arabs freedom of choice. However, this is not how it was perceived by the Arabs themselves. They viewed Israel's offer of broad autonomy as a shirking of authority, with the tacit understanding that this void would be filled by the Jordanian government in Amman. The upshot of the change in Israel's stance toward East Jerusalem's Arabs – from treating them as Israelis to treating them as Jordanians – was a stronger sense of identification with their brethren in the West Bank. Overall, this policy shift only deepened the impression that Israel was reluctant to impose its government and symbols of sovereignty in East Jerusalem, and this had wide-ranging political consequences.

Essentially, the Israelization policy supported by Prime Minister Levi Eshkol, Finance Minister Pinhas Sapir as well as the foreign minister and police minister meant that Jerusalem's Arabs were destined to be separated from the Arabs in the territories. The Jordanization policy supported by Defense Minister Moshe Dayan and Mayor Teddy Kollek meant just the opposite – linking the fate of Jerusalem's Arabs with that of the Arabs in the territories.

The debate over the status of East Jerusalem residents reflected an even deeper division between those who advocated parting with the West Bank and those who wished for Israel to remain there permanently. Moshe Dayan, Menachem Begin and Teddy Kollek envisioned a future in which the West Bank would be administered by a cooperative partnership with Jordan in which Israel would hold on to most of the territory and Jordan would govern most of the Palestinians living there. In their view, autonomy for the Arabs of the territories, and for the Arabs of Jerusalem, would eventually make possible a type of joint rule with Jordan. As Shlomo Gazit, who was appointed at the time by Dayan to head the Unit for the Coordination of Operations in the Territories, writes: "Their assumption was that even if a Jordanian government arose in the territories, the land would remain undivided."[21]

As autonomy was increased, the bond between Jerusalem's Arabs and Jordan grew stronger, and all with the support of the defense ministry and the mayor. Israel allowed King Hussein to continue managing from afar the daily affairs of Jerusalem's Arabs in the fields of economics, welfare, religion, education and more. All the government ministries in Amman had special departments assigned to deal with the residents of East Jerusalem, and hundreds of Arabs in East Jerusalem continued to receive salaries as employees of the government in Amman.

Like Gazit, some members of the government and other experts on the Jerusalem issue cautioned that the 'governmental partnership' between Israel and Jordan in East Jerusalem could affect Jerusalem's future political standing and the prospects for keeping the city united. But in those days of euphoria and self-confidence, no one paid these warnings any attention.

The more Israel retreated from the Israelization policy in East Jerusalem, the stronger King Hussein's hold became there. In 1972, Hussein announced a plan to create a federation between the West Bank and East Jerusalem. This plan indicated that once the West Bank was liberated from the Israeli occupation, the two areas would be united and their residents given equal national rights. The plan also called for a special status to be given to Jerusalem, different from what it had under pre-1967 Jordanian rule. Now King Hussein wanted it to serve as the capital of the West Bank, on an equal standing with Amman.

In a secret meeting held that year, Golda Meir and King Hussein were unable to reach any agreement on the future of the territories and Jerusalem.[22] However, they did agree that, for all practical purposes, the Arab residents of East Jerusalem would be under Jordanian governance; Hussein was permitted to extend them his patronage and to support them economically and administratively. In this way, his unofficial influence upon the Palestinian establishment in East Jerusalem received an official seal of approval from the Israeli prime minister; administration in the spheres of economics, religion and education was now centered in Amman. The welfare and charity services in East Jerusalem became subordinate to the welfare ministry in Amman and could thus receive direct assistance from Jordan; international aid from the Arab states and the UN welfare organizations was to be transferred via Amman, too. Jordan began putting money into East Jerusalem schools, colleges, cemeteries and a variety of economic and cultural projects. On top of that, the king donated $8.2 million of his personal fortune to restore the golden Dome of the Rock and commissioned a multiyear plan to renovate the 180 mosques in East Jerusalem. Thousands of public employees in East Jerusalem received their monthly salaries from Amman and inspectors from the Jordanian education ministry freely visited the Arab schools in East Jerusalem to oversee the Jordanian matriculation exams. By various estimates, in the 1970s, Jordan invested something on the order of $100 million in East Jerusalem, a sum ten times larger than the Israeli government had put into that part of the city.

In their 1991 book *Living Together Separately* anthropologists

Michael Romann and Alex Weingrod[23] contend that Israel's shirking of its governmental responsibility for the needs of East Jerusalem residents in the 1970s exacerbated their ethnic and political isolation and diminished the emblems of Israeli sovereignty in that part of the city. Israeli governments of the time concentrated exclusively on one aspect – territorial control of East Jerusalem – and were hardly concerned by the steady erosion of Israel's political control there.

A Policy of Discrimination

In the early 1970s, as Golda Meir's government moved away from the Israelization policy, government investment in the Arab neighborhoods of East Jerusalem dwindled sharply until it dried up almost completely.

This gave rise to a tremendous discrepancy in the standard of living between East and West Jerusalem. Romann and Weingrod[24] detailed the disparity in the level of services and infrastructure and show that the Israeli government made no attempts to narrow these gaps. This was particularly evident in the rural areas of East Jerusalem where, from the outset, going back to the period of Jordanian rule, there were no modern services whatsoever. Romann and Weingrod maintain that once Israel transferred governmental responsibility for East Jerusalem to Jordan in the early 1970s, it no longer felt obligated to bring services there up to par. Their data shows that as the development of the new Jewish neighborhoods in East Jerusalem gained momentum, municipal budgets and resources for the Arab neighborhoods shrank. From a high of 15 percent of the municipal development budget in 1968, investment sank to 10 percent in the early 1970s, to 5 percent in the late 1970s and to just 3–4 percent in the 1980s.

And the more the government ignored its responsibility to the Arab residents, the more the Arab minority ignored the Israeli government and its representatives. In the 1970 Jerusalem mayoral election, thousands of East Jerusalem residents turned out to vote for Teddy Kollek, who won 20 percent of the overall Arab vote. But in the years that followed, as Palsetinization took hold, the rate of Arab voters declined until, by the end of the 1980s, Jerusalem Arabs stopped going to the polls altogether. In the 1990s, when the Israeli government gave them the option of voting in Palestinian Authority elections, the city's Arabs exercised that right and voted for PA candidates they felt represented them.

For many years, Teddy Kollek denied that he had failed to keep his promises to the Arab population and found all kinds of excuses to explain why the budgets for East Jerusalem had shrunk so dramatically. Only in October 1990, on one of the toughest days of the first intifada, following

the killing of Arab rioters on the Temple Mount, did he frankly acknowledge this in a newspaper interview:

> We said again and again that we would make the Arabs' rights equal to
> the rights of the Jews in the city. Empty talk. They were and remain
> second and third class citizens. For Jewish Jerusalem, I did something in
> the past 25 years. For East Jerusalem? Nothing. What did I do?
> Schools? Nothing. Sidewalks, nothing! Old age homes, nothing! Yes,
> we did install a sewage system and improve the water supply. You
> know what? You think that was for their benefit? For their welfare?
> Think again! There were a few case of cholera there and the Jews were
> afraid it would reach them so a sewage system and water network were
> put in.[25]

The dimensions of the government neglect in East Jerusalem were
revealed to the public in 1989, during the first intifada, following the
formation of a municipal committee to equalize services and infrastructure in East Jerusalem. Teddy Kollek appointed me to head this committee
then. This was the first time that Kollek was ready to admit that previously only a token budget had been allotted for development in East
Jerusalem.

Before the committee was established, it was impossible to obtain any
idea of what the actual municipal budget was, or the rate of government
investment in East Jerusalem. This information was hidden amid myriad
vague clauses and sub-clauses, a situation that enabled Kollek to say that
the allocations for East Jerusalem were not 'designated specifically' for
Arabs but rather part of the overall development budget for the east of the
city. And indeed, hundreds of millions of shekels were invested annually
in East Jerusalem, but 99 percent of these funds were spent on infrastructure for the Jewish neighborhoods. This piece of information was
concealed from both the Jewish and Arab publics.

As head of the committee I requested a special report from the city trea-
surer on the scope of municipal investment in East Jerusalem. After I
received the report, and discovered that the rate of investment did not
exceed 3 percent of the total municipal development budget, I was asked
by Teddy Kollek, who I believe was also surprised by the low figure, to
keep this data confidential. I agreed – in return for his promise that he
would double the investment the next year. This promise was not kept, of
course. Throughout the 1980s and early 1990s, the city budgets for development of the Arab neighborhoods never exceeded 4 percent of the total
development budget, even though Arabs comprised close to a third of the
city's population.

Every couple of years during the 1970s and 1980s, Kollek would prepare a 'development plan for the Arab sector' and present it at a press conference. All of these plans made grand promises but nothing ever came of them. Meanwhile, the disparity in the level of services and infrastructure in the two parts of the city became ever more glaring.

In 1986, Kollek called a press conference and at which, for the umpteenth time, he presented another 'development plan for the Arab sector' (very similar to the one presented in 1982). Members of the foreign press reported on the plan to the whole world. Before long, major infrastructure work appeared to be getting underway in the Old City and it looked as though this time the promises were finally being translated into action.

However, few people knew that this time, too, the 'development plan' was no more than a ruse intended to quiet the growing criticism of the national and city government's poor treatment of East Jerusalem; only a few people were aware of a secret addendum to the plan, which stated: "Development in the Arab sector has great significance for the 'display window' effect, and therefore those projects with the highest visibility were given the top designation of 5 in the plan. Projects with no visibility shall be designated with a 1 in the plan and should be kept to a minimum."[26] At the end of the 1970s, the Israeli government announced a national neighborhood rehabilitation project that included Arab neighborhoods in mixed city centers in Israel. Approximately $160 million was allotted to help Jerusalem's more impoverished neighborhoods. But the municipality did not earmark any of this money for any of the poor Arab neighborhoods, all of which lagged far behind even the poorest Jewish neighborhoods.

Nor did anything change in 1990, when the committee I headed published its findings that Israel had invested only $4 million in the Arab neighborhoods while having collected $7.5 million in municipal and other taxes from the Arab residents.[27]

In 1994, after he lost the mayoral elections and vacated his office, Kollek was scathingly critical of government policy towards the city's Arabs: "Whatever Israel's governments could do to make life harder for the Arabs in Jerusalem, they did. Whatever Israel's governments could do to prevent them from developing, expanding, building and improving the quality of their housing, they did."[28]

Paradoxically, it was Ehud Olmert of the Likud, who succeeded Kollek as mayor in 1993, who exposed the true dimensions of the neglect of East Jerusalem. Olmert was genuinely concerned about the increasing disparity in services and infrastructure between the different parts of the city. He understood that if this continued, Israel's hold on East Jerusalem would be weakened. For the first time since 1967, the mayor asked for a detailed report on the state of the infrastructure in the Arab section of the city.

When the report was released in 1995, the public finally got a real glimpse at the years-long neglect. A disparity in services was occurring in four areas: 1. Welfare – Over half the city's Arab residents were living below the poverty line, double the poverty rate for the Jewish population; 2. Housing – Housing in the Arab sector was over twice as crowded as in the Jewish sector; 3. Infrastructure – The quality of roads, water, sewage systems, sidewalks, street lighting and so on was far below that in the Jewish part of the city; 4. Services – Social services, sanitation, fire stations, postal service and so on also lagged behind.[29]

The report stated that, to close the gaps, a concerted government effort was necessary – costing $62.5 million the first year and $67 million in the ensuing stages.[30] Olmert asked Prime Minister Benjamin Netanyahu to allocate the resources required for the first stage at least, saying, "The government must cooperate with the municipality in building an infra-structure that will bring a dramatic improvement in the quality of life of the Arab residents . . . so that we will be able to stand firm, with determi-nation, and make clear that there can be no diplomatic and political compromise regarding the status of the entire city as the capital of Israel."[31] In wake of the pressure from Olmert, in early 1997 the govern-ment acknowledged the serious disparity and allocated the unprecedented sum of $32.5 million for services and infrastructure.[32] The dovish Labor governments of the preceding years had never offered anything close to that for East Jerusalem.

In 1997–1998, government funds began flowing to the municipality and Olmert launched development projects amid much media fanfare. The Arab residents, too, were amazed by the sudden attention being paid to their needs. But it soon became apparent that the Likud government's plan, like those of Labor before it, was nothing more than hollow slogans. Within a few months, the government announced that this development budget was being slashed to just $20 million, and by the following year the government had only transferred $7.5 million.[33]

Since then, the municipality has allocated no more than 5 percent of its budget to the Arab population, and the national government has not allotted anything for Arab East Jerusalem.

How did Israelization become Palestinization?

In December 1987, with the eruption of the first intifada, a new chapter began in Israel's relations with the Palestinians. It is hard to exaggerate the impact the intifada had on Jerusalem, which soon found itself squarely in the middle of the Palestinians' uprising. For them, at least one consequence of the intifada marked an important political achievement. It took the

Jordanian option off the agenda, and effectively brought to an end the historic, nearly two-decade episode of joint Israeli–Jordanian administration in the city. The partner for discussion about Jerusalem's future was no longer Jordan, but the PLO, the body representing the Palestinians. From this point until the Camp David summit in 2000, Israel would futilely attempt to keep the Jerusalem issue out of any final status talks with the Palestinians.

A year before the outbreak of the first intifada, a final opportunity to reach an Israeli–Jordanian accord on Jerusalem was missed when Prime Minister Yitzhak Shamir rejected the proposal for an international conference on the matter. Throughout that year, 1986, Israel's national unity government had been plagued by ceaseless personal clashes between Shimon Peres and Shamir. The rejection of the so-called "London Agreement," put forward by Foreign Minister Peres and King Hussein, with American backing, led to the break-up of the unity government.

In those days, Shamir considered an international conference a dangerous prospect, and preferred an autonomy agreement for the Palestinians in the territories, in the hope that the residents of the territories, under Faisal Husseini's leadership, would accept such an arrangement. Shamir also refused to accept any accord reached in an international conference or in a forum in which the PLO had any representation in the autonomy talks. The diplomatic stagnation that resulted from Shamir's obstinacy was one of the key factors behind the outbreak of the intifada a year later.

Until 1987, Israel had managed to keep the city relatively free of Palestinian terror. The economic dependence of the city's Arabs on the one hand and the 'joint administration' with Jordan in the city on the other contributed to the political quiet in Jerusalem. However, it was precisely the preferential status enjoyed by Jerusalem's Arabs in terms of freedom of movement, employment possibilities and economic benefits that led members of Jerusalem's Palestinian elite to take a leading role in the intifada and become some of its main political players. Israeli law and their blue Israeli IDs afforded the intifada's unofficial leadership in the city much more leeway for activity. From its base in Jerusalem, the intifada's united leadership printed broadsides for the uprising that were distributed all over the West Bank and Gaza;[34] it was also simple enough to send a fax with the same content to Europe, and from there, on the same day, to the PLO headquarters in Tunis for approval.

By the end of 1987, popular resistance in Jerusalem to the occupation had melded with the waves of violence of the intifada in the West Bank and the Gaza Strip. Israel had hoped that its efforts during the 1970s and 1980s to strengthen its rule and to keep order and security in East

Jerusalem would prevent such outbursts of violence in the city, but it was sorely disappointed.

Jews and Arabs alike see the first intifada as the turning point in the history of majority–minority relations in the city after 1967. The intifada intensified and cemented the segregation between the Arab minority and Jewish majority and essentially erased Israel's two decades of effort to unify the city.

The first intifada reached a climax on October 8, 1990: Following an announcement by the Jewish Temple Mount Faithful organization that its members planned to ascend the Temple Mount and lay the cornerstone for the Third Temple, a crowd of inflamed Muslim worshipers began hurling stones at Jews worshipping at the Western Wall. The Israeli security forces who stormed the Temple Mount were met with a barrage of rocks, to which they responded with live fire, killing 17 Muslims. In the aftermath of this incident, Jerusalem was inundated by a wave of violence, which began with a series of knife attacks: A young Arab, Said Abu Sirhan, stabbed to death three Jewish residents of Jerusalem's Baka neighborhood as 'revenge for the Al Aqsa massacre'; in the following months, there were more attacks of this kind, as well as suicide bombings whose perpetrators were admired as 'martyrs' by their people. According to journalist Danny Rubinstein: "This slaughter contained the first signs of the religious struggle for Jerusalem, which led to the phenomenon of the suicide bombers which was unprecedented in our conflict and perhaps also in other family conflicts throughout the world."[35]

Mayor Teddy Kollek succinctly summed up the painful new reality in Jerusalem: "Co-existence is dead."[36] With violence on the rise, the vision of co-existence continued to fade.

In a conversation I had with Faisal Husseini in the late 1990s, he remarked on the political significance of the violence in Jerusalem: "On the Jerusalem issue, the intifada brought us our two biggest political achievements: It proved to the Israelis and the entire world that the city is not united, and it made us, the Palestinians, the potential partners in its fate."[37]

In September 1996, the violence reached new heights. Prime Minister Benjamin Netanyahu, at the urging of Mayor Ehud Olmert, inaugurated the Western Wall tunnel. This event, too, like the massacre at Al Aqsa, was perceived in terms of the religious struggle and reverberated far beyond the city borders: 70 Palestinians and 16 Israelis were killed in the disturbances that broke out in the city and around the West Bank.

All of these events, which occurred next to the site holy to Muslims, added a new religious dimension to the national conflict, which now became a struggle to defend the Islamic holy places in Jerusalem. On September 28, 2000, opposition leader Ariel Sharon staged a visit to the

Temple Mount. The visit was undertaken with government permission, despite requests from Arafat and Husseini that it be blocked, as it would be seen as a provocation, and with the worst possible timing: right after the collapse of the Camp David talks and with scattered incidents of violence already starting to erupt in the West Bank and Gaza.

The next day, Friday, September 29, which was also Rosh Hashana eve, Palestinian youths who had come to pray on the Temple Mount began throwing rocks at the Jewish worshipers and police officers in the Western Wall plaza. In the ensuing riots, 7 Palestinians were killed and about 200 Muslim worshipers were injured. Palestinian radio broadcasts described the confrontation as an Israeli attack on the worshipers at Al Aqsa. Within a few hours, the clashes had spread from Jerusalem to the West Bank and Gaza Strip. Once again, the Temple Mount was the spot where the match was lit, this time for what would come to be known as the Al Aqsa intifada.

In wake of the violent events of the second intifada, physical barriers were put in place between Jerusalem and the West Bank. The continuation of terrorist attacks in Israel motivated Ariel Sharon's government to erect the separation fence. In Jerusalem, this had far-reaching significance not only in terms of security but in terms of the precedent it set for a physical division of the city. Currently nearing completion, this barrier is perhaps the final nail in the coffin of the slogan of 'United Jerusalem.' Almost forty years after the wall that divided the city until 1967 came down, the process of physically dividing it began again. A tall cement wall about 90 kilometers long now separates nine Arab neighborhoods (some of which are still villages) from the city in which approximately 60,000 Arab residents carry Israeli identity cards.

The World's Most Polarized City

The combination of the increasing violence of the two intifadas and the Palestinian Authority's growing political strength in East Jerusalem gave rise to two distinct rival entities, or what is known in the scholarly literature as a 'polarized city.' The premise held by the policy-makers in Jerusalem, i.e., that the passage of time would work in favor of co-existence and unity, turned out to be completely mistaken. As the years passed and the Israeli–Palestinian conflict worsened, so did the polarity within the capital. And as this happened, Israel's hold on East Jerusalem was weakened and the 'unity' of the city became little more than a hollow slogan.

In their book,[38] Romann and Weingrod described the two main types of rifts that arose as a result of these developments. The first is a "horizontal" rift between the two groups, the residents of East and West Jerusalem, which was evident in numerous spheres. Social ties, housing, economics, employment, trade, transportation, education, health and medicine, public and political administration. In all these, the degree of segregation was so great that in effect there was a clear ethnic boundary which neither group would cross. And this separation was found to be much more extreme than in other polarized cities.

The second is the "vertical" rift between the Jewish majority and the Arab minority, in terms of access to resources and political power. The Arab side is unavoidably dependent on economic cooperation, which primarily takes the form of dependence on the Jewish employer who dictates the terms, and the economic disparity between the two societies which, was large to begin with, is steadily growing. Nor can the Arab minority compete with the Jewish majority's ability to "establish facts in the field." However, over the years, the Arabs did come to present a geographic and demographic threat, thereby creating a political draw in which neither side was able to exert decisive control.

From all the research on polarized cities, it appears that Jerusalem may present the most striking case of a municipal conflict being a more extreme reflection of a national conflict. Scholars of the subject divide such cities into groups according to the degree of polarity and division in them. Cities in which the conflict is not national, but rather ethnic or cultural belong to a group in which the dividing lines are not as sharply drawn; these are referred to as 'mixed cities.' The category of 'polarized cities,' in which there is a higher degree of division, includes Jerusalem, Nicosia and Belfast – and a comparison of the three can be quite illuminating.

Nicosia, the capital of Cyprus, is at the center of the ethnic, religious and national conflict between the Greek and Turkish Cypriots. In 1974, the Turkish army invaded the island, and subsequently it was physically divided into two entities – The Turkish Republic of Northern Cyprus (recognized only by Turkey) and the Republic of Cyprus in the south, under the control of the large Greek majority. The capital, Nicosia, was divided by a wall separating the Turkish part from the Greek part. The military posts on either side of the wall, the fences and the different falgs all recall Berlin before the fall of the Berlin Wall, or Jerusalem before 1967.

Despite the unresolved conflict there, both parts of Nicosia attempt to maintain a degree of co-existence and normalization that does not exist in united Jerusalem. Within the framework of the normalization arrangements, goods and people are allowed passage between the two parts of the city. The electricity supply to the entire city is handled by a power station on the Greek side, while the water supply to the Greek side is provided by pumping stations on the Turkish side. City planning is coordinated by both municipalities and there is a mutual agreement to maintain quiet and calm in the divided city. Since 1974, both sides have scrupulously upheld this agreement and there have been no violent incidents.

The conciliatory attitude of the city's Greek majority is also pointed up by the readiness to preserve the memory of the pre-1974 united city. In contrast to what occurred in Jerusalem, the Greek majority has preserved all the Turkish names of the streets and plazas and neighborhoods in its section of the city.[39]

Belfast, until recently, was also at the center of an ethnic, religious and national conflict. The Protestant majority, British in origin, that governs Northern Ireland was seeking to perpetuate and preserve its independence by maintaining the connection with the United Kingdom. The Irish Catholic minority viewed the Protestant majority as an occupier and wished to be annexed to the Republic of Ireland. The often violent struggle of the Catholic minority with the Protestant majority had been going on since 1969 and left its mark on Belfast, the capital. As in Jerusalem, a geopolitical division is still apparent between the two parts of the city. In Belfast, the Protestant majority was seeking to ensure its political control and demographic hegemony. The demographic concern stemmed from the Catholics' high birth rate, which could have led to a Catholic majority in the capital. In Belfast, compared to Jerusalem, the polarity and separation is not as acute. The minority takes part in the government and gives it legitimacy. It participates in municipal elections and a decade ago, the city elected its first Catholic mayor. There are also social ties and even mixed marriages of Catholics and Protestants. The Protestant majority, seeking normalization and political quiet, has avoided an imbalance in city planning, and both national and city policies strive to ensure an equitable distribution of resources and services between the two communities. This policy even includes 'affirmative action' measures intended to aid the Catholics who are the poorer group in the capital.[40]

In both Nicosia and Belfast, efforts have been made to alleviate tensions, and the patterns of segregation and polarity in these cities are less acute than in Jerusalem. Hence, Jerusalem can claim the dubious top honor of being the most polarized city in the world.

Another interesting and perhaps more relevant comparison can be made with another capital city – Rome. The conflict over Rome as the capital of Italy is long forgotten now, but at the time bore many similarities to the conflict over Jerusalem as the capital of Israel. The solution that was found to that conflict is also intriguing. In the 19th century, the struggle between the Papal state that encompassed part of Italy, including the city of Rome, and the rest of Italy was no less bloody and violent than what Jerusalem has experienced in modern times.

When the Italian states were at last united into a single kingdom in 1866, with the support of France, the Papal kingdom with its capital in Rome refused to cede the city to Italy. This state of affairs was also connected to the wider European conflict that pitted France, the Pope's supporter and defender, against Prussia and Britain.

In 1870, following Napoleon III's defeat in the Franco-Prussian War, the Italians took advantage of the opportunity and conquered Rome. They annulled the rule of the Papal kingdom and transferred their capital from Florence to Rome. But the conflict didn't end there. The Pope did not recognize the Italians' conquest of the city and barricaded himself in the Vatican palace, which the Italians were reluctant to attack. He imposed an international ban on Italy, and the conflict endured for nearly 60 more years. It wasn't until 1929 that Pope Pius XI and Prime Minister Benito Mussolini were able to resolve the 'Rome problem' with the signing of the Lateran Treaties in which the Pope recognized the Italian conquest of Rome and annulled the international Catholic ban on Italy. In return, he received Italian and international recognition for the Vatican State and sovereignty over a part, however tiny, of Rome, and legal standing for the religious education system in Italy.

And so today, the borders of a single city – Rome – contain two capitals: the capital of Italy and the capital of the Vatican State.

CHAPTER SIX

The Failed Attempts
to Bring Peace

What do you care about a flag – an Arab flag?! All we're asking for is something outward, something symbolic. That's all. Who knows what will be five years from now? You will be there. No one is going to remove you from there. Just give this and you'll see how all the Muslim states join us.

(Egyptian Vice-President Hosni Mubarak, at the Egypt–Israel peace talks, 1977)

Jerusalem in the Peace Process: The Jordanian Option

Since 1978, when the peace agreement was signed with Egypt, Israel has continued to seek peace agreements with its Arab neighbors and a final status accord with the Palestinians. Of all the issues that have come up in this process, the thorniest is surely the issue of Jerusalem.

From the start of the process in 1977 through the second Camp David summit in 2000, the parties have held divergent positions: Israel seeks to present the issue of the holy places as secondary while the Arabs wish to make it central; Israel pushes for 'Jerusalem last' while the Arabs push for 'Jerusalem first'; Israel defines the problem from an administrative perspective of municipal autonomy and control of the holy places, while the Arabs define the problem from a political perspective of sovereignty and division of the city.

Just over a decade passed from the unification of the city to the peace agreement with Egypt, the first agreement ever signed by Israel with an Arab state. For all these years, Israel's governments believed that it was possible to reach a peace agreement with Arab countries and with the Palestinians without ceding or dividing Jerusalem. However, during the peace process with Egypt, these assumptions – that the Jerusalem issue could be considered secondary and postponed until the end of the process, or reduced to a debate about religious and municipal autonomy – were proven wrong.

Anwar Sadat, president of the largest, strongest and most important of the Arab states, made clear in his speech to the Knesset on November 21, 1977 that the peace process with the Arab states and the Muslim world required that Israel give up the dream of unified Jerusalem if it truly desired peace and reconciliation in the Middle East. He suggested that rather than postpone the Jerusalem issue to the end of the reconciliation process with the Arab countries, Israel should start off the peace process with a historic compromise on Jerusalem. On the Jerusalem issue, Sadat saw himself as representing the Arab and Muslim world as a whole and not only Egypt. He emphasized in his speech that Israel's rule in the Old City epitomized the Israeli occupation not only in the eyes of the Palestinians or the Arabs, but of all Muslims everywhere. Meaning that even the most moderate Arabs would never accept the annexation of the Old City to Israel. As Sadat saw it, the path to a broader peace had to pass through Jerusalem, and the time for this was now, as Egypt was preparing to sign its peace agreement with Israel.

Sadat knew, of course, that signing a peace agreement with Israel would isolate Egypt politically and elicit severe censure from the Arab world. Nevertheless, he was determined to proceed. The report he received from his aide, Hassan Tuhami, about the secret preliminary talks with Moshe Dayan, Begin's foreign minister, gave him reason to expect that he would be able to present the Arab world with a major pan-Arab and pan-Muslim achievement: an accord on Jerusalem.

The secret contacts between Tuhami and Dayan took place in Morocco in September 1977, for the purpose of clarifying the parties' positions on two issues – the Sinai and Jerusalem. As far as the Sinai, Dayan made it clear that, within the framework of a peace agreement, Israel was prepared to cede to Egypt the entire peninsula; with respect to Jerusalem, once Dayan explained Israel's position to Tuhami, Sadat felt he would be able to reach a satisfactory accord there as well.

The obvious question is: Just what did Moshe Dayan say that led Sadat to believe he could obtain an agreement on Jerusalem?

Dr. Eliahu Ben-Elissar, who was the director-general of Prime Minister's Office and a close associate of Begin's for many years, revealed in his book the details of the discussions between Tuhami and Dayan, and the reason why Sadat imagined that a solution for Jerusalem, a matter that was so crucial to him, was indeed attainable. According to Ben-Elissar, Tuhami explained to Dayan that the Arab states' sensitivity on the Jerusalem issue would come to the fore in the prospective Egyptian–Israeli accord. Thus, Begin had to know that this subject would arise in the peace talks. When Tuhami requested an assessment of the chances for an accord on Jerusalem, Dayan replied as follows: "We have inalienable rights . . . the Western Wall, the Jewish Quarter, the Mount of Olives and the [Hebrew] University." Dayan said not a word about the rest of the Old

City or the Temple Mount, implying that Israel made no claim to them. However, Ben-Elissar also writes: "Dayan cited the geographical and urban changes that Israel had made in East Jerusalem" – referring, evidently, to Israel's claim to the newly constructed neighborhoods in the eastern part of the city. Dayan is also said to have asserted: "A solution to the problem of the holy city may be easily found, to the satisfaction of all the parties."[1] In Ben-Elissar's view, Tuhami found Dayan's response sufficient to serve as a basis for the launching of official peace talks with Israel.

It is unclear whether Dayan's statements were made in coordination with the prime minister. It is known that Dayan was very loyal to Begin. Dayan's position on this issue, i.e., that the Israeli interest in East Jerusalem was limited to the Jewish Quarter, the Western Wall, the Mount of Olives and Mount Scopus, is also well known. This had consistently been his stance since June 1967, when he served as defense minister in the Eshkol government, and even much earlier, in 1948, when he conducted negotiations with the Jordanians on behalf of Ben-Gurion. Yet the question of whether Begin shared Dayan's view and supported all he said to the Egyptians remains. It does not seem very likely, considering that, later on, in the Camp David talks, Begin's position on this issue was quite unyielding. He was against negotiating over Jerusalem in the context of the accord with Egypt, and opposed any concession whatsoever in the Old City.

When the talks began, Sadat proposed a solution for Jerusalem that included the following elements:

- The city would retain its physical and municipal unity
- Sovereignty in East Jerusalem and in part of the Old City would be Jordanian, since all the Arab residents there held Jordanian citizenship
- Municipal administration would be handled jointly with the Palestinians, who would be part of the Palestinian autonomy in Judea and Samaria (the West Bank)
- The Temple Mount (Haram al-Sharif) and its mosques would come under Muslim control via representatives from Egypt, Morocco or Saudi Arabia
- The places cited by Moshe Dayan – Mount Scopus, the Western Wall, the Jewish Quarter and the new Jewish neighborhoods – would remain under Israeli rule

Egyptian vice-president Hosni Mubarak pressed the Israeli delegation to accept the proposal and thereby create an opportunity for a historic reconciliation with the Arab world. He made no attempt to hide the fact that an Egyptian achievement on the Jerusalem issue would redeem his country from its isolation within the Arab world. Mubarak insisted that an Israeli compromise on Jerusalem would be purely symbolic, as Ben-Elissar reports:

> We can't let them accuse us of having entirely given up on Jerusalem. You have to help us with this . . . You have to do something. It's psychological. Jerusalem will not be divided again. What do you care about a flag, an Arab flag? All we ask is for something outward, something symbolic, that's all. Who knows what will be in another five years? If you will be there, no one will remove you from there. Just give us this and you'll see how all the Muslim countries join us – Bangladesh, Pakistan, Indonesia, even Saudi Arabia . . . They'll be satisfied with something outward. They're waiting for an opportunity, for an excuse, to join us. They need to be given this excuse. A flag will suffice.[2]

Ten years after its rejection of the Jordanian option proposed by Egypt, Israel was forced to grapple with the 'Palestinian option' in Jerusalem, under much worse conditions. Possibly, a peace agreement with Egypt that included the Jordanian option would have enabled Jordan to join the peace process already in the late 1970s and have negated the Palestinian option in the West Bank.

In his speech to the Knesset in response to President Sadat, Begin refrained from elaborating on his position regarding Jerusalem. He said only that the Jerusalem issue was open to future negotiations: "Don't say no, that there will never be negotiations on a particular thing. I suggest, like the decisive majority in this parliament, that everything will be open to negotiation."[3] Later on, during the talks, Begin took a firmer stance on Jerusalem. Yet he did show a surprising readiness to compromise on the Temple Mount issue. At the time, Begin was not willing to let this be made public, and did not inform Sadat, but only the American president, Jimmy Carter, to whom he sent a letter outlining his position. Ben-Elissar also says that in his talks with Carter, Begin was unexpectedly willing to consider certain compromises in regard to the holy places. He floated a 'temporary' and 'non-binding' proposal that 'the holy places be made subject to the self-administration of each religion and its representatives' and that the Temple Mount be administrated by a number of Muslim countries in cooperation with a Palestinian representative from the autonomy's administrative council. Writes Ben-Elissar: "Begin was prepared to accept that, in addition to the confrontation states, the governing body on the Temple Mount would also include representatives of states that do not border Israel, such as Saudi Arabia, Morocco and Iran." When Carter asked him whether he meant that the arrangement for the Temple Mount should be similar to that of the Vatican in Rome, Begin replied: "We will consider all kinds of possibilities. We have not yet decided."[4]

Although qualified as 'temporary' and 'non-binding,' Begin's proposal shows that "he was ready to admit that Israel did not have sole political claim to Jerusalem, and that he was prepared to allow political representatives of the Arab states unofficial standing in the body administrating the Islamic holy places in Jerusalem," says historian Menachem Klein. Begin apparently recognized the political as well as religious significance of these sites. Moreover, he appeared ready to grant representatives of the Palestinian autonomy equal standing to that of representatives of official countries, thus, says Klein, leaving an opening for another political entity in Jerusalem in addition to Israel. Klein adds that if the Vatican model were to be applied to Jerusalem, sovereignty over the holy places would be independent and not as envisioned by Begin's autonomy plan. The Autonomy was not supposed to be independent in the international arena, which would not have been the case with an extraterritorial 'State of Islam' in Jerusalem. Secondly, citizenship in the Vatican State is acquired solely on the basis of one's function in the Vatican and not in the conventional sense of citizenship. Applying to Jerusalem the model of the relations between Italy and the Vatican would mean that in the very heart of the Old City a separate category of citizenship would be in effect. Applying the Vatican model to Jerusalem would require the removal of Israeli sovereignty from the Islamic holy places in Jerusalem and granting the Islamic sites in the city a higher standing than Begin's plan accorded to the rest of the 1967 territories.

The mere fact that Begin did not absolutely rule out the possibility of "Vaticanization" signaled a significant change in his position. In 1967, Begin had rejected the proposal put forward by Yigal Allon, that Jordan be given religious standing on the Temple Mount. Begin explained at the time that granting Jordan any sort of standing on the Temple Mount would necessarily extend it a degree of sovereign status that could undermine Israel's sovereignty over the site.

Begin's proposal had far-reaching political implications, which he must surely have understood: It meant ceding the Temple Mount to a different sovereignty and the existence of a foreign sovereignty in the heart of Jerusalem. Begin was well aware that Italy had no sovereignty over that small part of Rome occupied by the Vatican State. And he was prepared to consider the idea of establishing in Jerusalem a "State of Islam" along similar lines, at the expense of Israel's sovereignty there. Perhaps he saw it as a chance to open a new chapter with the Muslim world and to take a step toward peace with the rest of the Arab countries. But Begin felt that the time was not yet ripe to publicly raise this idea with an Arab leader, and for the time being would only share his thoughts about it with the American president.

Later on, during the talks, Jerusalem became a major obstacle that almost led to the break-up of the first Camp David summit. But Begin, in his tenacity, was able to delay the discussion of the Jerusalem issue. Not for long, though: In the years to come, it continued to be a central bone of contention despite repeated efforts by Israel's prime ministers to postpone it until the final stage of the peace process. It came up again in the autonomy talks, and then at the Madrid conference, in the Oslo Accords, in the peace agreement with Jordan, until finally, it became the main stumbling block at the second Camp David summit, in the summer of 2000.

Over the years, Israel was dismayed to see the position of the United States, its close ally, drift increasingly in the direction of the Arab positions on this issue. For the first decade following the city's unification, the Americans maintained a neutral position, but in 1978, for the first time, President Carter took a clearly pro-Arab stance on the question of the solution for Jerusalem. He stressed that the United States viewed East Jerusalem as 'occupied territory,' putting it on an equal footing with the rest of the territories. From that point on, US policy on Jerusalem has leaned toward the Arab position. Twenty-three years later, at the second Camp David summit, President Clinton made this perfectly explicit when he outlined a prospective division of Jerusalem on the basis of the demographic distribution.

In the 1980s, the 'Jordanian Option' was revived in two other peace initiatives. In both cases, an accord might have been reached on Jerusalem, akin to what Sadat proposed at Camp David, but they were rejected by the Israeli governments headed by Begin and then Shamir.

The first initiative was proposed on September 1, 1982, when US President Ronald Reagan announced his plan for peace in the Middle East. Not only was Reagan one of the friendliest presidents to Israel, he was the only one who made no attempt to hide his "personal" view that Jerusalem should not be divided and must remain completely under Israeli sovereignty. The Reagan plan called for Israel and Jordan to forge an interim agreement whereby a Palestinian autonomous zone would be established in the territories and East Jerusalem. After five years, Israel and Jordan would conduct negotiations to reach a final status accord on the territories and Jerusalem. This plan was designed to satisfy Begin, who advocated autonomy, and Hussein, who wanted to get the PLO out of the negotiating picture. The Reagan plan essentially provided an opportunity for Jordan and Israel to jointly administer the West Bank and East Jerusalem.

King Hussein consented in principle to the plan, on condition that in the course of the five-year transition period, Israeli settlement projects in the territories cease. Arafat, however, reacted furiously. He thought the proposal spelled a death sentence for any future possibility of a Palestinian state, and certainly did not wish to see the PLO neutralized as a negotiating partner with Israel. The other Arab states were also stunned by the Reagan plan, which would have restored King Hussein's rule in the West Bank, if only partially.

President Reagan's plan envisioned that a peace agreement with Jordan would prompt most of the world to immediate recognize Jerusalem as the capital of Israel, and that at least two Arab embassies – of Egypt and Jordan – would open in Jerusalem. Nonetheless, Israel was not ready to embrace it. Prime Minister Begin was concerned about the uncertain outcome of the negotiations after the initial five years, and was also unwilling to halt settlement construction during the transition period. And he was also upset with Reagan (a friend of Israel who had tried to tailor the proposal to suit Begin) for having publicized his plan without consulting with him first.[5]

In April 1987, the Jordanian Option came up one last time. Foreign Minister Shimon Peres, who was serving as Shamir's deputy prime minister in the unity government, came to an agreement with Hussein, with the knowledge and blessing of the Americans. The so-called 'London Agreement' called for the convening of an international peace conference with the participation of a Jordanian–Palestinian delegation, with the aim of obtaining a peace agreement on the basis of Palestinian autonomy in the territories under Jordanian patronage. The Jerusalem issue was left open to negotiation, on the basis of an understanding that King Hussein would be 'the guardian of the Islamic holy places in Jerusalem' and be allowed to fly a Jordanian flag on the mosques of Haram al-Sharif. The London Agreement essentially boiled down to 'territories for Jerusalem.' Hussein would regain control of most of the West Bank and Israel would retain control of united Jerusalem, apart from the Temple Mount and the Arab neighborhoods, which were to be connected to the West Bank by a Jordanian corridor.

Arafat reacted just as angrily to the London Agreement. Again, he saw it as a death knell for any independent Palestinian state, and objected to Israel retaining even partial control over East Jerusalem. And to top it off, the coveted role of 'guardian of the Islamic holy places in Jerusalem,' to which Arafat felt he was entitled, was to be permanently transferred to the royal Hashemite family. Acceptance of the London Agreement would have spelled the end of the PLO's role in the Palestinian struggle and its exit from the political stage.

Yitzhak Shamir rejected the London Agreement. He was unwilling to seek a peace agreement with Jordan in the framework of an international conference, for fear of the pressure to which Israel would be subjected in such a setting. And he was also livid at Peres for reaching this agreement behind his back.

1987: The 'Amirav–Husseini Affair' – A First Israeli–Palestinian Attempt to Agree on a Division of Jerusalem and Find Peace between the Two Peoples

In the summer of 1987, a great uproar arose over an effort that was viewed by many Israelis and Palestinians alike as a momentous missed opportunity, a sad failure of a first-of-its-kind dialogue that aimed to forge an almost impossible connection between opposite ends of the political spectrum from both peoples. The *Yedioth Ahronoth* newspaper later described it as "an attempt that, had it succeeded, would have brought Moshe Amirav and Faisal Husseini the Nobel Peace Prize."

In retrospect, I see this episode as the planting of the first seed of a peace dialogue between two Jerusalemites, inhabitants of the same city, who contracted 'Jerusalem Syndrome' and managed eventually to be cured of it and to formulate a logical compromise to the problem of the city so cherished by them both. Unfortunately, this compromise was proposed too soon, before conditions for it were sufficiently ripe. It would take another two decades of violence for both of the peoples and their leaders to arrive at exactly the same idea.

That summer, I was an active member of the right-wing Likud. I served in various roles on the party's central committee and was considered one of the party's prominent young ideologues. My closeness to party leader Yitzhak Shamir, who was serving then as prime minister, created opportunities for ideological and political discussions between us, and he frequently expressed respect for my views. In these talks, in which two of my close friends, Dan Meridor and Ehud Olmert – who were Knesset members and also very close to the prime minister, also took part, I brought up the subject of the possibility of a peace accord with the Palestinians, and hence the question of what sort of political arrangement could be found for Jerusalem was also discussed. Shamir's view was that Shimon Peres' ideas for a solution in the framework of a Jordanian Option with King Hussein were not feasible. And he repeated his opposition to an international conference, which he expected would seek to impose upon Israel an accord that ran counter to its interests.

In one of these talks, the possibility of establishing an extensive Palestinian autonomous zone, a quasi-state, in the West Bank and Gaza, was raised. Upon hearing this suggestion, Yitzhak Shamir said to me and to Dan Meridor, who was also present: "If the Palestinians come, without the PLO and without Yasser Arafat [whom Shamir viewed as an enemy bent on Israel's destruction] to direct talks with me – I'd be ready to consider extensive autonomy." When I asked him why he didn't put forward such an initiative right now, with Arafat in Tunis and his standing in decline, and the possibility that a decent offer of this kind could encourage a split between the residents of the territories and the PLO terror organization, Shamir replied: "There's no reason to hurry. For twenty years now, the Palestinians have been sitting by quietly, not rising up in revolt or resorting to terror, and so the cost of ruling them is low, even worthwhile, from our perspective . . . " Dan Meridor, agreeing with Shamir, added: "You know, it is surprising how quiet the Palestinians are being, considering the fact that they're under occupation . . . "

After that conversation, I got in touch with Professor Sari Nusseibeh. Nusseibeh, a Palestinian intellectual and scion of one of East Jerusalem's most distinguished families, was astonished when informed that I wanted to meet with him. Meetings between Israelis and Palestinians for the purpose of political dialogue were a real rarity in those days, and a meeting with a member of the Likud, who was a close associate of the prime minister and a major proponent of the 'Greater Israel' vision, was, at the time, just about inconceivable. Through the mediation of a mutual friend, we met for the first time to get acquainted.

At our very first encounter, Nusseibeh asked me whether Yitzhak Shamir had indeed abandoned the Jordanian Option and was prepared to speak directly with the Palestinians as preferred partners for a political accord. When I said yes, he said to me: "Then you must meet with Faisal Husseini, who is the unofficial leader of the Palestinians in the territories, and in Jerusalem in particular, and essentially represents the PLO. Talking with him would basically mean starting a dialogue between the Likud and the PLO."

At the time, a special Knesset law prohibited meetings between Israelis and members of the PLO, and in my case, a meeting with Husseini would not only be a violation of the law, it would be interpreted throughout the world as a precedent implying that a Likud prime minister was willing to begin a dialogue with the PLO, which still did not recognize the State of Israel and whose charter called for Israel's destruction.

I relayed the details of my talk with Nusseibeh and his suggestion to Yitzhak Shamir, who agreed to it, with some qualifications: "If Faisal Husseini is prepared to part ways with the PLO and to represent the Palestinians in such a dialogue, I am willing not only to have you speak with him, but also to invite him to speak with me, if he'll come with a top, reputable team of Palestinian leaders in the territories, and to start talking with them tomorrow morning."

Thus began a series of secret meetings between myself and Faisal Husseini, which stretched over an entire summer. In these talks, we both suggested far-reaching mutual concessions, and at the end, we signed a joint declaration of principles.

At the end of June 1987, I met with Faisal Husseini for the first time, at my home in the Ein Kerem neighborhood of Jerusalem. We were both excited at the mere thought of the occasion. Husseini – the son of Abdel Qader Husseini, a Palestinian leader who fell in the fighting against Israel in 1948, and the grandson of Musa Qassem Husseini, the former Jordanian mayor of Jerusalem, and a relative of Hajj Amin al-Husseini, who was the Grand Mufti of Jerusalem and led the 'Great Revolt' against the British in the 1930s – was a well-known figure in the Arab world and highly respected among the Palestinians.

Husseini began the conversation by saying in Hebrew: "I have never met with Israelis before, aside from the Israeli jailers in your prisons. Because of my time in prison, I learned Hebrew, but I always saw you as an enemy to be spoken with on the battlefield, since we really don't have anything to talk about. Both we and you want the same thing: I, a member of the PLO, espouse the ideal of Greater Palestine, while you, a member of the Likud, espouse the ideal of Greater Israel. If that's the case, then what is there for us to talk about?"

To which I replied: "I have never met with members of the PLO, aside from those I met on the battlefield in Jerusalem in 1967 and in Karameh in 1968. I killed some of your comrades there, while you killed some of my best friends. But why don't we talk about our children's future? You have a son you named Abdel Qader, after your father, the Palestinian leader, in the hope that he would perpetuate the legacy of the national struggle. I have a son whom I named Iri ("my city") after unified Jerusalem, which I helped to liberate, and my hope was that it would become a city of peace. Both our children, Abdel Qader and Iri, are the same age and they live in the same country, in the same city, even. What will be their fate? Is it possible to find for their sake – not for ours – hope for peace in this city, which has seen more wars than anyplace else on earth? Are the two of us capable of reaching a compromise that will guarantee them a better future than one of prisons and battlefields? This is what we ought to talk about!"

I'll never forget the lengthy silence that fell then in the room. Husseini glanced around the house, an Arab house in the village of Ein Kerem where a Palestinian family had lived until 1948, when it fled the military onslaught. And now I, the victor, was hosting the vanquished in this house. Perhaps Husseini expected to hear from me the conditions for surrender that Yitzhak Shamir wished to dictate to his people . . . Instead I began:

"What I'm offering you is partnership over this country and this city. I am prepared to part with the dream of Greater Israel and united Jerusalem under Israeli rule, if you are prepared to part with the dream of

Greater Palestine and to give up Jaffa and to suffice with a part of Jerusalem, but not all of it. If you are ready for that – then we do have something to talk about!"

"Did Yitzhak Shamir authorize you to say these things?," Husseini asked.

"No," I answered. "I am not authorized to speak on anyone's behalf but my own. But if we do agree on something – we shall bring it to Shamir and to Arafat and try together to convince them that this is the basis for a historic compromise between the two peoples."

And so began a series of secret meetings that took place over the course of that summer – at my home in Ein Kerem, at his home in East Jerusalem, and at the Institute for Palestinian Studies at Orient House.

Little by little, we built up mutual trust, which grew into mutual respect and eventually into genuine friendship – an amazing friendship that each of us deeply appreciated. During those long nights of discussions, we both felt the bonds of 'Jerusalem Syndrome' lifting; we became able to strip away all the myths and dreams surrounding this city and to treat it as a place where people have to live together, and not die together.

One day, I showed up for a meeting at Husseini's home with my eleven-year-old son Iri. I explained to Husseini that my son wanted to meet his son. The two boys went into another room to chat as best they could in broken English, while Husseini and I continued conversing in Hebrew about the outline for a historic compromise. For the first time in the history of the conflict, it seemed that 'understandings,' as we called them, were beginning to take shape. And the main understanding was this: two states for two peoples with one city as the shared capital of both.

Our talks that summer went beyond a discussion of broad principles and understandings; we also delved into details like national symbols, mutual recognition of the suffering inflicted by each side upon the other, open borders and a joint Jerusalem city council for both peoples with two mayors – one for the east and one for the west. At times, we would catch ourselves and wonder if we weren't going too far, and by just what authority we imagined so easily dispensing with a dispute that, up to now, had appeared completely irresolvable.

During that summer, I reported to Yitzhak Shamir about the talks in general terms, while Husseini relayed detailed reports to Arafat in Tunis. At first, Shamir seemed quite intrigued by the possibilities. Defense Minister Moshe Arens and MKs Meridor and Olmert, who were also in on the matter, viewed this dialogue as an interesting but non-binding intellectual exercise and warned me against any attempt to involve the PLO in Tunis. Shamir stressed to me: "Husseini is a partner, but not Arafat!" Arafat, as I learned from Husseini, was most enthusiastic. He was constantly asking Husseini to compose together with me a memorandum of understandings in English, Hebrew and Arabic, and said he would be satisfied if just the two of us, Husseini and I, signed it.

As July approached, I was ready for this, too. I knew that Shamir would be opposed. However, having gone as far as I had already, I said to myself: "Moshe, this is a historic opportunity! Don't miss it and don't be afraid! Pursue it to the end!"

And so, at the end of July, Husseini and I signed a joint document that laid out for the first time the principles for peace between the two peoples, with an emphasis on the idea that the Likud government had to forgo the dream of Greater Israel and that the PLO had to recognize the State of Israel.

One morning, a few days after we'd relayed copies of the document to Yitzhak Shamir and to Yasser Arafat, I received a phone call from the Prime Minister's Office. Shamir was requesting an urgent meeting with me. I was in his office within the hour. I imagined that Shamir would be angry, and so I arrived all prepared to explain that this was a non-binding document that could form the basis for future negotiations, that it was an intellectual and not a political paper, and so on. But I was in for quite a surprise. Shamir seethed with rage:

"I did not give you permission to sign a joint document! Do you even have any idea what happened with your innocent little document?"

"It got to Arafat" – I answered, and started in with my explanations in the hope of assuaging his fury.

But the prime minister cut me off to inform me, to my great astonishment, that the document was already on the desk of the Romanian leader Ceausescu, who was close to Arafat, and that he had invited the two of them, Arafat and Shamir, to Bucharest in order to begin secret negotiations on the basis of Husseini's and my paper.

"It's a trap that Arafat set for you!" the prime minister shouted. "Now Arafat will use this document to obtain the United States' recognition of the PLO's status as a partner to the discussion, while I naïvely thought that our partner would be Husseini and the Palestinians in the territories . . . "

"Then maybe you ought to travel to Bucharest anyway?" I suggested to Shamir. "Maybe this is a historic opportunity to begin negotiations with the PLO. What's more, I know that you agree with most of the things we wrote in the document . . . "

"Absolutely not!" said Shamir sternly, "And I demand that you immediately suspend the talks with Husseini and inform him that you are removing your signature from the document!"

"Mr. Prime Minister," I replied, "I will not suspend the talks or remove my signature, and if you do not wish to continue on this course – then history will judge you for missing this opportunity . . . "

The tough conversation with Shamir left me quite upset. When I arrived home, and had yet to calm down completely from that highly charged meeting, I got a phone call from Husseini:

"Arafat wants to meet you the day after tomorrow in Geneva. He's ready to start talks with Shamir and wants to make sure that Shamir is ready for it," he told me.

"I'll get back to you soon," I said.

I immediately called my friend Dan Meridor and told him about the conversation with Shamir and about Arafat's invitation. Meridor was horrified:

"I suggest that you do not go to Geneva and that you halt all the talks. If this gets out – it will only cause damage to the Likud and to the government, so don't publicize anything of this!"

I called Husseini back to tell him that I wouldn't go to Geneva and about Shamir's reaction. He wasn't home. His wife told me that just a few minutes earlier, he had been arrested by members of the security forces and taken to an unknown location for detention.

That night, I couldn't sleep a wink. I read the document over and over again, and resolved to make it public. The next day, all the news programs in Israel opened with the story of the 'Amirav–Husseini affair,' which continued to be a focus of the Israeli and international media throughout that fall.

Husseini was being held an Israeli prison and I couldn't even convey to him my apologies and my regret for what had happened. Sari Nusseibeh, who had brought Husseini and me together, was badly beaten by Palestinian students at Bir Zeit University where he taught, and hospitalized with a broken hand. The students accused him of having betrayed the Palestinian dream and denounced him for having contacts with someone from the Likud who was close to the prime minister. Many Palestinians thought I'd laid a trap for Husseini, and many Israelis believed that Husseini had laid a trap for me, calling me a naïve academic.

Suddenly I found myself at the center of a tumultuous debate that swept up the Israeli public. Some saw me as the lone "sane man" in the Likud; but many more viewed me as a traitor to my country. The political uproar was echoed in arguments that raged throughout that autumn in Likud branches all over the country. I went to all those places and spoke about the need to shelve the dream of Greater Israel, to divide the land between us and the Palestinians and to make Jerusalem a shared capital. In some instances, fists even began to fly when devout Likud members tried to physically attack me.

Nor was my family spared: Anonymous phone calls were made to the house, threatening my life. My wife and children were genuinely frightened. But, hardest of all for me was the reaction of my father, a veteran Likudnik who did not hide his anger over my conversations with a member of the PLO. All my attempts to explain to him what we'd talked about were of no avail.

Before long, the affair had grown to such proportions that Yitzhak Shamir was unable to control what was happening. He understood that Husseini's arrest was not enough, and ordered that I be tried by the Likud court. Tzahi Hanegbi, the prime minister's aide (and later an MK and a minister), filed a motion to have me removed from the Likud for 'ideological deviation.'

In a trial that was covered by both the Israeli and international media, I was accused of disseminating ideas contrary to the ideology of the Likud. Before the court could rule, I took matters into my own hands and, in a symbolic act, tore up my party membership card and announced that I was leaving the movement that had been my political home since I was fourteen years old. My departure from the Likud made big waves, but it did not trigger an ideological crisis. Close friends who had previously been supportive of my ideas got cold feet and toed the party line, while I continued to preach my views from every possible public platform.

For the Palestinians, the episode was a source of great disappointment in the Likud. The Palestinian press wrote that Shamir's stubborn refusal to conduct negotiations with the PLO would lead to a popular uprising and to waves of violence: "Only by force shall we liberate Palestine" screamed the headlines in East Jerusalem. And indeed, just three months later, in December 1987, the first intifada began. The Palestinian popular uprising, which Shamir predicted would never happen since nothing like it had occurred in the previous two decades, erupted full force throughout the Gaza Strip, the West Bank and Jerusalem.

Hanna Siniora, a leading Palestinian figure, declared about a week after the outbreak of the intifada: "The only way to stop the violence in the territories is to start talking with the Palestinians on the basis of the Amirav–Husseini document." Sari Nusseibeh, who had been present at nearly all of my meetings with Husseini, embarked on a public relations campaign on behalf of the Amirav–Husseini document. He was arrested, too, on charges of being an organizer of the intifada.

In a phone call a few months later, Abu Mazen, who held the Israel portfolio in the PLO at the time, said to me:

"This was Shamir's last opportunity to reach an accord with the PLO without bloodshed. From now own, the violent intifada is what will bring about peace between the peoples."

Following the intifada, a historic change occurred in the PLO's position, as it agreed to recognize Israel's existence and to seek a peace agreement with it. In 1988, the PLO annulled the Palestinian charter that called for Israel's destruction and effectively adopted the position that was set down a year earlier in the Amirav–Husseini document.

In wake of the intifada, Yitzhak Shamir finally agreed to attend an international peace conference with the Palestinians in Madrid. Faisal Husseini, whom Shamir had released from prison for the purpose of attempting to reopen a peace dialogue with him, headed the Palestinian delegation. Husseini announced in Madrid that the Palestinian people's representatives to the talks were Arafat and the PLO, and that he was acting as their emissary at the peace conference.

In the years to come, Husseini and I would cross paths numerous times. We became comrades in arms – fighters for mutual recognition: by the PLO of the State of Israel and by Israel of the Palestinians' right to a state of their own and a capital in Jerusalem.

A New Player on the Jerusalem Stage: The Palestinians

With the Palestinians moving from the sidelines to the center of the political stage in Jerusalem, and some of the historic 'players' being pushed aside, the issue changed from 'Who has sovereignty over Jerusalem?' to 'Whose capital will Jerusalem be?'[6] Israel argued 'It's all mine,' while the Palestinians said 'It must be divided – with the west as your capital and the east as our capital.' The objective set by the Palestinians – 'two capitals in one city' – derived from the national goal they had defined in the late 1980s: 'two states in historic Palestine. Israel, and Palestine alongside it.'

Until 1967, the Palestinian struggle for Jerusalem and for an independent state appeared hopeless. The division of the land and of Jerusalem between Israel and Jordan, and the international community's de facto acceptance of the results of the 1948 war in Jerusalem, made it difficult for the Palestinians to define their national struggle as one for the 'liberation of Jerusalem.' The situation in the years in which the Old City was under Arab sovereignty, and the Islamic holy places were under Muslim control, caused the Palestinians to stress the 'liberation of Palestine' from Israel, to a great degree at the expense of the 'liberation of Jerusalem,' a term they refrained from using so as to avoid a confrontation with Jordan. However, after June 1967, once the Old City and its Islamic holy places had fallen into the hands of 'the Israeli enemy,' the emphases shifted. From this point on, the struggle to liberate Jerusalem became a very powerful impetus within the larger goal of liberating Palestine.

However, even after 1967, the Palestinians were still perceived as 'supporting players' on the margins of the struggle for Jerusalem, while Jordan still held onto the leading role vis-à-vis Israel as far as the demand to liberate Arab Jerusalem. Jordan's strength in this regard had two origins: the loyalty of the city's Arab residents to Jordan, which, with

Israel's consent, paid the salaries of many city officials; and the international – and primarily American – view that the city's final status would be determined in an accord between Israel and Jordan. One example of this could be seen in the first American attempt at mediation in the region in 1970, when the US Secretary of State, William Rogers, proposed, as part of a comprehensive peace plan, a solution for Jerusalem that was based on 'the Jordanian option.'

Nonetheless, the Palestinians set a clear strategic goal: to take Jordan's place as the 'leading player' and as a partner for negotiations with Israel on Jerusalem, and to replace the Jordanian option with a Palestinian option. In the 1970s, this goal still appeared to be very far off.

For the sake of this objective, the PLO developed strategies to be applied in three different spheres – the international sphere, the Muslim-Arab sphere and the Israeli sphere. In the first, the Palestinians sought to obtain international recognition for their primary standing on the Jerusalem issue while divesting Jordan of its standing. In the second, they sought legitimation for their standing in regard to the Islamic holy places. And in the third, they sought to halt the Israeli policy of 'creating facts on the ground.'

The lion's share of the PLO's effort in the first sphere was directed at the United States, because of its status as a superpower and Israel's patron. Getting the Americans to support the Palestinians rather than Jordan as the main player on the Jerusalem issue would be the very apogee of international recognition. And by the late 1980s, the United States' readiness to recognize the PLO brought about just such a state of affairs. As international recognition grew for the PLO acting as the representative body for West Bank residents in their demand for self-definition, support for the Palestinians as the leading player on the Jerusalem issue increased accordingly.

In wake of the intifada and Israel's willingness to attend the Madrid conference, the US Secretary of State advocated a new policy: The Palestinians, and not the Jordanians, would be Israel's 'partner' in any discussions about Jerusalem. This process continued throughout the 1990s. In 2000, when the Clinton administration formulated its proposition for an accord in Jerusalem, it was based on the idea of a division of the city between Israel and the Palestinians. The Jordanians no longer had any standing on the matter.

On the inter-Arab level, the Palestinians also managed to gradually gain precedence over Jordan in terms of political status in Jerusalem, and then religious status, too. In the early 1980s, largely in reaction to the passage of the Basic Law: Jerusalem, the Palestinians were able to obtain legitimacy from the Summit of the Arab League for their claim to sole sovereignty in the city. By the 1990s, they had earned pan-Arab and pan-

Muslim support for their senior standing in regard to the Islamic holy places.

For the Palestinians, all of these changes meant that three decades' worth of efforts to attain primacy in Jerusalem, at the expense of Jordan, had paid off.

In the third, Israeli, sphere, the Palestinians launched two strategies. The first was of 'popular resistance,' which meant boycotting the Israeli government and staging a moderate civil rebellion. The aim was to thwart Israel's ongoing attempts since 1967 to create a state of 'normalization' in the city and the 'Israelization' of its Arab inhabitants. During the first intifada, which erupted in December 1987 and quickly swept through the territories, it was in East Jerusalem (despite the relatively low level of violence there) that the most important political turnabout occurred. The uprising put the lie to the twenty-year-old Israeli myth of Jerusalem as a unified city where Jews and Arabs co-exist in peace.

In the face of the Israeli attempt to loosen the Arabs' physical and symbolic grip on Jerusalem, the second Palestinian strategy during this period was to 'create counter-facts' – physical, demographic and symbolic – in response to those created by Israel. This approach, spearheaded primarily by Faisal Husseini, could be summed up in one word: *sumud*, or the ideal of clinging steadfastly to one's land. By rallying the Palestinians around numerous national and autonomous institutions, with Orient House being the most prominent, the groundwork was laid for the 'capital in the making.'

From the early 1990s on, the Palestinians were gearing up for the eventual discussion of a final status accord in the city. Their goal was to create cracks in the Israeli consensus concerning the 'unity of Jerusalem' and to come up with practical models for a division of the city.

Meanwhile, during the 1990s, the brunt of Israel's diplomatic efforts shifted from an attempt to obtain legitimacy in the international arena to a tenacious struggle to halt the Palestinians' attempts to 'create facts on the ground.' But this effort, too, was doomed to failure. By the late 1990s, the Palestinians had managed to establish numerous physical and symbolic 'facts' in Jerusalem. Most important of all: The eastern part of the city had become 'the Palestinian capital in the making.'

In the Oslo Accords, Israel pledged not to impede the activity of the Palestinian institutions in East Jerusalem, and even to encourage it.[7] But even before the signing of those accords, Israel had allowed dozens of Palestinian institutions, such as the chamber of commerce, professional associations, workers' federations, charitable organizations, colleges and councils to operate in Jerusalem. These institutions assisted the populace in a wide range of areas, such as housing, tourism, health, research, journalism, culture and more. The Palestinians were able to have autonomy in education and transportation, and also with their religious institutions, such as the Supreme Muslim Council, the Muslim Waqf and the Shari'a Court. All of these served as an organizational basis and a legal precedent for the Palestinians' new policy in Jerusalem: the establishment of national institutions that were intended to constitute the infrastructure for 'the capital in the making.' Foremost among these were Orient House and the Palestinian security forces.

Orient House, in the heart of East Jerusalem, not far from the American Colony hotel, functioned in the 1990s as the unofficial Palestinian foreign ministry. The place originally served as a center for academic research and as a meeting place for members of the foreign media, and in 1979 Faisal Husseini had founded the Arab Studies Society, and under this aegis, in the 1980s, he worked to coordinate support for the PLO in Jerusalem. Activity here included recruitment and public relations, as well as the disbursal of funds for different national causes. As of March 1991, the activity here also had Israeli government approval. The Shamir government's consent for Orient House to be the headquarters for the work of the 'technical committees' – committees of experts who prepared the working papers and position papers for the Palestinian delegation to the negotiations at the Madrid conference – drew strong criticism from a number of ministers, including Ariel Sharon. However, Prime Minister Shamir was determined to allow Orient House to operate freely as a governmental center for the Palestinians, in the hope that it would eventually serve as a counterweight to the PLO in Tunis.[8] But Shamir's expectation that he would be able to separate the 'internal PLO' (Husseini) from the 'external PLO' (Arafat) was very soon disappointed.

From 1991 until 1994, when the PLO established its headquarters in Gaza, Orient House operated as the PLO's unofficial extension in Jerusalem, and a Palestinian flag was flown on top of the building. Between the time of the Madrid conference and the declaration of principles between Israel and the Palestinians, 47 diplomatic meeting were held in Orient House with representatives from the United States, France, Britain and Russia. Subjects related to the negotiations were discussed, and aid agreements were signed.[9] Between the signing of the Oslo Accords and the summer of 1995, representatives from 29 more countries, including one prime minister, two deputy prime ministers, five foreign ministers, two deputy foreign ministers, nine ministers and many ambassadors paid visits to Orient House.[10]

Gradually, a 'government' or 'municipality' in miniature developed at Orient House. Different departments dealt with municipal matters, with obtaining permits to visit relatives in Arab countries, with the construction and renovation of schools, with the economic development of East Jerusalem and with legal matters such as resolving civil disputes and approving land deals. And all of this was done by circumventing the Israeli legal system. Orient House also coordinated the elections for the Palestinian National Council, housed the Palestinian Center for Statistics and prepared working papers for the Palestinian Authority on the Jerusalem issue in anticipation of the final status talks in 2000.[11]

In ten years of essentially serving as the Palestinian government center, Orient House achieved its goal: creating a Palestinian governmental infrastructure in Jerusalem. However, after Faisal Husseini's death in 2001, Orient House practically ceased functioning and its profile plummeted as the governmental functions now shifted to the Palestinian Authority in Gaza.

The Taboo of the 'Unity of the City' is Broken

From the late 1970s until the Camp David talks in 2000, the Palestinians' goal was to undermine the Israeli consensus regarding the unity of Jerusalem. Israel's refusal to discuss the Jerusalem issue in either the interim or final status negotiations stemmed from an ostrich-like, head-in-the-sand approach: If we keep putting it off, maybe time will work in our favor and alter the harsh reality. But, starting in the 1990s, more and more Israelis became willing to begin a dialogue on the basis of the principle of 'dividing Jerusalem,' and in 2000, there was also an Israeli government that was ready to do so.

Starting in the early 1990s, when the Palestinians still could not conduct talks with Israel's governments on any sort of arrangement regarding Jerusalem, Israelis and Palestinians began holding unofficial talks in the framework of working groups, with the participation of hundreds of Israeli experts, researchers and public figures. From the Palestinians' perspective, these dialogues had two objectives: The first and most important was preparing Israeli public opinion for the shattering of the taboo about the unity of the city. The second was to seriously examine potential models for a division of the city. The Israelis, for their part, sought to clarify just how much the Palestinians were ready to concede in the city.

These unofficial meetings did indeed help to create fissures in the Israeli consensus about the 'unity of Jerusalem,' and at the same time they helped to create a common political and professional language that made possible the joint formulation of potential solutions to the Jerusalem question. The fruits of this dialogue were reaped at the Camp David summit, where the official delegations reached agreement on a majority of the issues related to Jerusalem. The models developed by these dialogue groups were of benefit to both the Israeli and Palestinian delegations.

The Palestinians who took part in these dialogues had very limited information about Jerusalem. The Palestinian leadership, which was head-quartered in Tunis at the time, was not very well-acquainted with the city. Better versed on the subject were a number of Palestinian scholars in Jerusalem and academics at universities abroad. By the time the Palestinians came to the Camp David talks, they were equipped with extensive knowledge and had firm ideas about the final status accord they wished to obtain in the city. The grandiose, radical political slogans that called for a division of Jerusalem along the 1967 lines, for evacuating the urban settlements – the new neighborhoods that were built in East Jerusalem – and the return of the Arab neighborhoods that were conquered in 1948, such as Katamon, Baka and Musrara, were now replaced by a 'practical' Palestinian approach based on transforming the de facto reality in Jerusalem into a de jure reality, i.e., acceptance of the 'facts' that were created after 1948 and after 1967. The models were based on principles of cooperation and separation: the idea of a city that is undivided physi-cally but serves as a joint capital for two nations.

Academics, experts and politicians from both sides participated in these dialogues; however, their political standing was completely different. The Palestinian participants had a direct affiliation with the PLO administra-tion in Tunis, and in this sense they represented it, while the Israeli side was made up of people identified with the 'peace camp,' who were ready to break the taboo of the 'wholeness of Jerusalem.' They did not represent the Israeli government, the Jerusalem municipality or even the Zionist parties, who were reluctant to state clearly that Jerusalem must be shared. Even the extreme left party Meretz was speaking only in vague terms about such a possibility then.

The first attempt to hold such a dialogue about Jerusalem's future, on the premise that it had to serve as a 'dual capital' for Israel and Palestine or, in other words, 'two capitals for two peoples,' was made in July 1991 at Stanford University in California. The academic setting made it possible to circumvent the law that prohibited political meetings with PLO members. The conference was organized by Faisal Husseini, in his capacity as head of the Center for Palestinian Studies at Orient House, Hanna Siniora, editor of the *Al-Fajr* newspaper, Professor Moshe Ma'oz, head of the Truman Institute at the Hebrew University, and me (at the time I was a member of the administration of the Jerusalem municipality). Arafat approved the participation of the Palestinian side and even sent a senior representative – Dr. Nabil Sha'ath, the chairman of the PLO political committee. For the Palestinian participants, the goal was to examine whether agreement could be reached that would adequately prepare Israeli public opinion for the prospect of breaking the Israeli consensus on the 'unity of Jerusalem.' The Palestinian side also included academics like

Professor Rihad Issawi and Dr. Bernard Sabella, and the Israeli side was comprised of Professor Moshe Ma'oz, Brigadier-General (res.) Giora Furman, the former air force commander, Professor Galit Hazan-Rokem, Brigadier-General (res.) Oded Megiddo and myself. Participating on behalf of Stanford University was Professor Lee Ross, a world-renowned psychologist and head of the university's Center for Conflict Resolution. The discussions were moderated by Harold Saunders, a former aide to US Secretary of State Henry Kissinger.

During the conference, Arafat was in daily contact with the Palestinian participants and instructed Nabil Sha'ath from afar on the positions he should present on behalf of the PLO. The Palestinian position on Jerusalem, as presented at the conference, was based on the following four principles: (1) The city must be open and not divided by any physical barrier; (2) The area of the city must be expanded to create 'metropolitan Jerusalem' with Arab and Israeli sub-municipalities (this plank called for the Israeli expansion to encompass the outlying communities of Givat Ze'ev and Ma'aleh Adumim as well); (3) The Old City and the holy places would be subject to a special regime; and (4) Jerusalem would serve as a joint capital for the Palestinian state and for Israel.

These principles, which were agreed to by both sides in a document signed by Nabil Sha'ath with Arafat's blessing, and for the ten years that followed, served as the basis for the Palestinians' position on the final status arrangement in Jerusalem.

At a joint press conference in Jerusalem, Faisal Husseini and I presented the decisions reached at the conference regarding a two-state solution with two capitals in a single open city. In Tunis, Dr. Nabil Sha'ath presented the decisions from the conference to the PLO executive committee. The committee approved it, and expressed the hope that this initial crack in the Israeli consensus about the unity of Jerusalem would eventually widen and reach the Israeli government and the broader public.

In the year after the Stanford conference, Hanna Siniora, the American researcher Dr. Cecilia Albin and I developed, under the aegis of the Truman Institute and in collaboration with Stanford University, a model for a final status accord in Jerusalem based on the discussions at the conference.[12]

Though the conference did not herald a change in Israeli public opinion, the mere fact that it took place helped to open up an Israeli–Palestinian dialogue about Jerusalem. Hanna Siniora and I started IPCRI – the Israel Palestine Center for Research and Information – through which, in the early 1990s, at the Notre Dame Monastery in Jerusalem, we held dozens of secret meetings between experts in various fields. Between 1990 and 1993, about two hundred Israeli and Palestinian city planners, sociologists, economists, engineers and security personnel took part in these Notre Dame talks. The material they prepared provided as a basis for expanding the public discourse about the possibilities for a solution in Jerusalem.[13]

Between 1993 and the Camp David talks in 2000, more than 30 Israeli–Palestinian discussion groups worked on formulating the outlines for final status arrangements in the city.[14] By the end of the 1990s, almost all the Israeli research institutes that deal with conflict resolution had joined the Israeli–Palestinian dialogue. Most notable was the Jerusalem Institute for Israel Studies, which built a database and devised alternative solutions to the Jerusalem question that were used by the policy-makers in preparation for the Oslo Accords, and by the Barak government.

In May 2000, the Jerusalem Institute published a paper entitled 'The Peace Accords in Jerusalem,' in which a practical and detailed plan for a division of Jerusalem was presented. It proposed that the city remain open and comprise two capitals, with the Old City coming under a special administration.[15] Up to this point, the idea of dividing the city had only been put forward by fringe groups. But the publication of the findings of the Jerusalem Institute, the most highly respected of institute in this field and one identified with the center of the political map, brought the idea to the center of the academic consensus. Subsequently, many in Israel came to see a 'division of Jerusalem' as a necessary, even desirable, solution, both from the urban and the national perspective. The advantages it offered over a continuation of the current situation came to be a matter of agreement among most of the academics studying the possibilities for a political solution in the city.

Since 1990, Faisal Husseini and I had headed numerous discussion groups about the future of Jerusalem, and we had covered a large range of the topics: new perceptions of sovereignty, the desired economic regime for the city, territorial exchanges and connections between the neighborhoods, administration of the holy places, joint operation of the local Atarot airport as an international airfield, a joint police force for the seam areas and the Old City, and more. As the Camp David talks approached, it was only natural for the official delegations of Prime Minister Barak and of PA Chairman Arafat to include many of the people who had been involved for years in a dialogue concerning a potential final status arrangement for the city. Hence, at Camp David, I headed Barak's team of experts while Arafat's team was headed by Professor Manuel Hassassian and Faisal Husseini.

Camp David 2000: Israel is Willing to Divide Jerusalem

The issue that Israel tried for years to push off until the very end quickly became the central and paramount issue in the talks. This time, the attempt to put aside the issue failed largely because of the United States' insistence on a detailed discussion and progress on the matter in tandem with any possibility of progress on all the rest of the core issues – borders, refugees, settlements and security arrangements.

Long before this, in October 1995, Prime Minister Yitzhak Rabin had presented his government's position on the final status accord, namely that Jerusalem in its present borders would remain united under Israel's sovereignty. Rabin defined the objective as 'metropolitan Jerusalem,' which would also encompass Ma'aleh Adumim, Gush Etzion, Efrat, Beitar Illit and Givat Ze'ev. He steadfastly refused to reveal what concessions he would be ready to make in Jerusalem, and preferred to leave vague Israel's consent to a 'compromise' in the city until a later date, once agreement had been reached on all the rest of the core issues.

The installation of the Barak government in May 1999 accelerated the attempts to reach a final status accord. In the Sharm el-Sheikh Memorandum, January 2000 was set as the target date for the signing of the framework for the final status accord. Ehud Barak believed that within the framework of a true peace that would bring the historic conflict to an end, it would be possible to find an agreed-upon solution for Jerusalem. Barak envisioned that the outlying Arab neighborhoods would come under Palestinian sovereignty and that their capital would also be located in one of these areas – Abu Dis. In the Old City, Barak was prepared for the Islamic and Christian holy places to be granted extraterritorial status.

The Israeli preparations for the second Camp David talks were still shadowed by the public and political taboo about the possibility of a division of the city. Barak was careful not to give away too much about his positions on the Jerusalem question. He believed that at the end of the process, once understandings had been reached on all the other issues, the sides would be prepared for historic compromises on Jerusalem, too.

Meanwhile, Barak instructed his team to conduct a public opinion survey to see just how ready the Israeli public was to part with the concept of 'unified Jerusalem.' He was not surprised to find that a majority of the Israeli public no longer viewed its capital as united. The public's readiness for concessions in Jerusalem, too, encouraged him to seek creative solutions that would enable Israel 'to share the pie' while still leaving it whole and united.'

Attorney Gilad Sher, who was Barak's bureau chief at the time and one of the people closest to him, described in his book the feeling of the Israeli delegation members at Camp David when it became apparent, within the first two days of the talks, that the Jerusalem issue could not be put off until the very end, and that the question Israel had to answer was: 'Is it ready for a division of Jerusalem?':

The Israelis who at Camp David took a step of decades in less than a week began to grasp that the slogan 'Jerusalem must not be divided,' in whose shadow they'd lived for over a generation, need not be interpreted in the most extreme manner and that creative solutions could be considered that would give sufficient expression to the national ambitions of the two peoples. Within Jerusalem it is certainly possible to contemplate two capitals for two sovereign states, each one homogenous in terms of its inhabitants. The Arab world and the Palestinians also began to truly recognize the emotional religious attachment that Israelis, religious and secular alike, have for their capital. Leaders in the Arab world now understood that it was not the refugee issue, or even the territorial dispute, that would prevent the achievement of a final status accord in the Middle East, but rather the Jerusalem question. Everyone searched for creative solutions, formulas and directions.[16]

Prior to Camp David, the Palestinian leadership resolved that the final status arrangement in Jerusalem had to be based on international legitimacy and on UN Resolution 242. The problem with this, from their standpoint, was twofold: The international community interprets international legitimacy as the implementation of UN Resolution 181 and not only UN Resolution 242. According to UN Resolution 181, the city is supposed to be a *'corpus separatum'* – an internationally administered body, separate from the Arab and Israeli states.

The second problem was the reality that Israel had created in East Jerusalem: About half the city's Jewish population at the time – 190,000 people – were living there in nine large neighborhoods. Since restoring the previous situation and evacuating these neighborhoods was not feasible, the Palestinian leadership preferred at Camp David to present a tactical stance as a starting position, and a strategic stance as a 'red line.' The Palestinian tactical position, which was presented as being the 'historically just' position, demanded a return to the 1967 borders in Jerusalem. It also reopened the so-called '1948 file,' regarding a series of Arab neighborhoods – Baka, Katamon, Ein Kerem, Malha and others – that cover about 60 percent of West Jerusalem. In these neighborhoods, the Palestinians documented over 20,000 homes that were abandoned in 1948 and later inhabited by Jews.

Faisal Husseini had always insisted that this was the 'just' opening position for the Palestinians. However, in order to be practical and make a peace accord possible, the Palestinians were ready to retreat to strategic positions on various issues: Regarding the neighborhoods that were conquered in 1948, they were prepared to accept financial compensation for the Arab homeowners in West Jerusalem, and they expected that, as a sign of goodwill, Israel would also allow some owners of abandoned homes, in places like Lifta, for example, to return to live in them. In the territorial sphere they were ready to cede about a third of the territory of East Jerusalem, which Israel had already annexed for the construction of the new neighborhoods, and in return to receive other territory on a 1:1 exchange basis. And as far as the Old City was concerned they were ready to give up the Jewish Quarter and the Western Wall. But in regard to the Temple Mount, or Haram al-Sharif, they would not agree to cede sole sovereignty.

The 'practicality' of the Palestinian offer, as Husseini described it, derived from the balance it created between the two sides in terms of concessions. Husseini also stressed that Israel stood to gain more from accepting the Palestinian offer than from perpetuating the status quo.

The Palestinians cited four incentives for Israel: First and foremost, an end to the historic conflict over the land, which would be impossible to reach without an accord on Jerusalem. Second, international recognition for Israel's sovereignty in West Jerusalem. Third, the recognition that there was no going back to the 1967 borders, and Israel being able to retain about a third of the annexed territory of East Jerusalem. And fourth, Jerusalem would not be physically divided, but rather remain an open city so that its deteriorating economy could be revived.

On Barak's explicit orders, the Israeli side had not prepared position papers or alternatives regarding the Jerusalem issue prior to the arrival of all the participants at Camp David. The Palestinians, on the other hand, had prepared quite thoroughly. The 'Jerusalem and Homeland Building Committee,' which was established in 1996 as a subcommittee of the Palestinian National Council under Faisal Husseini, prepared the negotiation files at Orient House.

The Camp David summit was held July 11–24, 2000. The more it went on, the more it became the 'Jerusalem summit.' Towards the end, it could even have been called the 'Temple Mount summit,' for this was perhaps the sole substantial issue that remained in dispute, once Israel had accepted the principle of dividing the city. Near the end of the summit, the Americans formulated their proposal, which reflected the Israeli agreement to a division of Jerusalem. In it, they suggested what they considered a feasible compromise in three areas of dispute: On the territorial front, it was proposed that the Palestinians be given reduced sovereignty or functional autonomy in the inner neighborhoods, and full sovereignty in the outlying neighborhoods. The inner neighborhoods consisted of Sheikh Jarrah, Wadi Joz, Salah a-Din, Sultan Suleiman, A-Tur, Ras al-Amud, Silwan and Abu Tor. This proposal reflected Israel's consent to part with almost all of the Arab neighborhoods in Jerusalem. Barak's instruction to the negotiating team was that of the 240,000 Palestinians in the Jerusalem area, no more than 12,000 would remain under Israeli control.

For the Old City, the Americans proposed a special regime; this part of Jerusalem, comprised of just one square kilometer, would not come under Israeli or Palestinian sovereignty, but would be subject to joint administration. Alternatively, the Americans proposed a division of the Old City, with the Muslim and Christian quarters going to the Palestinians and the Armenian and Jewish quarters to Israel.

With respect to the Temple Mount, the Americans proposed qualified sovereignty for the Palestinians. They called this 'custodial sovereignty' in order to please the Israelis, but in fact, it meant full sovereignty over the area of the mosques. The Americans proposed that Israel have 'residual sovereignty' for the area under the Temple Mount.

The Americans also raised another option: Postponing a final agreement on Jerusalem for up to five years. This delay could apply to just the Old City or to all of Jerusalem. However, the Palestinians rejected the idea outright.

Between the Camp David summit in July 2000 and the Taba talks in January 2001, the attempts to find a compromise for the Temple Mount continued, but without success.

Throughout September and October 2000, the Israeli and Palestinian delegations continued their efforts to bridge the gaps between the parties on the core issues.

At the end of September 2000, the Temple Mount issue was transformed from a theoretical question into a burning political issue. On September 28, opposition leader Ariel Sharon ascended the Temple Mount. The visit was held with the government's approval, despite requests from Arafat and Husseini to prevent it. The next day, Friday, September 29, 2000, the eve of Rosh Hashana, Palestinian youths, in reaction to Sharon's visit, began hurling rocks at Jewish worshipers at the Western Wall. In the disturbances that ensued, seven Palestinians were killed, and about 200 Palestinians and seventy Israeli policemen were injured. Within hours, the violence that began on the Temple Mount had spread throughout Judea, Samaria and Gaza. Once again, the Temple Mount had become the focal point of the national conflagration. This was the start of the second intifada – the Al Aqsa intifada, named for the most important mosque on the Temple Mount.

In addition to intensive meetings and discussions between the delegations (about 35 meetings by Sher's count), October and November brought unprecedented violence. In December, in a last-ditch attempt to rescue the deteriorating negotiations and halt the bloodshed, US President Bill Clinton tried – too late, in the opinion of many – to present the parties with a take-it-or-leave-it 'presidential proposal' that could not be amended in any way.

On Wednesday, December 20, 2000, a preliminary meeting was held in which the participants were Yasser Abed Rabbo, Mohammad Dahlan and Saeb Erekat on the Palestinian side, and Shlomo Ben-Ami, Gilad Sher and Pini Meidan on the Israeli side. Both sides spoke of the need to reduce the violence and to make a concerted effort to reach an accord. Abed Rabbo, speaking on behalf of Arafat, expressed a commitment to reach an agreement in the coming weeks, though he stressed at the same time that "the question of Haram al-Sharif is critical."[17]

On Saturday, December 23, Clinton presented both parties with his proposals on the issues of territory, security, refugees and Jerusalem. The proposal for Jerusalem was based on the principle of 'Palestinian sovereignty for the Arab areas and Israeli sovereignty for the Jewish areas.' For the Old City and the 'Holy Basin,' the president proposed a special regime. On the Temple Mount, the Palestinians would have sovereignty over the Islamic holy places, and Israel would have sovereignty over the Jewish holy places; the mosques and plaza would be under the sovereignty of Palestine, while the Western Wall would be under the sovereignty of Israel. Alternatively, the parties were offered joint functional sovereignty over the excavations beneath Haram al-Sharif and behind the Western Wall.[18]

At the first Camp David summit in 1978, President Carter, as the third party, chose to dictate a possible compromise. In the end, this method led to peace between Israel and Egypt. This time, however, five months after the failed 2000 Camp David summit, and after many weeks of intense violence and mounting distrust that had prompted deeper entrenchment and mutual recriminations, there was hardly a chance that the parties would wholly embrace the Clinton plan. Though Prime Minister Barak responded positively to the proposal, he requested certain clarifications and cited a few reservations. Arafat also responded positively, though not in such a straightforward way, and he, too, requested clarifications and expressed reservations.

On January 23, 2001, in Taba, the Palestinians and Israelis made a last attempt to reach an accord. The atmosphere at Taba was already pessimistic: The imminent elections in Israel and the growing violence in the territories effectively undermined any chance of reaching a quick agreement. Nevertheless, the progress the parties made was still of some value.

In retrospect, in analyzing the reasons for the failure,[19] the Palestinian order of priorities dictated by Arafat may be discerned. And it is evident that the Palestinian readiness for flexibility occurred in descending order: On the Temple Mount issue, the Palestinian demand was uncompromising, but on all the other core issues, the Palestinians displayed a readiness for concessions, from their point of view at least.

At the top of the order of priorities was Haram al-Sharif; the Palestinians left absolutely no room for compromise on the issue of sovereignty here. They demanded full sovereignty over the Temple Mount, while consenting to allow Jews freedom of worship and access there. The only concession they were willing to make had to do with the Western Wall, which they consider a part of the Temple Mount. Second on the scale of priorities was the refugee problem. The Palestinians demanded unequivocal recognition of the right of return, and the concession on their part on this issue was to take the form of acceptance of just a symbolic realization of this right, i.e., the return of just 200,000–400,000 refugees. Third in order of importance was the Jerusalem issue. The Palestinians demanded Palestinian sovereignty over all the Arab neighborhoods and over three of the four quarters of the Old City. They were ready to compromise on the Jewish Quarter and the Western Wall and to cede the new Jewish neighborhoods, which cover about a third of the territory of East Jerusalem. Fourth on the scale of priorities was the issue of borders and territory. The Palestinians staked a claim to 95 percent of the West Bank. The compromise here, as they saw it, was in their readiness to let about 80 percent of the settlers remain in three settlement blocs that comprise about 5 percent of the West Bank. At the bottom of the order of priorities were all the rest of the issues, and on these the Palestinians were ready to show much more flexibility.

Ehud Barak Tears the Mask off the Idea of United Jerusalem

I met Ehud Barak through his chief of staff, retired general and former Mossad chief Danny Yatom. I had known Danny since our childhood in Netanya. We served together in the paratroops and over the years we have had countless conversations about the political and security situations. When he first introduced me to Barak and suggested that the prime minister take me on as his advisor on Jerusalem affairs in anticipation of the final status talks with the Palestinians, Danny launched into a long speech about my talents as 'an expert on Jerusalem.' Barak just smiled and cut him off: "You don't need to go on and on, I know who he is, I know about his great contribution to Jerusalem and his expertise in this area." He turned to me earnestly: "I hereby appoint you advisor to the prime minister on Jerusalem affairs. Alright now – Form a team of experts and get down to work. Times a wastin' . . . "

And so our acquaintance began. Barak quickly and astutely grasped the most complex issues connected to Jerusalem. He was a conscientious student who assiduously read and thoroughly mastered all the material. I came to admire his strategic vision and his willingness to give up the fixed ways of thinking that had characterized policy-making in Jerusalem for so many years.

But in assessing his actions, with the gift of hindsight, admittedly, despite our friendship and the experience of working together, I must also be critical. I publicly expressed some of this criticism when the talks failed.[20]

My chief criticism had to do with the faulty preparation for the Camp David summit. I believed then, and I still believe today, that the Jerusalem issue, which was likely to become the toughest of all the core issues to be discussed at the summit, was not adequately prepared for. As a matter of fact, it was not prepared for at all. Israel's delegation and Foreign Minister Shlomo Ben-Ami were instructed by Barak not to prepare any position papers for a solution to this issue. This was not the case with all the rest of the issues, which were properly prepared by Barak's bureau chief Gilad Sher and a large team of advisors. And it compares even more poorly to the first Camp David summit in 1977, for which the Israeli and Egyptian delegations had reached preliminary understandings in a meeting between Foreign Minister Moshe Dayan and Egyptian Deputy Prime Minster Hassan Tuhami before Sadat ever came to Jerusalem.

Barak also failed to correctly gauge the importance of Jerusalem, and of the Temple Mount especially, on Arafat's scale of priorities. As noted, for Arafat, this was the most crucial of all the core issues. In my view, the lack of preparation and absence of basic prior agreement on the Jerusalem issues was what doomed the 2000 Camp David summit to failure.

I must also comment on Barak's fickleness on the Jerusalem issue during the summit. His inconsistence encouraged the Palestinians to conclude that, on the Jerusalem issue, the Israeli prime minister had no red lines. They became certain that the pressures of time or pressure from the Americans would induce Barak to retreat from the red lines that were presented the day before. They rightly accused Barak of conducting negotiations 'Oriental bazaar'-style, when from the start they had clearly outlined their own red lines concerning Jerusalem.

Another obstacle was Barak's condescending attitude during the summit. He was openly disdainful of the Palestinians' firm adherence to their demands and was sure that, with American pressure, he would be able in the end to get them to make further concessions. When this didn't happen and the summit ended in failure, Barak accused Arafat of being too stubborn, and went so far as to charge that Palestinians never really wanted an agreement in the first place. Barak's triumphant declaration that he had 'unmasked Arafat' created the impression in Israel and elsewhere that, from the start, Arafat had been looking for a pretext to sabotage the summit – a charge that I believe is unfounded. The Palestinians did want an agreement. However, they did openly present their red lines regarding Jerusalem, and made clear from the beginning, even prior to the summit, that the Temple Mount issue could not be resolved as long as the Israelis insisted on claiming full sovereignty there. At the first Camp David summit between Begin and Sadat, in which Jerusalem was also the key point of dispute between the leaders, neither side felt that the other did not respect its positions. The arguments between them never devolved to the point of personal contempt or outright hostility as was evident in Barak's treatment of Arafat. Arafat's insistence on his positions, on the Temple Mount issue in particular – the only one where he was not prepared to make any compromise whatsoever – angered Barak and led him, almost from the day one, to play 'ego games' whose purpose was to teach Arafat a lesson and humiliate him. The way Barak spoke about Arafat to the Israelis and Americans present only added to the tense atmosphere and made the summit all the more difficult. Foreign Minister Shlomo Ben-Ami criticized Barak's scornful conduct, when the prime minister declined all of Arafat's requests to meet with him, and told him: "The problem isn't the gap between your positions, but the cultural gap. Arafat may be the ostensible leader of a people, but deep down he has an insatiable longing for respect, and he senses that you're mocking him."[21]

Another tactical mistake by Barak was putting the Temple Mount issue on the negotiating table. Barak would have done better to postpone the discussion of this issue by courageously declaring that it was a religious rather than a political question, and that a solution to it would be discussed in a different, religious and not political, setting. Then, perhaps, it would have been possible to avoid the preoccupation with the sole issue at the summit for which, from the outset, there was no chance of reaching a political accord. The discussion of the Temple Mount question had to come down to a 'zero sum game' in which one of the parties has destined to lose. That wasn't the case with the rest of the core issues, where the parties' positions had come within 'touching distance,' to quote Gilad Sher. Paradoxically, while earlier Israeli and Zionist leaders had been ready to concede sovereignty over the Temple Mount with little hesitation, it was Ehud Barak, the one leader who was prepared to divide Jerusalem, who insisted on not conceding the Temple Mount.

However, there can be no denying Barak's boldness in taking a sharp pin to the inflated and meaningless balloon known as the 'unity of Jerusalem.' There can be no denying his courage in cutting this Gordian knot that had entangled Israel since 1967.

By consenting to divide the Old City, Ehud Barak took his place alongside two great leaders: Theodore Herzl and David Ben-Gurion. Both, in their respective eras, understood that the establishment of a Jewish state, peace with the Arab world and the attainment of international legitimacy for Jerusalem as the capital, were much more critical objectives than the kind of hollow 'sovereignty' that Israel has enjoyed in East Jerusalem since 1967.

Ehud Barak gambled and lost at Camp David. And the Israeli public did not forgive him for it. The right painted him as the 'divider of Jerusalem' while the left saw him as 'the saboteur of peace.' For him, the consequence was being booted from power; for the country – it was the terrible bloodbath of the second intifada.

On the day that peace finally arrives and Jerusalem is divided, and the inherent contradiction between the 'unity of the city' and 'peace in the city' is resolved, history will undoubtedly judge Ehud Barak as having been one of the most courageous people in the annals of the State of Israel. It wasn't Arafat's mask that Barak tore off at Camp David, but the mask concealing the common national lie: 'united Jerusalem under Israeli sovereignty.' Jerusalem is not truly united and Israeli sovereignty in the city has never been recognized. As was made plain at Camp David, the condition for recognition of Israel's sovereignty is a division of the city.

Peace in Jerusalem: The Failure

In the forty years since Jerusalem's unification, Israel has tried in vain to achieve a peace that would include international legitimation for its rule over the entire city. In 1967, following the conquest of the Old City, the years-long process of achieving recognition for the city as Israel's capital was summarily brought to a halt. This process had gained momentum in the 1950s and 1960s as more and more countries began to accept the 'facts in the field' established by Ben-Gurion, who declared Jerusalem the capital in defiance of the UN resolution, and 23 embassies eventually opened there. But from 1967 on, this trend reversed, largely because of mistakes on the part of Israel's governments and a failure to seize opportunities for an accord that would have entailed a division of the city. Such opportunities occurred in the negotiations with Egypt in the late 1970s, with Jordan in the 1980s, with the Palestinians in the 1990s and at Camp David in 2000. It is impossible, of course, to know for certain whether readiness on Israel's part to divide Jerusalem, as proposed by Sadat, King Hussein and Arafat in turn, would in fact have brought about worldwide recognition of the city as Israel's capital, though it is quite likely. This assessment was further reinforced during the 2000 Camp David summit, when the international community, the Arab world and the Palestinians were very close to recognizing Jerusalem as Israel's capital in the framework of a peace agreement that would divide it between Israel and the Palestinians. At this summit, it became absolutely apparent to the Israelis that a division of Jerusalem was not only a condition for international recognition of their capital, but also a key condition for any possibility of peace with the Palestinians and the Arab world.

The failure to achieve international legitimacy for the unification of the city under Israel's sovereignty could lead one to conclude therefore that policy-makers in Israel from 1967 to the present, including the participants in the Camp David negotiations, were unwilling to pay the price of dividing the city and of losing control of the Temple Mount. The Israeli public, for the most part, was also captive to the conception of the 'unity of the city' and was not psychologically ready for such concessions, even in return for peace and international recognition of the city as Israel's capital. Public opinion surveys show that only after 2000 did a shift away from this begin.

The Israeli effort to create 'established facts' by means of settlement activity and the construction of Jewish neighborhoods in East Jerusalem on the assumption that the world would come to terms with these actions and eventually recognize unified Jerusalem, was a complete failure. More and more countries, foremost among them the United States, Israel's ally, came to regard a division of the city as an essential condition for recognition of Jerusalem as Israel's capital.

An examination of the assumptions from 1967 to the present reveals the analogical trap in which the policy-makers were caught. Looking to the Zionist policies of an earlier era, the policy-makers figured that time was on their side. However, the opposite turned out to be true. One could even say that, as time passed, policy-makers also became aware of their error, but found the price of admitting to it intolerable. Meanwhile, as the years passed, the price tag for peace and international recognition of Jerusalem as the capital continued to rise. Had Israel accepted the Rogers Plan in 1970, the price in Jerusalem would have been lower than what it was asked to pay in 1977 during the peace negotiations with Sadat; had Menachem Begin accepted Sadat's proposal, the price in Jerusalem would have been less steep than the price requested by King Hussein some years later; had Prime Minister Yitzhak Shamir accepted the London Agreement in 1986 and reached an accord in the framework of the 'Jordanian option,' the price in Jerusalem would have been lower than what Israel was asked to pay as part of the 'Palestinian option' in the late 1990s. If only and if only and if only . . .

The Israeli assumption that time was on its side insofar as Jerusalem was concerned became the foundation for a decades-long policy in the city. This assumption was based on two conceptions: *The first conception* is the analogical approach that relies, ostensibly, on historical experience and draws conclusions from it in regard to the present. From 1967 on, the policy-makers presumed that the future reality in Jerusalem would be identical to the international situation in the 1950s – when a steadily increasing number of countries recognized Israel's annexation of areas of the Galilee and the Negev that were outside the original Partition borders. They also presumed that David Ben-Gurion's success in making West Jerusalem the capital in 1949 would be repeated in East Jerusalem in 1967. The error lay in the faulty analogy between places that do not involve the same level of sensitivity, like Acre and Nazareth, which were annexed in 1949, and the Old City in Jerusalem. The policy-makers believed that the world would gradually grow accustomed to and come to accept Israel's takeover of the Old City, just as it had with Acre and Nazareth.

The second conception that characterized Israeli policy in Jerusalem since 1967 is what I call 'Jerusalem Syndrome' – the feeling of euphoria arising from the renewed encounter with the Old City, which triggered an irrationality in which the 'unification of Jerusalem' was perceived to be a consequence of 'historic determinism,' a political inevitability explained by a myth. Some went as far as to say that the 'hand of God' had intervened in the military and political events for the sake of the Jewish people.

'Jerusalem Syndrome' prompted policy-makers to liken themselves to historic figures from the city's past. In their minds, their deeds rivaled those of past heroes – from King David all the way to Ben-Gurion. And as more and more 'facts' were established in Jerusalem, the harder it became to retreat from them without a serious political crisis and a crisis of consciousness. Even when they could see that time was not working in favor of the objectives they had set, and that the measures they had taken had brought about the opposite of the desired results, they did not stop for a single moment to try and find alternatives to the failed policy. There was a denial or a suppression of the unwanted reality. Finally, when the 'moment of truth' arrived, it became apparent that not only had the policy failed to achieve its goals, but the results also went against Israel's interests in Jerusalem.

Such a moment of truth came at the Camp David summit in 2000, when two things became clear beyond all doubt: (1) The Israeli policy of 'establishing facts' in Jerusalem for almost forty years had not meaningfully altered the geopolitical reality in Jerusalem in Israel's favor; (2) Without a division of Jerusalem and the abandonment of the conception of the unified city, it would not be possible to attain peace, and international legitimacy for Israeli's sovereignty in the city could certainly not be expected.

Bill Clinton, one of the friendliest American presidents Israel has ever known, presented Israeli policy-makers at Camp David with the dilemma of the price that had to be paid for international recognition and legitimacy of Jerusalem as Israel's capital. He told Barak that dividing Jerusalem would enable Israel to at last obtain international legitimacy for its capital. He repeatedly stated that a solution in Jerusalem would bring instant recognition from the United States of Jerusalem as the capital, and he promised to move the US Embassy from Tel Aviv to Jerusalem. All the other embassies were sure to follow suit, he said.

It took the failure of the talks and the bloody intifada (635 terror attacks were carried out in Jerusalem from the start of the second intifada until January 2006, in which 211 Israelis were killed and 1,643 wounded) that followed for this recognition to finally sink in with policy-makers and the Israeli public.[22] In January 2006, the Jerusalem Institute for Israel Studies (JIIS), as part of its ongoing research, conducted a public opinion survey to examine the Israeli public's readiness to divide Jerusalem: 63 percent of the respondents expressed a willingness to divide the city within the framework of a peace agreement.[23]

In the summer of 2006, Costa Rica and El Salvador, the last two countries that still recognized Jerusalem as Israel's capital, announced that they, too, were transferring their embassies to Tel Aviv. Not a single foreign embassy remained in the city.

After forty years of diplomatic efforts to achieve Israel's two main objectives following the Six-Day War – peace and recognition of united Jerusalem as Israel's capital – the extent of the disappointment and failure is apparent: Not only did Israel fail to gain international support for its standing in Jerusalem, but the exact opposite occurred. Over the years, as a result of the failed policy, the embassies that were in the city departed one after the other. And as of now, peace with the Palestinians appears to be farther off than ever.

The recognition of the contradiction between a 'unified city' and 'peace' has begun to sink in with most Israelis. As it makes another attempt to sign peace agreements with the Palestinians and the Arab states, Israel now understands that the condition for peace and international recognition of its capital is a division of the city between it and the Palestinians.

CHAPTER SEVEN

The Struggle Over the Holy Places

If you do not relent in Jerusalem, the sword will not cease to hang over the Holy City, for Christianity has not relented and Islam will not relent.

(The Vatican Cardinal to director-general of the Prime Minister's Office, Yaakov Herzog)

The Dome of the Rock

Few monumental buildings go beyond the aesthetically pleasing to the genuinely stirring. One such building is an octagonal structure with a majestic golden cupola: The Dome of the Rock on the Temple Mount in Jerusalem. Also known as the Mosque of Omar, after Omar ibn al-Khattab, the 7th-century conqueror of Jerusalem, it is the oldest extant example of Islamic architecture. Its golden dome rises forty-three meters, to about the height of a fourteen-story building. Built by the Caliph Abdel Malik in the year 691 CE, it has become the most widely recognized symbol of Jerusalem.

Viewed from any perspective – from the surrounding hilltops, from close up in the vast Temple Mount plaza, or from the inside, winding along the circular path to the enormous white rock for which it is named – the overwhelming beauty combined with the legend of the Foundation Stone evokes a rush of excitement.

The Jewish Sages wrote in the Midrash Tanhuma (Kedoshim 10): "The Land of Israel dwells in the center of the world and Jerusalem in the center of the Land of Israel and the Holy Temple in the center of Jerusalem and the Holy of Holies in the center of the Holy Temple and the Holy Ark in the center of the Holy of Holies and before the Holy Ark, the Foundation Stone upon which the world was established."

I'll never forget my first visit to the Taj Mahal. I arrived there at sunrise and remained glued to the place until sunset. The thrill I felt while gazing at the stunning white marble mausoleum with its magnificent dome and turrets was partly inspired by the poignant story of Shah Jahan, the Moghul emperor who built this 'Temple of Love' as a tomb for his beloved who died giving birth to their son. For four hundred years, the beauty of

Queen Mumtaz and the intensity of her husband's love for her have moved millions of people from all over the world. No image is more synonymous with the vast country of India than the spectacular Taj Mahal.

In much the same way, the dazzling beauty and glorious legend of the Dome of the Rock touches all humanity, and not only the Muslims who built this 'Temple of the Faith.'

When the Crusaders conquered Jerusalem in the 12th century, they set about destroying all the mosques in the city to wipe out any trace of the 'infidels.' But the awe that gripped them at the sight of the Dome of the Rock prevented them from razing it, too. Instead, they turned the place, which in the past had been the site of the Jewish 'Temple of the Faith' and later the Muslim 'Temple of the Faith,' into a Christian 'Temple of the Faith. They converted the building into a church, which they called Templum Domini ('The Lord's Temple'), installed a huge gold, diamond-studded statue of Christ and erected a giant gold cross, brought from Europe, atop the dome. The Order of the Templars subsequently adopted the octagonal, domed form as a model for its churches throughout Europe. One of the best known examples of is the Temple Church in London.

The Christians weren't the only ones awestruck by the Dome of the Rock. In the 14th and 15th centuries, the structure was a central motif in Jewish art: in manuscripts, books and Passover haggadahs, on the curtains covering the holy ark in synagogues, on carpets and sukkah decorations. On all of these things, the Dome of the Rock appears with the word 'Zion' or 'Jerusalem' underneath.

The Caliph Abdel Malik, builder of the Dome of the Rock, brought to Jerusalem the finest artists and architects of the late Byzantine Empire and the newly victorious Islamic Empire. The result of this collaboration was so breathtaking that legend has it that when construction was completed, the Caliph ordered the artists' hands cut off so they would never be able to produce similar buildings for other rulers.

As with the Taj Mahal, the secret to the building's beauty lies in its perfect proportions and the way it fits in the surrounding landscape. The peak of Mount Moriah, which in Herod's time was transformed into an immense plaza occupying about a quarter of the area of the Old City, is the platform upon which the Dome of the Rock stands. And this in turn is surrounded by Mount Zion, Mount of the Anointing, the Mount of Olives and Mount Scopus – as the Psalm says: *yerushalayim harim saviv lah*.

Contrary to popular notion, the Dome of the Rock is not a mosque. Rather, it is a monument to the Foundation Stone (*even hashtiya* in Hebrew or *quba as-sakhra* in Arabic). It is not used by the Arabs as a mosque, although they pray both inside it and next to it.

Jewish tradition ascribes the site of the rock to the place where

Abraham prepared to sacrifice his son Isaac. Muslims associate the site with the prophet Mohammed's 'night journey' and point to a certain spot in the rock as the place where the prophet stepped.

Nowhere else in Jerusalem have empires and religions gone to such lengths to bolster their standing. Often, this took the form of acts of destruction aimed at erasing all traces of the vanquished infidels, and the construction of monumental structures by the victors atop the losers' ruins: Having burned the second Jewish Temple down to the foundations, the Romans built a Temple of Jupiter in its stead. The size and splendor of the new temple were meant to signify paganism's triumph over Judaism. The Byzantine Christians who followed had the same idea: They demolished the pagan temple and built the Church of the Holy Sepulchre nearby as a *memoria*, similar to other structures throughout their empire, such as the San Vitale cathedral in Ravenna, Italy and the Hagia Sofia church in Istanbul. The latter two buildings were also purposely erected on the ruins of Roman temples to symbolize Christianity's triumph over paganism. All three feature an octagonal structure and impressive dome. Later on, the Caliph Abdel Malik built the Dome of the Rock as a counterweight to the Church of the Holy Sepulchre. Its features are very similar to those of the Christian monumental buildings, except for its larger and more ornate dome, which was essentially a visual declaration of the new religion's supremacy and its triumph over Christianity in Jerusalem.

Personally, when I gaze at the Dome of the Rock, I think about the conqueror who, for me, will always be one of the city's greatest heroes: His story is one of peace and compromise, of modesty and generosity – exceedingly rare qualities in Jerusalem's long, blood-soaked history. As one who has spent many years seeking a path to peace, I feel duty-bound to share the story of the second Islamic Caliph, Omar ibn al-Khattab, the first in history to conquer the city without bloodshed. And as a Jew, I am indebted to him for his benevolence in permitting Jews to return to Jerusalem after they had been forbidden entry to the city for five hundred years. He offered the Jewish Quarter as an eternal gift, even though, in the eyes of his religion, the Jews were 'unbelievers.'

Having studied the history of the numerous battles for the city, and having fought in one myself and witnessed up close the cost of its liberation in 1967 – hundreds of dead and over a thousand wounded – I have always been amazed at the way the Caliph Omar conquered Jerusalem: In order to avoid the kind of bloodshed that had characterized the advent of the ancient Hebrews, the Assyrians, the Babylonians, the Greeks, the Romans and the Persians before him, Omar proposed a 'peace pact' to Sophronius, the Christian patriarch of besieged Jerusalem. As part of this pact, Omar promised the Christians not only to spare their lives, but also that they would not be taken into slavery. He further pledged that no harm would come to the city's Christian inhabitants: They would not be forced to convert to Islam against their will, their property would not be confiscated and their churches would not be destroyed or turned into mosques. The sole obligation that Omar insisted upon was the payment of the *jizya* tax, and he was prepared to exempt anyone who chose to convert to Islam. However, his generous offer came with a stern warning attached: "For if it is not so, then I shall bring upon you men whose love of death is greater than their love of drinking and eating pork, and I shall give you no respite until I have destroyed, by God's will, those who fight for you, and I shall take your sons as slaves."

Surprised by the Caliph's offer, Sophronius commanded his soldiers to lay down their weapons while he himself went to the city gate to greet the Muslim conqueror, whose reputation preceded him throughout the Christian world: His modesty and ascetic lifestyle stood in stark contrast to the hedonistic and ostentatious ways of the Byzantine leaders. And he was just as renowned for his military prowess, having led his horsemen from the Arabian desert to unprecedented triumphs that extended the Islamic Empire from India to Spain.

I learned later about a lesser-known side of the Caliph Omar: his treatment of the Jews and their holy places in Jerusalem. In 2000, I served as the adviser on Jerusalem affairs to Prime Minister Ehud Barak, and in this capacity I headed a large team of experts that studied possible alternatives for a political accord in the city. For this purpose, I held many talks with Faisal Husseini, who held the Jerusalem portfolio in the Palestinian Authority and coordinated all the preparations for the talks on its behalf. Husseini and I already had a friendship that went back many years, to the early 1980s when we first held a political dialogue with the aim of finding a peaceful solution for Jerusalem. During the talks I conducted as head of the team of experts, the issues of the Temple Mount and the sites there that are sacred to Islam and Judaism naturally came up. One day I suggested that we go up on the Temple Mount together to closely examine a proposal we were preparing jointly to present to our respective leaders – Arafat and Barak.

On that visit, whose purpose was the political future of the place, it was impossible to avoid talking about the past. As we sat companionably near the Dome of the Rock, sensing the wings of history beating at the mere fact of our coming together here in this place, the conversation rolled around to the topic of the Caliph Omar. Husseini was surprised that I knew about the pact Omar had made with Sophronius, which I cited as an example of magnanimity and political wisdom that 1,300 years ago had averted a lot of bloodshed in this city. He was even more surprised when I told him what I'd learned about the Muslim Caliph's readiness for compromise in regard to the sites sacred to both religions.

"Why isn't Arafat ready for a compromise like the one that was accept-able to Omar, Mohammed's successor as Commander of the Faithful in the world?", I asked him. "I'm not familiar with this compromise," Husseini replied. "Why don't you tell me about it?"

And so, as we relaxed in the shade of the cypresses next to the magnif-icent structure named for the Caliph, I found myself, an Israeli Jew, telling Husseini, a Muslim Arab whose ancestors arrived in Jerusalem in the 7th century, about the second Caliph, Omar ibn al-Khattab. I felt a little awkward telling him about something that most Muslims are hardly aware of nowadays, though my chief historical sources were the writings of Muslims of that period, including members of the Caliph's own entourage!

This is what I told him: "When Omar came to the Temple Mount and saw what a refuse and dung heap it had become after generations of neglect, he was horrified. Some say that he ordered Sophronius, as punish-ment for disrespecting the place, to crawl on his belly through the dung. He commanded the city's inhabitants, as well as a group of Jews that had joined him on his journey to Jerusalem, to clean up the place and uncover the rock – the Foundation Stone.

"When the rock was exposed, an interesting dialogue took place between the Caliph and a member of his retinue, a Jew by the name of Ka'ab al-Ahbar who had converted to Islam." At this point I quoted directly from the writings of at-Tabari, a Muslim historian of that period: Omar Ibn al-Khattab asked Ka'ab: Where should we pray? He said: towards the Rock. Omar replied: Oh, Ka'ab! You are glorifying Judaism. I saw you remove your shoes [due to the holiness of the Rock]. Ka'ab said: I wanted to touch it [the Rock] with my feet! Omar replied: I understand [your true intention] but I will make the Qibla of this *masjid* at its front just like the Prophet of Allah made the Qibla of all our *masajid* at its front" (from *Tarikh al-Tabari*, Chapter: *Fath Bayt al-Maqdis*).

The 'true intention' of Ka'ab, the Jew who had become a Muslim, was clear: To permanently establish a site sacred to Islam on the spot that, from time immemorial, had been sacred to Judaism, and thereby proclaim Mohammed the successor to Moses. The Caliph's intention was clear, too: He would not dispossess the Jews of the Foundation Stone so they could eventually rebuild their Temple there, and would suffice with the southern-front section for the site sacred to Islam.

In those days of discussions between the two delegations, the idea of building a synagogue on the Temple Mount had been raised, and now I told Husseini that, in fact, on the spot where the Al Aqsa mosque now stands, the Caliph Omar had erected a temporary wooden structure and that it wasn't until fifty years later, in the time of the Caliph Abdel Malik, that the two permanent structures were built: the Al Aqsa mosque where the Caliph Omar prayed, and the Dome of the Rock – right on the spot

that Omar had sought to reserve for the Jews. Husseini listened very atten-
tively. He seemed a bit taken aback. At last, he said: "Why did you tell me
this story? Does this mean that you want the Dome of the Rock for your-
selves?" "No," I answered. "But I told you this so you can tell it to Arafat,
who denies that we have any historic connection to the Temple Mount
plaza. Who could be a better witness to our connection here than the
greatest Caliph in the history of Islam?"

Husseini smiled and nodded as if to say, "I'll be sure to tell him," and
then he said he had a story about the Caliph to tell me, too: "You told me
about the interesting dialogue between the Muslim Caliph and Ka'ab the
Jew that took place here, right where we're sitting, 1,300 years ago. Now
I'd like to tell you a story about another dialogue that took place – also
on this very spot – between the Muslim Caliph and the Christian Patriarch
Sophronius. Let's see what conclusion you draw from it!"

This is what he told me: "I'm sure you know that for five hundred years,
following the destruction of the Second Temple, the Christians banned
Jews from entering Jerusalem, and executed any Jew who violated this
prohibition. The Christians saw the removal of the Jews from the city as
a punishment for their refusal to accept Jesus as the messiah, and any
attempt by the Jews to return was looked upon as a challenge to
Christianity's supremacy. Hence, Sophronius wanted the peace pact to
contain a clause absolutely forbidding Jews from coming to live in
Jerusalem. Omar at first consented to this demand, wishing to assuage the
Christian Patriarch. However, when he entered the city, Omar was accompanied by a group of Jews who upon setting foot there began weeping with
heartrending cries. They pleaded with the Caliph to renege on his promise
to the Christians and to allow them and their families to move down from
Tiberias to Jerusalem. Moved by the Jews' request, Omar summoned
Sophronius on the pretext that he needed his advice on an important
matter. He then told the Patriarch about the entreaty put to him by the
Jews who wanted permission to return en masse to Jerusalem. Omar said
he was aware that he could not grant their request, because of his promise
to the Patriarch. However, he did want to make some symbolic gesture to
the Jews and permit just a small group to come to the city – and this was
why he wanted to consult with the Patriarch, over the precise number. The
Patriarch, who felt intimidated by the Caliph, agreed to allow entry to just
fifty families. Then the Caliph summoned the Jews and asked how many
families wanted permission to come to the city. Two hundred families, he
was told. Omar went back to Sophronius and asked him to allow entry to
more families. And so began a long discussion between the victorious
Caliph and the defeated Christian leader, until a compromise was finally
reached and it was agreed that seventy Jewish families would be permitted
to move to the city. Both sides – the Jews and the Christians – emerged

satisfied. And not only that," Husseini added, "but Omar also allotted to the Jews as a gift the southern section of the city, which is close to the Temple Mount and the site of the Temple. The area was known then as 'The Jews' Market'. We know it today as the Jewish Quarter. The Caliph also allowed them, for the first time in centuries, to build a synagogue and a study hall near the site of the Temple, where they could recite their prayers. And so the Jewish presence in Jerusalem was restored, and with the exception of the Crusader period, when the Jews were again banished from the city, all of the Muslim rulers kept the Caliph Omar's promise to allow the Jews to live in the Jewish Quarter and to recite their prayers at the Western Wall . . . "

When he finished, I asked him: "Why did you tell me this story?" "So you could tell it to Ehud Barak and to the Israeli delegation, and to demonstrate to you that our history, the history of Muslims in this city, began in peace and not in war, with compromise, not confrontation, and that even though we were the victor, we sought to live in coexistence and respected your faith," he answered. "There's no reason it shouldn't be like that in the future!"

The story's ending is well known. Our dream of a City of Peace evaporated at Camp David, and a new war, the so-called Al Aqsa Intifada, soon followed. Husseini passed away and is buried near the Dome of the Rock in the same plot as his ancestors, including some who came here with the Caliph Omar, the conqueror of Jerusalem.

Living in Jerusalem, not a week goes by without my seeing the golden Dome of the Rock. Whenever I look at it, I can't help recalling the wise Caliph who had the temerity to think that Jerusalem does not belong exclusively to its conquerors and that there is room enough and more in the city for all who love her. Indeed, he was even prepared, despite his victory, to concede one such place, the Foundation Stone, to others (unbelievers yet!) so that Jerusalem could at last become a City of Peace.

The Places Holy to the Three Major Religions

Jerusalem is packed with sites that are sacred to Judaism, Christianity and Islam. A study published in 2000 found that there were 326 places considered holy to one of the three major religions, and that most were concentrated in a small area of about three square kilometers in and around the Old City. That same year, the city was also home to 1,198 synagogues, sixty-nine mosques, 158 churches and seventy-two monasteries.[1]

For Jews, Jerusalem is the holiest city in the world and their historic capital since the time of King David. More than the "royal seat" and political capital, it has always been the religious focal point, due to its status as *mikdash melekh*, as the site of the Holy Temple. Accordingly, the holiest site in Jerusalem for Jews is the Temple Mount, where the Holy Temple once stood. Jewish tradition ascribed a special sanctity to this place many centuries before it became the site of the Temple, for it was identified as Mount Moriah where Abraham prepared to sacrifice his son Isaac. The first Temple was built here by King Solomon and later destroyed by the Babylonian king Nebuchadnezzar. The second Temple was later built on the exact same spot by Babylonian exiles upon their return. In the year 20 BCE, King Herod built a new, much larger and more elegant building for the Temple. This Temple was destroyed during the great revolt against the Romans in the year 70 CE. Ever since the Second Temple's destruction, the holiness of the Temple Mount has been expressed in the Jewish belief that this is the eternal dwelling place of the *Shekhina*, the Divine presence – even in the absence of the physical structure. For this reason, in 1967, Israel's Chief Rabbinate issued a ruling prohibiting Jews from setting foot on the Temple Mount. Following the destruction of the Second Temple, the Mount of Olives (until the 16th century) and the Western Wall (from the 16th century on) became the alternative prayer sites for Jews. Contrary to popular notion, the Western Wall is not part of the Temple itself, but rather a supporting wall of the Temple Mount that was built during the Second Temple period or, according to other theories, by one of the Roman emperors.

For Muslims, the holiness of Jerusalem derives from the sanctity of the Temple Mount, which they call *Haram al-Sharif* ("the holy and exalted place"). This is third most important site in Islam, after two in Saudi Arabia – the Ka'aba stone in Mecca and the Mosque of the tomb of the prophet Mohammed in Medina. Jerusalem is not specifically mentioned in the Koran; however, in two traditions that developed in the 8th century, Al Aqsa is described as 'the farthest mosque' in the southern section of the Temple Mount. According to the Koran, this is the place where the prophet Mohammed arrived on his night journey, and from which he ascended to heaven. Muslims say that a certain mark in the rock inside the Dome of the Rock is the footprint left by the prophet during that event. At the time of the construction of the Dome of the Rock and the nearby Al Aqsa mosque by the Caliph Abdel Malik, the entire area was sanctified as Haram al-Sharif.[2]

To Muslims, Jerusalem, with its combination of holiness, historic tradition and national symbolism, has a unique nature that sets it above anyplace else in Palestine. Muslim proverbs and sayings, as well as works of literature, reflect the belief that Jerusalem, unlike Jaffa, Haifa, Gaza and the other cities of Palestine, is 'holy ground.' 'Whoever dies in Jerusalem is as if he died in heaven,' says one Muslim tradition, and only Jerusalem is said to be guarded by 'twenty thousand angels.'[3] To Muslims, Jerusalem is Palestine. While most places in Palestine are already lost to the Palestinians and relegated to the past, Jerusalem embodies a vision of the future.[4] It alone can serve as the capital of the Palestinian state, if and when one is established. As the Sudanese poet Muhammed Miftah al-Fayturi wrote in his poem *Shahid Diyan* ("Eyewitness"): "The Jew may take from the Palestinian Muslim or Christian all he has and leave him naked, but he can never take from him Jerusalem and the olive tree of Al Aqsa and the bell of the Church of the Holy Sepulchre." This bond with the city is not only a collective religious or national bond; it also takes the form of a deep personal-moral commitment. The poet Majd Abu-Ghosh expresses this in an erotic poem in which Jerusalem is compared to a beloved woman: "Would you bring someone else besides me into your *mihrab*? I am certain you would not![5]) In light of this belief, one can understand the pain felt by the Muslim world when Jerusalem was conquered by Israel in 1967, and the mobilization of the Muslim countries in the struggle to liberate it. The compromise that the Arab world was prepared to accept from the early 1980s onward was the 'concession' of the western city as the capital of Israel. But such a compromise was always contingent on East Jerusalem becoming the capital of the Palestinian state.[6]

For Christians, Jerusalem is second in importance only to Rome, because of the belief that Jerusalem was the site of significant events in the history of Christianity and of all humanity. Events connected to the life and death of Jesus have imparted holiness to a number of places, the most important being the sites of his crucifixion (Golgotha) and burial, both located inside the Church of the Holy Sepulchre. Over the years, other places in Jerusalem also became sacred to Christianity, such as the route leading to the Church of the Holy Sepulchre – the Via Dolorosa ("Way of Agony") – upon which Jesus strode to his death, bearing the cross; Mount Zion which was the site of the Last Supper; the Mount of Olives, from which, according to Christian tradition, Jesus ascended to heaven; and the grave of his mother, Mary, in Gethsemane.

Added to all this is the significance that millions of believers from all three major faiths ascribe to Jerusalem as the city where the apocalyptic events of the End of Days, the Day of Judgment, the coming of the Messiah and the resurrection of the dead are expected to occur.

At the same time, a key factor in Jerusalem's importance for each of the major religions was the political struggle over the city. This struggle began in the 8th century, when Muslims and Christians vied for control of Jerusalem. As the Church of the Holy Sepulchre grew in importance to Christians, so the importance of Haram al-Sharif rose in the eyes of Muslims, and vice versa. The conflict between the religions reached a peak a few centuries later, with the Crusades, whose aim was "to liberate" the

Christian holy places from the 'infidels.' In modern times, too, while religion has receded in the face of nationalist secularism, religious motifs in Jerusalem continue to be exploited by politicians who wish to reinforce their colonial or national claims upon the holy places.[7] This teeming continuum of fierce rivalries, religious wars and political conflicts has cost millions of lives and been dominant in shaping Jerusalem's history.

The standard view today in the field of political and cultural geography is that the holy places are the source of the conflict, in part because of the fear that 'the other side' will deny and conceal the political and cultural identity of the Jew, Muslim or Christian. In such a conflict, you get a clash of varying, frequently contradictory narratives about the same place, all of which are meant to strengthen the claim of a particular ethnic, national or religious group to that place while suppressing the other side and erasing its history.[8]

While much bloodier struggles may be occurring elsewhere in the world, the Middle East conflict has a special resonance because of the profound cultural and religious connection felt by millions of people to a place that is 'theirs, too.'

Indisputably, Jerusalem has been the site of dramatic and formative events for all three major religions. Hence the archeological "evidence" that is continually brandished by the various parties locked in a political struggle for the city is not of any decisive relevance.

1967: A Choice of Options for Control of the Holy Places

Following the IDF's military triumph in the Six-Day War, Israel held every part of Jerusalem. With its exhilarating conquest of the Temple Mount and Western Wall, the Jewish state faced an unprecedented situation – control of numerous sites holy to Christianity and Islam. It's no wonder that this provoked disagreements among the ministers in the Eshkol government as to East Jerusalem's future political status, and the status of the holy places in particular: Should they be annexed and made subject at once to Israeli sovereignty, or should they be assigned another political status that would satisfy the Arab world and the international community?

Some ministers, caught up in the euphoria sparked by the brilliant military victory, pressed for this historic opportunity to annex the Christian and Islamic holy places to be exploited even if it meant defying the international community and the Arab world. Others pushed for the perpetuation of the nearly century-old Zionist policy, which rejected the prospect of controlling the Christian and Islamic holy places for fear of the conflict this would generate with the international community and with Muslims and Christians the world over.

The ministers deliberating the matter had to grapple with two main questions, which would also trouble every Israeli government that followed:

1. Doesn't control of the Islamic and Christian holy places hurt the chances of uniting Jerusalem and of obtaining international legitimacy for Israel's sovereignty there?
2. Won't control over Haram al-Sharif, which is sacred to Muslims, preclude the possibility of reconciliation and peace with the Arab world?

Coupled with the euphoric atmosphere, the brief time that policy-makers had to reach a decision made it difficult for them to exercise cold and rational judgment.

A striking illustration of the hesitations involved came from Defense Minister Moshe Dayan, as he stood with Command Uzi Narkiss atop Mount Scopus while the paratroop forces were surrounding the Old City. With the battle nearing its end and the Jordanian Legion beating a hasty retreat, Narkiss requested permission for his troops to enter the Old City. To which the defense minister abruptly replied: "Absolutely not! What do we need all this Vatican for?!⁹ Dayan expected within hours to see white flags raised over the surrounded city, and therefore saw no reason for the army to enter it. His reluctance to send in the troops did not stem from a fear of incurring casualties in a possibly unnecessary battle, but from wariness of the heavy political price Israel could pay in the long term. But in the end, under pressure from some of the ministers, particularly Allon and Begin, Dayan gave the order to enter the Old City.¹⁰

In the days that followed, as the cabinet heatedly debated the future of East Jerusalem, many people warned against imposing Israeli law on the holy places, and suggested alternative moves. One prominent proposal among the many submitted to the government prior to the June 11th cabinet meeting was part of a position paper that had been hastily prepared, at Prime Minister Levi Eshkol's request, by a team of experts from Jerusalem's National Academy of Sciences that included Professor Avigdor Levontin, an expert on international law; Near East scholar Uriel Hed and historian Yaakov Talmon. They proposed the creation of a governmental framework that would satisfy Israel's national interests while taking into account the international community and the Muslim world.¹¹ Their memo foresaw difficulties from three points of view – Muslim, Christian and Jewish – that could arise if Israeli sovereignty were imposed on the entire Old City.

The key concern was the reaction of the Muslim world to Jewish control of Haram al-Sharif:

The Muslim problem will be very serious, when, a few hours from now, from Karachi to Tehran to North Africa they begin to publish photographs of Haram al-Sharif with Israeli soldiers standing beside it, or pictures of the Mosque of Omar with the Israeli flag on top. The seed of future jihad will be planted in this way. A situation will arise in which we beat the Arabs but at the same time enraged all the Muslims against us.[12]

The Christian reaction was predicted to be much less severe, since the Vatican's standing was already weak and on the decline, and it was expected to adjust, as it had in the past, to the fact that Christian holy places were not, and would not be, under Christian control.

From the Jewish perspective, the team raised several concerns:

Extremist circles will start to claim that since the Temple Mount is in our hands the time has come to take radical action, such as rebuilding the Temple or expanding the Western Wall – at the expense of its Muslim sections. With the heated atmosphere today in Israel and among the Diaspora Jewry, the government is liable to get caught up in the belief that this is 'the psychological moment' to issue a solemn proclamation as to the absolute unity of all parts of Jerusalem. If this occurs, the difficulties and dangers cited above will remain unresolved.[13]

The team headed by Professor Avigdor Levontin recommended the unification of the two parts of Jerusalem with the application of full Israeli sovereignty to the Jewish Quarter and the Western Wall, and the internationalization of the rest of the Old City, or at least the holy places. This option included a proposal to establish two international councils, one Muslim and one Christian, with each to have responsibility for its holy places.[14]

On June 14th, a team of senior Foreign Ministry personnel also submitted a position paper in which it warned against surrendering to the passion of public opinion, which favored immediate annexation. The team recommended that before any government decision on the unification of the city, an independent, demilitarized Palestinian state should first be established as a solution for the West Bank; its security matters would be left to the IDF, while internal policing would be the job of a Palestinian police force. The team also proposed the establishment of an Arab sub-municipality in East Jerusalem and the granting of special status to the Christian and Islamic holy places, which would not come under Israeli sovereignty. The authors urged the government to implement this plan right away, while a state of confusion still prevailed in the Arab world and the international community, in order to achieve strategic benefits for Israel.[15]

At the June 11th cabinet meeting, at least some ministers were not in favor of imposing Israeli sovereignty upon the Old City and the Christian and Islamic holy places. Minister Eliahu Sasson proposed instead a municipal unification of Jerusalem without applying Israeli sovereignty to the eastern part of the city. Justice Minster Yaakov Shimshon Shapira, a leading opponent of unification, proposed that East Jerusalem be given the same status as the territories that Israel now held. Ministers Sasson, Barzilai and Bentov also opposed annexation for fear of how it would affect Israel's international standing and the chances for peace with the Arab world. Some ministers raised the possibility of unilaterally implementing what Israel had advocated for many years: functional internationalization of the holy places. Interior Minister Moshe Haim Shapira argued: "What's wrong with internationalization of the entire Old City, as we would then have access to our holy places without responsibility and control over their holy places?[16]

Education Minister Zalman Aran also expressed vehement opposition to annexation, based on the experience of the not-so-distant past:

> I'm concerned that governments in the east and west are calling for the internationalization of Jerusalem. I clearly remember Ben-Gurion at the time of the Sinai Campaign, when he declared that we would not withdraw. I'm afraid of a Knesset decision on Jerusalem to the effect of 'We shall not budge' only to be followed by our relenting to pressure. A Knesset declaration of the annexation of Jerusalem followed by a retreat from it spells doom. Alternatives to annexation must be sought, such as guaranteeing Jews access to the holy places and to Mount Scopus. I'm quite amazed that the foreign minister supports annexation.[17]

Seven ministers opposed annexation of the Old City – Sasson, Yaakov Shimshon Shapira, Haim Shapira, Barzilai, Bentov, Aran and Dayan. However, the majority, which included Prime Minister Levi Eshkol and ministers Yigal Allon, Menachem Begin, Eliahu Carmel and Yisrael Galili, was in favor. As Uzi Benziman writes: "The government was suffused with the feeling that it could stand up to the world's anticipated opposition . . . The ministers were filled with the sense that it was their duty to the history of their people to decide in favor of adding East Jerusalem to the State of Israel."[18] Here, too, the majority chose to rely on analogies to the successes of the War of Independence rather than consider Israel's more recent diplomatic failures in the aftermath of the Sinai Campaign.

In the view of some researchers, Eshkol's position on this issue was largely influenced by criticism he received from David Ben-Gurion and other political circles, which castigated him for excessive caution and hesitation. Ben-Gurion, still ruing the lost chance to liberate the Old City in 1948, came to the Knesset in the late hours of Monday, June 5, 1967 with the aim of prodding the government to press ahead to conquer the Old City, arguing that this time "the hour is not to be missed."[19] At the cabinet meeting, Levi Eshkol said: "Just as East Jerusalem was under Jordanian rule, it will now be under Israeli rule. The chances of peace are equal in both cases."[20]

Several ministers asked to postpone the discussion so as to avoid making hasty decisions, but Eshkol rebuffed them, explaining that Foreign Minister Abba Eban, who at that moment was in New York at the United Nations General Assembly, had told him: "Speed matters. Facts must be created . . . "[21] Eshkol put his basic proposal for the unification of the Old City with the new city to a vote, and it passed by a large majority, with just four votes against – from ministers Aran, Sasson, Barzilai and Bentov. Despite his qualms, Moshe Dayan voted in favor.

Lieutenant Colonel Yaakov Salman, who was close to Dayan, was appointed as the IDF deputy military governor in Jerusalem then. In a paper he wrote some years later, Salman analyzed the government's decision-making process on the unification issue. After interviewing all the ministers who were part of that government, he concluded that the prevalent feeling of urgency and public pressure had got in the way of in-depth thinking, and if not for those things, the unification of the city would have been accomplished differently.[22] He quotes one minister who told him: "The decision was made on an emotional basis, without serious thought. It was a policy of reaction that was shaped by the pressure of the political environment, the favorable climate of public opinion and the sympathetic mood in the media. The long-term implications were not considered." Another minister explained that "The reality and the environment influence you in such a way that you decide not to think and just to let the matter evolve." Aware of Dayan's view, Salman asked him after the vote why he had raised his finger in favor. Dayan's response: "If I voted against the decision, I wouldn't have a finger left . . . "[23]

Vatican Policy on the Holy Places

From the start of the Zionist movement's activity in Palestine in the late 19th century, great efforts were made to attain cooperation with the Christian world so as to win its support for the establishment of a Jewish state. In the first half of the 20th century, when it possessed significant influence in the League of Nations, and later over many of the UN member countries, the Vatican's position was quite important. However, this trend reversed in the second half of the 20th century as the Vatican's power declined while the strength of the Arab-Muslim bloc in the UN grew, causing the international political emphasis to shift from the Christian holy places to the Muslim holy places.

In the 1920s, the Vatican exerted much influence on the decisions of the League of Nations as to who would receive the Mandate over Palestine and just what authorities this would entail. The Vatican wished to keep the British from being awarded the Mandate, fearing that their pro-Zionist policy would curtail its influence in Jerusalem.[24] It preferred a regime of internationalization in which it, or at least a Catholic nation like France, would have senior standing. Sir Herbert Samuel made a special trip to meet with Pope Pius XI to allay his worries – which were shared by France – that under the Mandate the British would lay the foundations for a Jewish state that would eventually rule over the Christian holy places. Only after receiving assurances that Christian interests in the city would be given priority did the Vatican finally agree to support the granting of the Mandate to the British.

In 1947, as the British Mandate was nearing its end, the Vatican objected to all three proposals for the future of Palestine that were raised simultaneously in the UN: the establishment of an Arab state, the establishment of a bi-national Arab and Jewish state, or the partition of the land into two states – Jewish and Arab.

The proposal to internationalize the city, which was also put forward in the UN at the time, was largely intended to satisfy the Vatican's interests. Ben-Gurion supported this idea for two main reasons: fear of the possibility that the entire city would come under Arab rule, and the need to recruit the support of the Vatican and of the Catholic nations for the Partition Plan. The Arab states' opposition to internationalization helped Ben-Gurion on this. And in fact, when the battles in Jerusalem subsided and the city was divided between Jordan and Israel, the Vatican became the most avid supporter of territorial internationalization of the whole city, and rejected the idea of limiting this to functional internationalization of the holy places alone.

From 1948 to 1967, Israel assiduously pursued two goals: Vatican recognition of the State of Israel, and Vatican support for functional internationalization of the holy places. As early as September 1948, at the height of the UN debates over internationalization, Israel dispatched a foreign ministry representative, Yaakov Herzog, for talks with the Vatican. The purpose of these talks was to persuade the Vatican to support Israel's proposal of functional internationalization of the holy places, and to give up the idea of internationalizing the entire city. The Vatican would not comply with either request. Nor in the nineteen years that followed was Israel able to persuade the Vatican to drop its objection to recognizing Jerusalem as Israel's capital. The Vatican also refused to recognize Jordanian rule of the Old City and on more than one occasion criticized Jordan's treatment of the churches in Jerusalem.

Israel's conquest of the Old City in 1967 caused the slings of criticism from the Vatican to be redirected from Jordan to Israel. From then on, the Vatican spoke not only about the holy places, but about the Palestinian Christians in the Old City, who made up about half of the Old City's population at that time. As Pope Paul VI said in 1972: "The question of Jerusalem is not only a question of protecting the holy places. It is organically related to living faiths and communities of people in the Holy City."[25]

Now that Israel controlled the Old City, the Vatican may have expected it to submit a proposal in the UN for functional internationalization of the holy places, as it had done in 1948. Abba Eban's speech to the UN, in which he expressed Israel's readiness for this, also planted hope in the Vatican for a new internationalization arrangement or international guarantees that would grant the Vatican sovereign status in the Christian holy places in Jerusalem and Bethlehem. However, the Eshkol government did not initiate any such move, and later on, under Golda Meir, this option was completely taken off the agenda.

The legislation of the Basic Law: Jerusalem in 1980 exacerbated the Vatican's criticism of Israel and its actions in the city. Although it had hitherto refrained from taking a political stand on the Israeli–Arab conflict, the Vatican began to comment publicly on the issue and sided with the Palestinians. The terminology that had up to now defined the Palestinian problem as a refugee problem requiring a 'humane solution' also changed in the 1980s. During the first intifada, the Vatican began talking about the need for a 'political solution' to the problem of the Palestinian people. Michel Sabbah, the Latin Patriarch in Jerusalem, and other senior church officials in Israel, openly aligned themselves against Israel.

The Palestinians meanwhile played up the fact that a good portion of their political leadership was Christian-Arab. From the start of his political career, Arafat made a point of expressing positive sentiments about the Christian churches and of appointing Palestinian Christians to prominent posts: In the 1980s, he selected Hanna Siniora, a Christian, to represent the PLO at the beginning of the negotiations with the Americans, and in the 1990s, he picked another Christian, Professor Hanan Ashrawi, to be the spokesperson for the Palestinian delegation to the Madrid summit; Arafat also married a woman from a distinguished Christian-Arab family. The growing involvement of the Christian churches and their Christian-Arab leaders in Jerusalem in the Palestinian national struggle against Israel helped the Palestinians obtain the Vatican's support for their political demands.

As time passed, the Vatican gradually abandoned the idea of internationalization of the city or internationalization of the holy places, and began calling instead for a division of the city with East Jerusalem as the capital of the Palestinian state. In January 1991, for the first time, the Vatican made known its conditions for recognition of Israel, and in this context it termed the Israeli occupation of East Jerusalem an obstacle to recognition. In 1993, Israel and the Vatican decided to formalize their diplomatic relations, and the Vatican consented to recognize Israel even though the Israeli occupation of East Jerusalem had not ended. Nonetheless, its position in favor of international guarantees or some sort of international administration of the Christian holy places in Jerusalem remained unchanged.

So while during the first half of the 20th century, the Vatican made its recognition of the State of Israel conditional upon internationalization of the Old City, by the late 20th century, it had added two conditions for recognition of Jerusalem as Israel's capital: Palestinian rule in East Jerusalem and international guarantees regarding its standing in the Christian holy places.

The Arab View of the Temple Mount: From Religious to Political Paradigm

Both times in the 20th century that control of the Old City passed out of Muslim hands – to the Christian British Mandate in 1917 and to Jewish rule in 1967 – the attitude of Muslims, and Palestinians in particular, towards the Islamic holy sites led to a Muslim refusal to accept the situation. The British (from 1917 to 1948) and Israel (from 1967 on) both tried, in vain, to separate the issue of the holy places from politics.

The Palestinians have always linked the religious issue to a political solution. The first Palestinian leader to use the issue of the holy places to advance his political interests was the Mufti of Jerusalem, Hajj Amin al-Husseini. In the late 1920s, Husseini embarked on a fundraising expedition around the Muslim world for the sake of renovating the mosques on Haram al-Sharif. Beyond the purpose of safeguarding Muslim autonomy in the mosques, this trip was designed to bolster Husseini's political demand for an independent Palestinian state, which helps to explain why Husseini exploited the affair of the Jewish prayer at the Western Wall in 1929 to consolidate Palestinian national opposition to the British and the Jews.

The 1929 riots, which erupted after members of the Betar movement prayed at the Western Wall at the end of Yom Kippur, became a historic milestone in the Israeli–Palestinian conflict. In one week, 133 Jews were killed and 330 injured; the Hebron Jewish community, the oldest in Palestine, lost 66 people and its buildings were completely demolished. Briefly, the very survival of the Jewish Yishuv seemed endangered. Reeling from the events, the Zionist movement had to come to grips with the notion that its dream of a national homeland required a readiness for violent confrontation. Dialogue and diplomacy would no longer suffice.

The Mufti found the use of Haram al-Sharif as a pretext for confrontation with the Jews and the British over the independence of Palestine to be quite effective. Following the violent riots, in which 116 Arabs were killed and 230 injured, there was a changing of the guard in the Palestinian leadership; the nationalist extremists who called for an armed struggle against the British were now ascendant. The riots bolstered the Mufti's standing among the Palestinians as 'defender of the Islamic holy places in Jerusalem.'

In December 1931, Husseini hosted an international Islamic conference in Jerusalem. Representatives from 22 Muslim states took part. The issue of 'defending the Islamic holy places,' as the Mufti put it, would serve from now on as a tool to foster Arab and Muslim solidarity with the Palestinians' political struggle for independence. Jordan's conquest of the Old City in 1948 put an end, at least temporarily, to the Palestinians' attempt to use the Islamic holy places as political leverage in achieving independence.

Jordan's Hashemite regime, which now controlled the Islamic holy sites, made a distinction between the religious paradigm and the political paradigm. King Abdullah adopted the Saudi model, which differentiates between the country's religious capital (Mecca) and its political capital (Riyadh); he wore one hat as 'guardian of the Islamic holy places in Jerusalem' and another as the political head of the state whose capital was Amman.

On March 16, 1949, a ceasefire agreement was signed between Israel and Jordan, giving an official seal of approval to the partition of Jerusalem between the two countries. Jordan and Israel's disregard for the UN Resolution that called for the establishment of an international authority in Jerusalem (UN Resolution 181 from November 1947) created a convergence of interests between King Abdullah and Ben-Gurion; each had come away from the 1948 war with significant achievements in Jerusalem. Ben-Gurion won a political capital, and Abdullah won the Islamic holy places. It bears remembering that the fall of Islamic holy places into Jordanian hands was received with hostility by the Arab League; Pakistan alone recognized Jordan's rule in Jerusalem. The Arab League's stance was that Jerusalem should belong to Palestine, and as far as the holy places were concerned, it preferred a pan-Arab or pan-Islamic arrangement to Jordanian rule.[26] The Arab states' aversion to accepting Abdullah as 'guardian of the holy places' was so strong that the Arab League representatives at the UN stated their readiness to amend UN Resolution 181 from 'internationalization of the city' to 'internationalization of the holy places.'[27]

In the hearings of the UN Conciliation Committee on Jerusalem and the Holy Places, which began after the war, Arab League representatives again voiced a clear preference for internationalization over Jordanian control of the Islamic holy places. King Abdullah refused outright, declaring that 'an international authority in Jerusalem or the holy places will only be established over my dead body."[28] Israel's conquest of the Old City in June 1967 also did not bring about a change in the Arab stance at first.[29]

Not until the end of the 1970s did a change emerge in the pan-Arab position, which went from calling for 'functional internationalization' to seeking 'Muslim control' of Haram al-Sharif, now accorded a 'separate status' from the rest of the Old City. This distinction is discernible in Sadat's position in the peace negotiations with Israel in late 1977, and in the stance of Muslim states that the Arab part of Jerusalem must be returned to "Arab" sovereignty, while the Islamic holy places must come under "Muslim" control.[30] At Camp David, Sadat attempted to broach the idea of flying a Muslim flag on Haram al-Sharif. The Tenth Islamic Conference of Foreign Ministers, held in May 1979 in Fez, did not cite the political status of Haram al-Sharif or include it in the proposed framework for Palestinian sovereignty over the Old City.[31] Noted historian and political scientist Menachem Klein explains that this was because, "As is well known, Saudi Arabia, Jordan, Morocco and even Egypt see themselves as being destined to take part in the future alongside the Palestinians in the control and management of the Islamic holy places in Jerusalem.[32]

Haram al-Sharif in the Late 1980s: Impetus for the Palestinian Struggle

After 1967, the Temple Mount was administered by a "holy coalition" that included the Muslim religious establishment in Jerusalem, the Jordanian authorities and the Israeli government. What all three members of this coalition had in common was a desire to preserve the status quo.[33]

The Muslim religious establishment on the Temple Mount included hundreds of workers from the offices of the Waqf, the Supreme Muslim Council and the Mufti of Jerusalem. These workers received their salaries directly from the Jordanian Waqf in Amman, and were quite well paid in recognition of "the special effort required of them to work under conditions of occupation."[34] Israel was satisfied with this arrangement, as it produced a dual system: of supervision by the Israeli authorities and loyalty to the Jordanian authorities.

Thus, for two decades, until the outbreak of the first intifada in 1987, the working system there was able to neutralize radical political extremism in a place where everyone had something to lose. There were regular meetings between heads of the Muslim establishment and representatives of the Israeli government and the Jerusalem municipality for the coordination and administration of daily affairs on the Temple Mount.[35] Reports about these meetings and the agreements reached in them were relayed regularly to Amman for approval, and the direct superiors of the religious leaders would then instruct them on how to proceed with the joint activity.

Also involved to one extent or another in this "holy coalition," whose aim was to prevent politicization of the Temple Mount, were Arab states and international organizations. The most important of these was the Organization of the Islamic Conference (OIC). After the start of the Israeli occupation, government bodies, public councils and academic committees devoted to defending the holy places in Jerusalem sprang up in all the Arab states. In Muslim literature and poetry, too, the mosques of Haram al-Sharif enjoyed a glorious resurgence. Every radio station in the Arab world played Umm Kulthum's song 'Three Holy Cities' featuring this line about Jerusalem: "From the place where Mohammed ascended at night to the sky, from Jerusalem the pure and chaste, I hear a cry for help . . . I hear the sad stones wailing in the dark of night, poor Jerusalem that is in the hands of the aggressor."[36]

One of the Palestinians' chief goals in the 1980s and 1990s was to change the religious paradigm of the Temple Mount to a political paradigm. The way to do this was to take control of the religious establishment there and so obtain legitimacy from the Arab League and the OIC. Two developments contributed to the achievement of this goal: the first intifada in the late 1980s, and the peace agreement with Jordan in 1994. The first intifada, which erupted in 1987, shook up the 'holy coalition' that controlled the Temple Mount and sparked processes that eventually brought that coalition to an end. In the late 1980s and early 1990s, the religious paradigm that had been consolidated with much effort by Israeli and Jordanian officials, was replaced by a new, political, paradigm that placed the Temple Mount at the epicenter of the Palestinian political struggle against the Israeli occupation.[37]

The Palestinians notched another significant achievement as a result of the peace agreement between Israel and Jordan which was signed in Washington on September 25, 1994. In the agreement, the parties attempted to establish solid facts in regard to the holy places in Jerusalem.

The lack of clarity shown by the Arab states concerning the status of the Islamic holy places ever since the 1982 Fez conference, and a wariness of potential Palestinian claims to them, made King Hussein seek indisputable affirmation that he was the guardian of the holy places. Crown Prince Hassan put it this way: "Jordan has never abandoned and will never abandon its responsibility for the Islamic holy places in East Jerusalem."[38]

In the agreement, Prime Minister Yitzhak Rabin acceded to a personal plea from King Hussein to include a clause stating: "Israel respects the present special role of the Hashemite Kingdom of Jordan with respect to the Islamic holy places in Jerusalem. When the final status negotiations are held, Israel will grant high priority to the historic Jordanian role in these holy places."[39] (This clause was composed by Rabin and Hussein with the specific aim of separating the discussion of political sovereignty in the city from discussion of the religious status of the holy places.)

This personal gesture – promising Hussein the role of 'guardian of the Islamic holy places in Jerusalem,' a title he had dreamed of since 1967 – went against Israel's interest. It caused Israel substantial damage while the Palestinians ended up profiting from it considerably. Foreign Ministry personnel had tried to dissuade Rabin from making this commitment, asking: Why should we give priority to Jordan in relation to the Islamic holy places and not, say, Egypt, an older friend of Israel's that has also been wanting this for years, or to Saudi Arabia or Morocco, as part of a future peace agreement with them?[40]

Paradoxically, it was the Palestinians who benefited most from Rabin's foolish promise. The inclusion of this further inflamed the Arab world's anger at Israel, for having the gall to grant the second-most important role in Islam – after 'guardian of the Islamic holy places in Mecca – to Jordan. For many years, the king of Morocco, who headed the Jerusalem committee in the OIC, had sought this title for himself, as had the king of Saudi Arabia. Now that Israel tried to dictate to the Muslim world who would fill this important function, Arafat found more support for his arguments that he should rightfully be given the coveted role and proclaimed: "No Arab or Israeli leader controls the holy places in East Jerusalem. This right belongs to the Palestinians alone."[41]

Various mediation attempts by Arab states between the Palestinians and Jordan on this issue failed. Nor did Crown Prince Hassan get anywhere when he attempted in early November 1994 to convince the Palestinians that Jordan was serving as the emissary of the Arab and Muslim world in removing the holy places from Israel's hands, and therefore this was in the Palestinians' interest. Arafat was not persuaded and decided to bring the matter up before the Organization of the Islamic Conference. At the organization's December 1994 meeting in Casablanca, Jordan was supported only by Qatar, Yeman and Oman, while the

Palestinians won the backing of Saudi Arabia, Egypt, Morocco and all the other Arab states represented there. Some tried to talk Arafat into agreeing to a compromise. The proposed compromise called for the establishment of a committee from the OIC to relieve Jordan of custodianship of the holy places until the day when the Palestinians obtained control over East Jerusalem. However, this effort was thwarted by Saudi Arabia, which argued that the separation between religion and politics that Hussein wished to implement with Jerusalem was alien to Islam. The final statement put out by the conference showed that the Palestinians had scored a major victory. The statement said it was incumbent upon all the Islamic states to assist the Palestinians in future negotiations so that all authorities and jurisdictions in the occupied lands, including the Islamic holy places, shall come into the hands of the national Palestinian authority.[42] And in the interim, it called for authority over Haram al-Sharif to be placed in the hands of the PA and not Jordan. In essence, Arafat received the Muslim world's blessing to call himself the 'guardian of the Islamic holy places in Jerusalem.' These decisions dealt a severe blow to King Hussein, who stormed out of the summit before it ended.

So, as it turned out, Rabin helped Arafat attain what he had long dreamt of: Muslim legitimation for his standing in regard to the holy places in Jerusalem. Which may help to explain Arafat's stubborn refusal, at the 2000 Camp David summit, to cede any bit of Palestinian sovereignty over the Temple Mount.

The Temple Mount from the Israeli Perspective: From Religious to Political Paradigm

From 1934 on, following the enactment of the King's Order-in-Council, which codified the legal situation in Mandatory Palestine, the Mandate Government, like the Jordanian and Israeli governments that came after it, preferred the status quo religious paradigm over a political paradigm that only exacerbated the question of who should have sovereignty over the Temple Mount.

After Israel's conquest of the Old City in 1967, the government's instruction to the IDF not to fly Israeli flags on the Temple Mount, the transfer of administrative authorities there to the Muslim Waqf and the non-enforcement on the Temple Mount of certain Israeli laws, such as the Protection of Holy Places Law (1967), the Antiquities Law (1978) and the Planning and Construction Law (1965), all signaled to the international community, and to the Israeli public, that Israel had no desire to make an issue of the Temple Mount within the political discussion regarding a final status accord in Jerusalem.[43]

The scholar Amnon Ramon writes:

The most important consequence of the arrangement made by Dayan in 1967 was the distinction made in the consciousness of a majority of the Jewish public between the Temple Mount as a site of Muslim religious ritual, and the Western Wall. In the minds of many Israelis, religious and non-religious, the Temple Mount and its mosques became another land, and many have not set foot there since 1967.[44]

The Likud governments led by Menachem Begin, Yitzhak Shamir and Benjamin Netanyahu also did not try to alter the religious paradigm, which had come to be known as "the Temple Mount status quo." It endured for many years due to support from the courts and a ruling from the chief rabbinate prohibiting Jews from ascending the Temple Mount. These rulings were motivated in part by leeriness of a violent clash that could lead to loss of life, and by the fear that action that led to the rebuilding of the Temple by human rather than Divine imperative would change the character of Judaism, which had developed for the past two thousand years without a Temple.

Israel's governments embraced the religious paradigm, maintaining that for pragmatic reasons and the national good, Israel should not seek to fully assert its sovereignty over the Temple Mount. As Minister of Religious Affairs Zerah Warhaftig stated at the June 18, 1967 cabinet meeting: "There is no question that the Jewish People has the right to the Temple Mount, for it is the Holy of Holies of the Jews. However, as I understand it, the Jewish People has no intention of demanding the fulfillment of this right in our times."[45]

On numerous occasions since 1967, the courts have upheld government decisions in this area whenever groups or individuals have sought a change in the status quo. However, towards the end of the 1980s, and especially during the 1990s, public pressure for a change in the status quo on the Temple Mount steadily grew. And the political paradigm gradually undermined the religious paradigm.

Following the first intifada and increased attempts by the Palestinians in the 1980s to turn Haram al-Sharif into a national symbol, there was growing concern among the Israeli public that Israel would lose control of the Temple Mount. In 1991, the Lubavitcher Rebbe, Rabbi Menachem Mendel Schneerson, permitted his disciples to hold *simhat beit hashoeva* celebrations on the Temple Mount. This was the first time that such a widely revered rabbi had come out against religious ruling prohibiting Jews from ascending the Temple Mount. In 1992, Rabbi Shlomo Goren, a former chief rabbi of Israel, published a book whose thesis was the need for Jews to go up to the Temple Mount. He argued that the halakhic prohibition applied only to limited places, since the Temple had not covered the entire area.[46]

In February 1997, the Movement for the Rebuilding of the Temple staged a Temple Feast. It was attended not only by fringe groups like the Temple Mount Faithful headed by Gershon Solomon, but also by representatives of political parties like Moledet and the National Religious Party (NRP), and groups like the Committee of Yesha Rabbis and Professors for Political Strength. Messages of congratulations sent by government ministers appeared to reinforce the idea that Israeli public opinion was coming to accept the possibility of changing the status quo on the Temple Mount. Surveys bore this out: In 1981, about 70 percent of the Israeli public was opposed to conceding sovereignty on the Temple Mount or to seeing an Arab flag fly there or to internationalizing the site;[47] by 1995, that figure had risen to 93 percent, and even in a secular city like Tel Aviv, 82 percent of the respondents defined the Temple Mount as "extremely important."[48]

By the late 1990s, the activities of Jewish groups that wished to change the status quo, along with the actions of Palestinians concerning the Temple Mount, had greatly strengthened the political paradigm and the Temple Mount had taken center-stage in the political discourse. So it was no surprise that at the Camp David talks in the summer of 2000, its status was the key question, or that the issue of sovereignty there became the crucial test of the other side's intentions. Prime Minister Barak, who had agreed in principle to a division of Jerusalem, refused to make any concession on what he called 'the Holy of Holies.' Barak expanded the meaning of the term, which in the Bible refers to a very small section of the Temple in which the Holy Ark was kept, to take in the entire Temple Mount. He did so in order to justify his refusal to extend Palestinian sovereignty from the mosque compound (to which he had agreed) – to the subterranean area, where remnants of the Temple could be located.

The Main Stumbling Block at Camp David

The Israeli delegation arrived at the Camp David summit in July 2000 confident it would be able to separate the Temple Mount issue from the Jerusalem issue. Ehud Barak was certain he could arrive at an agreement that would combine "Muslim control" and "Israeli sovereignty" on the Mount. How greatly disappointed he was when the Americans demanded a compromise on the Temple Mount, too, and would not recognize Israeli sovereignty over the entire area.

The Palestinians, meanwhile, were upset by the United States' retreat from its long-held position that all of East Jerusalem was occupied territory and an inseparable part of the West Bank. They perceived America's willingness to allow Israel partial sovereignty over the Temple Mount, or over the area beneath the mosques, as evidence of the US having joined in an Israeli scheme to seriously diminish their status in connection to the mosques. Some on Palestinian side even viewed it as a ploy designed to plant the possibility of the Israelis one day demanding to rebuild the Temple right beside, or even in place of, the mosques.

As the Camp David summit proceeded, it increasingly became the "Jerusalem summit," and towards the end, the "Temple Mount summit." This was the final significant issue, and nearly the only one concerning Jerusalem on which real dispute remained, as Israel had already agreed in principle to a division of the city.[49]

Near the end of the summit, the Americans put forward a compromise proposal, based on Israel's consent to a partition of Jerusalem. The proposal dealt with three issues: the territorial issue, the Old City and the Temple Mount. For the Temple Mount, the Americans proposed that the Palestinians receive "custodial sovereignty" – which would in effect be complete sovereignty over everything related to the mosque compound, and that Israel be given "residual sovereignty" over the area beneath the mosques. The Americans also offered another alternative – postponement of a decision on Jerusalem or the Old City for up to five years. The Palestinians, who did not wish to put off an agreement on Jerusalem, accepted in principle the proposals concerning territorial matters and the Old City, but rejected the proposals concerning the Temple Mount.

On July 25, the day after the talks ended, it became apparent that, in fact, agreement in principle had been reached on most of the disputed issues related to Jerusalem. The final sticking point was the Palestinians' refusal to accept Israeli sovereignty over the area beneath the Temple Mount. Ehud Barak summed it up this way:

> The move [to try to reach a peace agreement with the Palestinians] was halted by the other side's demand for sovereignty over the Temple Mount to be transferred to it. If there is one point around which Israel's position may be united and consolidated, it is Clinton's proposal concerning a certain division of sovereignty over the Temple Mount, by leaving us with sovereignty over the subterranean area and leaving sovereignty over the mosques and the surface to the Palestinians, but even this proposal from the president was rejected by Arafat. This spells the end of one chapter and the start of a new chapter.[50]

The failure of the Camp David talks, and of the Taba talks that followed soon afterward, was largely due to the parties' inability to reach agreement over the Temple Mount. What made this issue insurmountable?

The answer lies in the evolution that occurred on both sides: The religious paradigm was replaced by a political paradigm that turned the conflict over the Temple Mount into a zero-sum game. In the years since Camp David, various explanations have been offered for the supreme status accorded the Temple Mount issue by the Palestinians. Having spoken many times with the Palestinian leader, I believe that the explanation for Arafat's stubbornness on the Temple Mount issue at Camp David and Taba was fueled by the readiness of the Arab League and the OIC to cede their status on the Temple Mount to enable Arafat to 'take things up a notch' and handle the Haram al-Sharif issue from a national, rather than a religious, perspective. It is possible that Arafat did not expect to encounter opposition to Palestinian sovereignty over the Temple Mount from an Israeli prime minister who was thoroughly secular and not bound to the place by any religious ethos. Arafat's bid for full sovereignty over the entire Temple Mount, and not just the mosque compound, perhaps derived from the idea that Haram al-Sharif would be the nascent Palestinian state's most important asset. Or maybe Arafat worried that the end of the Palestinians' heroic-revolutionary period, marked by the founding of an independent state, would diminish his international standing, as well as his standing within the Arab and Muslim world. He may have had misgivings about an independent Palestine having to face the challenges of nation-building within very tight (about 5,000 square kilometers) and resource-poor confines, from a position of weakness and inferiority in relation to its neighbors. In such a vision, Haram al-Sharif was the most precious asset left to him. With its historic, religious and symbolic significance, it would set Palestine apart from the rest of the Arab states and impart to it a unique standing within the Muslim world.

The quote that follows, from Klein's book *Shattering the Taboo* (published in Hebrew), concisely describes the impact of the Temple Mount's new standing in both the Israeli and Palestinian public discourse:

> The placement of the Temple Mount at the center of the Israeli–Palestinian dispute since Camp David has led to an extension of the public discourse concerning the Temple Mount and a change in the status quo. It has gone from being the topic of discourse among extremist religious elements in both national camps, Israeli and Palestinian, to a discourse being held by the national leaderships. The circle of discourse has been expanded and shifted from the margins to the center.[51]

Solution for the Temple Mount:
A Return to the Religious Paradigm

The fall of the Old City to Israel in 1967 sent major shock waves across the Muslim and Arab world. This wasn't the first time that the Muslims had lost Haram al-Sharif. Twice before they'd had to surrender it to Christian "unbelievers" – to the Crusaders in the 11th century and to the British in the early 20th century. Each of these losses sparked a great tide of anger which found expression in Arabic literature and poetry and in the hope of the masses for the imminent liberation Haram al-Sharif by the Muslim faithful. The events of 1967 again plunged the world's Muslims into an agony of despair, though this time it was tempered somewhat when Israel consented to hand administrative control to the Muslim Waqf, which traced its lineage directly to Jordan's royal Hashemite family.

In the 1980s, the scene of the battle for control of Haram al-Sharif shifted to the meetings of the Arab League and the Organization of the Islamic Conference, where the PLO and Jordan vied mightily for the title of "Defender of the Islamic Holy Places in Jerusalem," with the Palestinian Authority emerging the clear victor.

Israel's policy on the Temple Mount issue has always been complex and plagued by internal contradictions that weakened its position as a claimant to sovereignty over the place. The Israeli argument was undermined by a number of factors:

First is the historic position of the Zionist movement, which practically from its inception publicly disavowed any political demand for the Temple Mount. After the state's founding, Israel adopted this approach and was willing to accept internationalization of the site. After 1967, various Israeli governments were still prepared to give up sovereignty over the Temple Mount: Levi Eshkol right after the Six-Day War, Menachem Begin during the negotiations with Egypt in the late 1970s and Ehud Barak in the negotiations with the Palestinians in 2000 all showed a readiness to concede sovereignty, as they considered the site a valuable asset that could be bartered for peace with the Palestinians and the Arab states, and for a historic reconciliation with the Muslim world.

A second contributing factor was the chief rabbinate's ruling forbidding Jews from entering the Temple Mount or praying there. This prohibition sent a clear message to the world that Israel was not seeking this holy place in order to facilitate Jewish prayer there.

Also hurting the Israeli claim was the backing away by a succession of Israeli governments from any signs of sovereignty on the Temple Mount. "Sovereignty" classically entails a number of criteria, and Israel did not meet any of them. Foremost is international legitimacy. Since 1967, every

UN Resolution on the subject has denied Israel's claim to the place. And these Resolutions are also supported by Israel's strongest allies, including the United States. Another criterion is the application of a country's laws and symbols. As noted above, the three most relevant pieces of legislation are not enforced on the Temple Mount. Other signs of sovereignty, such as the state flag and other state symbols, are nowhere to be found on the Temple Mount plaza. Responsibility for the maintenance of public order, another sign of sovereignty, was transferred from the government to another body – the Muslim Waqf. Israel's security forces are deployed on the outer rim of the Temple Mount and do not enter the plaza itself, except in exceptional circumstances when worshippers at the Western Wall may be endangered.

The final criterion is how the government defines the Temple Mount in terms of its religious standing. The Protection of Holy Places Law, passed by the Knesset in 1967, authorized the Minister of Religious Affairs to institute procedures for its implementation. This was done in regard to the Western Wall, but not the Temple Mount.

Astonishingly, the Temple Mount does not appear on the official list of the Holy Places in Israel. In the absence of statutory legislation concerning the Temple Mount, the secular legislature is compelled to look to the religious authorities that hold sway there, i.e., the Muslims!

The further away the sides got from the religious paradigm, which allowed for compromise in the administration of the place sacred to both religions, the harder it became to achieve a solution. Reliance on the political paradigm made the question of sovereignty central and compelled the parties to negotiate in a zero-sum game framework in which no resolution is possible. And without a solution the Temple Mount issue, it is hard to envision an end to the Israeli–Arab conflict.

In my opinion, the only hope is to forgo the idea of national sovereignty for one of the parties. Then two alternatives could be proposed. First: Placing the site under 'Divine sovereignty,' meaning that administrative issues would be referred to representatives, Jewish and Muslim, of the religious establishment; second: placing the site under international sovereignty, and referring administrative issues to the international community, represented by the United Nations. Functional internationalization agreements that circumvented questions of 'ownership' or 'sovereignty' have previously been adopted by the international community. They include the 1957 Rome Convention, which partially bypassed the sovereignty issue and made possible the establishment of the European Union; the 1959 Antarctic Treaty; the 1977 Panama Canal Zone treaties; naval conventions from the late 1980s regarding the Falkland Islands, and others.

What then, are the odds of the parties to the conflict over the Temple

Mount finding a solution within the framework of the religious paradigm, which neutralizes the sovereignty issue?

Given the past positions of all the parties, I would say the odds are fairly good. The international community, the Muslim world, the Arab states, and the State of Israel have all at some time displayed a positive attitude toward a solution based on an international arrangement in which Muslim hegemony on the Temple Mount would be preserved. I believe that the benefit Israel would accrue from some type of international arrangement governing the Temple Mount would outweigh the damage caused by the symbolic loss involved. The main benefit for Israel would be reconciliation and peace with the Muslim world, the Arab states and the Palestinians, none of which will ever accept Israel's control of the place. In a way, as long as Israel holds the Temple Mount, the Temple Mount holds Israel hostage to a continuation of the conflict in the Middle East.

Which brings us to a certain Israeli–Palestinian attempt in 2000 to resolve the Temple Mount issue. As noted earlier, in my role as head of the team of experts that advised Prime Minister Barak at the Camp David and Taba talks, I met numerous times with Faisal Husseini, who held the Jerusalem portfolio as a minister in the Palestinian Authority and was responsible for preparing the Palestinian delegation's teams for the talks on Jerusalem. Together we drafted a document of principles for an accord that hinged on bypassing the issue of national sovereignty. Husseini was willing to forgo the Palestinian demand for sovereignty over the Temple Mount and to accept exclusive Israeli sovereignty over the Western Wall. We called our proposal, which bore a strong resemblance to the solution for the holy places once put forward by Theodore Herzl, a "Custodial Accord for the Holy Places." We deliberately chose the term "custodial" because it refers to an asset that is more precious than all the other assets we shall have to share, one that is not ours alone, but belongs to believers and civilized people of all nations, religions and eras. With our outline, Husseini and I sought to go beyond a political accord to challenge the two peoples to try, in this unique place, to find a common ground that is not to be found on any of the other issues in the conflict, for which we believed that the solution lay in separation. We agreed that no place was better suited to be the birthplace of peace or, rather, mutual acceptance, than here, at the heart of the conflict, on the Temple Mount.

Although we unfortunately were not able to translate our formula into reality, I have chosen to present it here. It boils down to three principles governing the partnership arrangement on the Temple Mount, and offers each side advantages it did not have before. Israel stands to gain in four ways: having a share in the joint sovereignty over the Temple Mount, where it did not have sovereignty before; obtaining international legitimacy for Jerusalem's status as the capital of Israel; obtaining Muslim recognition, for the first time in history, of the Jews' historic and religious connection to the Temple Mount, which the Muslim world has yet to acknowledge; and most importantly, achieving peace with the Arab states and the Palestinians.

These are the principles for the Custodial Accord for the Holy Places that were agreed upon by Husseini and me:

1. Divine Sovereignty

The special holiness of the Temple Mount would be given expression through exclusive "divine sovereignty" over the place. The importance of the place to believers of all faiths requires all the members states of the United Nations to guard it for them and ensure them free access, visitation, communion and prayer as they wish and in accordance with their faith.

2. International guardianship

The United Nations, as the body representing all the world's nations, will formulate an international charter for the administration of the site by a commonwealth of eleven states, as follows:

- Representatives of the five permanent members of the Security Council (the United States, China, Russia, France and Great Britain).
- Representatives of four states representing the Arab League (Egypt, Jordan, Morocco and Saudi Arabia).
- Representatives of the two states sharing Jerusalem (Palestine and Israel).

3. Custodial Arrangements:

Custodial arrangements and administration of the site shall be set down in the international charter, on the basis of the following principles:

- Each state holds a right of veto over any arrangement that is determined.
- The principle of freedom of access, visitation, communion and prayer for believers is fundamental and binding.
- The Organization of the Islamic Conference shall determine who serves in the role of 'guardian of the places in Jerusalem holy to Islam.'
- Representatives of Judaism shall determine the prayer arrangements for Jews on the Temple Mount.

- Archaeological excavations on the Temple Mount must be unanimously approved by the commonwealth of states.

Husseini was assisted by several members of the Palestinian delegation and I was assisted by several members of the Israeli delegation. Primarily, I received the blessing of Professor Ruth Lapidoth, an expert on international law and adviser to Foreign Minster Shlomo Ben-Ami. Lapidoth and Husseini's aides felt that this proposal could be a potential breakthrough on the issue. Shlomo Ben-Ami and Ehud Barak, to whom I submitted the proposal, viewed it positively, and without making any commitments, wished to know Arafat's reaction to it. Both were pessimistic and did not expect Arafat to embrace it. The proposal was also shown to Egypt and to the Americans, who welcomed it when they heard that Husseini was one of its authors.

Husseini met with Arafat and presented the proposal to him, but Arafat rejected it. When I asked why he had been so optimistic when he worked out the formula with me, Husseini answered that it was because Arafat had previously accepted its principles, and therefore, even though at Camp David he had toughened his stance calling for exclusive Palestinian sovereignty on the Temple Mount, Husseini hoped to convince him to go back to a "functional internationalization" accord. In such an arrangement, the Palestinians would attain preferential status and Arafat would preserve for himself the title of "guardian of the Islamic holy places."

Failure of the Inter-Religious Objective

Zionist and Israeli policy had always been predicated on the assumption that it was possible, and necessary, to remove the issue of the Christian and Islamic holy places in Jerusalem from the conflict over the land and over the city. The reasoning was that the Zionist movement, and later the State of Israel, would be better off limiting the dimensions of the struggle over the land to a confrontation with the local Arab inhabitants, and preventing it from expanding into a confrontation with the entire Muslim and Christian worlds. This premise was based on a sense of optimism that such a separation was indeed possible, a feeling prompted by recent historic precedents: 19th-century wars of national liberation and the founding of nation-states in the 20th century had supplanted the religious wars of earlier eras. It was against this backdrop that the Zionist movement adopted an "asset conversion strategy" where the holy places were concerned. It let the world know that in exchange for the asset most vital to it – a Jewish state with its capital in Jerusalem – it was prepared to make concessions on assets that were less crucial to it, but vital to the Christian and Muslim world: the holy places.

By virtue of its success in forging this separation, the Zionist movement was able to achieve its overriding national goal – the establishment of a Jewish state in Palestine. It was the Zionist movement's willingness to cede sovereignty over the places holy to Christianity and Islam, and to accept international control of them that led the Vatican, which wielded great influence over a significant portion of the UN member states, to withdraw its opposition to the establishment of a Jewish state.

Of course, from the inception of the State of Israel until 1967, Jerusalem's Christian and Islamic holy places were in Jordanian hands. This situation actually contributed greatly to a growing international acceptance during the 1950s and 1960s of the city's status as the capital of Israel. Israel's rule in Jerusalem without the holy places could be said to have achieved de facto recognition from most of the UN member states, and de jure recognition as evidenced by the location of 23 embassies in Jerusalem by 1967.

In 1967, amid all the jubilation triggered by Israel's overwhelming victory in the Six-Day War, Levi Eshkol's government missed a historic opportunity to realize the Zionist policy of separating the issue of the holy places from the political conflict over Jerusalem. The chance of obtaining international support, and even Arab and Muslim support, for the international status of the Old City or the holy places was quite high at the time. However, the Eshkol government, in thrall to a mistaken analogical approach and caught up in post-war elation, decided to impose Israeli control over the holy places. It expected the international community to come to terms with this just as, in 1949, it had accepted Israeli rule in west Jerusalem and the declaration of that part of the city as Israel's capital. Israel's governments also believed they would be able to obtain the Muslim world's consent to Israeli rule over the Islamic holy places in return for religious autonomy there.

For the past forty years, Israeli policy on the unity of Jerusalem has been based on the idea that the issue of a political accord on Jerusalem can be separated from the issue of the holy places, for which Israel has offered religious autonomy. Yet time after time, the policy-makers missed opportunities to achieve this separation, particularly in negotiations with parties other than the Palestinians: in the negotiations for the peace agreement with Egypt in 1978 and later in the secret contacts with Jordan in the 1970s and 1980s. By the time of the negotiations with the Palestinians at Camp David in 2000, the matter of the Islamic holy places was no longer a marginal issue that could be separated out from the rest, but rather the very core of the conflict. The Temple Mount had become the key to a potential peace agreement with the Palestinians, and more importantly –

the basis for legitimization and reconciliation with the Muslim world.

Over the past two decades, I have participated in dozens of international academic and political conferences. I met many Arab and Muslim leaders at these events, and spoke with them about the Temple Mount–Haram al-Sharif issue. Three of these conversations were particularly memorable:

The first took place in Stockholm in February 1990, where I gave a talk at a conference attended by politicians and academics from all over the world. Unexpectedly, PA Chairman Yasser Arafat also came to the conference, and was present at my lecture on "Jerusalem in the Zionist Movement's Order of Priorities." At the end of the conference, I had a brief talk with Arafat in the corridor of the convention hall. This wasn't our first meeting; I had met him before a number of times.

This time our conversation revolved around the Temple Mount. Arafat wanted to talk about the part of my lecture in which I analyzed the Zionist Movement's priorities in the 1930s and 1940s, when David Ben-Gurion served as head of the Jewish Agency. Arafat had listened quite intently to my talk, in which I maintained that all the Zionist leaders of those years had placed the Temple Mount at the bottom of their order of priorities, that Jerusalem was next to last, and that at the top was the goal of establishing a Jewish state. Ben-Gurion and the Zionist leaders were prepared to give up the Temple Mount, and even Jerusalem, for the sake of a Jewish state. They saw the Temple Mount as a burden that would impede the achievement of their national goals. I also argued that the position of Herzl and Ben-Gurion on the Temple Mount issue was an expression of their desire to separate holiness from politics, and to differentiate between what was of greater and lesser importance. They were not devout, and their position on the matter derived not from religious or ideological motives, but rather from pure political pragmatism. And it was this pragmatism that enabled them to eventually realize their goal – the founding of a Jewish state in Palestine.

Now Arafat wanted to make clear to me that he, too, had his priorities, and their order was the exact inverse of that of the pre-State Zionist leadership:

"For me, the approach is not pragmatic, but religious and ideological. Unlike them [Ben-Gurion and Herzl], I'm a religious man who is adamantly against separating religion and state, or religion and politics. To me, Haram al-Sharif is the top priority. After that comes the right of return, then Al-Quds (Jerusalem), and only at the end, a Palestinian state. So you should understand that my order of priorities is just the opposite of Ben-Gurion's and you should also understand that I will never be able to give in on the Temple Mount issue. I can make concessions on the other three – on the scope of the right of return, on part of Jerusalem and on some of the territories of Palestine, but I am absolutely unwilling to concede even the tiniest part of Haram al-Sharif."

At the time, I was somewhat surprised by what he said, but ten years later at the Camp David summit, I saw that, unfortunately, this was precisely the order of priorities upon which the Palestinian leader insisted.

The second conversation took place in Rabat, the Moroccan capital, in November 1998. I'd given a lecture there at the invitation of the Royal Academy of Morocco, at a conference of leaders of Arab parliaments, on the topic of possible solutions for the Jerusalem problem. At the end of the conference, Fathi Sorour, the speaker of the Egyptian parliament and chairman of the conference, invited me to his room, where we had an interesting chat – about the Temple Mount, of course.

Sorour reminded me that he was a devout Muslim and told me that since 1967, he felt humiliated whenever he saw on television Haram al-Sharif, the holy place so dear to him, in Israeli captivity: "As long as you hold on to the Haram," he said, "every single Arab country will feel humiliated by your hold on it. For us Egyptians, too, it is hard to see our holy place in your hands."

Sorour also told me of his amazement that in the Oslo Accords, Israel agreed, as one of the final status issues, to discuss the matter of Jerusalem solely with the Palestinians.

"Even if you agreed to that," he says, "I think that you should have, at least, demanded that there be other parties to the discussion, such as the international community, the Vatican and the Arab League, because the Jerusalem issue concerns them, too. Why didn't you take Haram al-Sharif out of the discussions with the Palestinians? With all due respect to the Palestinians, who number about five million, this subject affects 120 million Arabs and a billion and a quarter Muslims, and with all due respect to Arafat, he does not represent all the Arab and Muslim countries on this question. From the moment you allowed him in Oslo to be your sole partner on this issue, he put the rest of the Arab countries in an awkward position, and for some of them, like Jordan, Morocco and Egypt which have an interest in the Temple Mount, it was hard to keep from him what you, the Israelis, agreed to give him. I still think that if you remove the Haram al-Sharif issue from the final status accords with the Palestinians and give the place to the Muslim world or the Arab states, that a billion and a quarter Muslims will be very grateful to you. In 1967, you took our holy place by force; why don't you return it to its owners? You would gain a tremendous political benefit in that you would earn the recognition of the Muslim world and the Arab states for your sovereignty in Jerusalem. I just don't understand you Israelis!"

The third conversation took place in New York in April 2003, at an international conference (for which I was one of the organizers) on the subject of world terror. Among the invited participants was Abdurrahman Wahid, former president of the world's most populous Muslim country, Indonesia. Abdurrahman Wahid is a big friend of Israel and has visited the country several times, even though Indonesia still does not formally recognize the Jewish state. On one of his visits to Israel, I introduced him to Prime Minister Ariel Sharon. The meeting, which was supposed to last half an hour, went on for three hours at the behest of Sharon, who was full of admiration for the Muslim leader. One topic of their conversation was Israel's standing in Indonesia. Wahid promised Sharon that if he was reelected president (at the time he planned to run again, but he later pulled out of the race), Indonesia would recognize Israel and establish diplomatic relations.

At our meeting in his New York hotel room, Indonesia's Muslim leader repeatedly stressed his positive view of Israel. During our talk, which centered on the rise of Islamic terror, Wahid surprised me by bringing up the issue of the Temple Mount, which he contended was closely linked to fundamentalist Islamic terror:

"In my country," he said, "there are 200 million moderate Muslims. They don't know where Israel is and have barely heard of Jerusalem. But they all know that the holy place from which the prophet Mohammed ascended to heaven is under Jewish control, and as long as it is not liberated, a black stain will hang over you in Israel. The war against the infidels which is being fanned by the extremists, whose actions I oppose, is fueled by the fact that you are defiling this place that is holy to Islam just by your control of it . . . You ask me what must be done to weaken Islamic fundamentalism, and I say: Stop giving it a pretext for terror! Haram al-Sharif is one of many pretexts. Why not return it to Islam and then the extremists won't be able to accuse you of defiling this holy place? This is the kind of propaganda that is easily taken to heart by many millions of Muslims in my country. If you return the Temple Mount to the Muslims, you'll gain legitimacy for your rule in Jerusalem – not just from the 200 million Muslims in my country, but from the billion and a quarter Muslims all over the world."

CHAPTER EIGHT

Epilogue

From City of the Dead to City of Peace

Jerusalem is besieged by an army of the dead. I wander among the tombstones until I begin to think myself possessed.

(Herman Melville, 1860)

Five Thousand Years of War

Jerusalem has many names. One that is mentioned in the Bible is *Ir Shalom* ("City of Peace"). I find this name most ironic, since no other place in the world has been the site of so many wars.

Situated at the nexus between East and West, the city overlooks the Judean Desert, home to the prophets who fled there for the quiet it afforded them. They prophesied a future of peace for Jerusalem, but as Jesus said in his sermons, Jerusalem became a "city that kills its prophets," which proved true for him as well, for it was in Jerusalem that he was crucified and ascended to heaven.

The struggle for Jerusalem is one of the longest in human history; in its five thousand years, the city has seen more wars and bloodshed than any other city on the face of the earth. Its recorded history tells of over forty nations who conquered it, more than 200 battles that were fought in it and hundreds of thousands who died for it. They came from all over the world to die in Jerusalem, guided by a faith that in redeeming the city from their 'infidel' predecessors, they would thereby redeem their souls.

Each one of the nations that conquered Jerusalem believed that this was the final battle for the city and that thereafter it would become a 'city of peace.' 'The same holds true for the Israelis who conquered it forty years ago, and continue to wage an unyielding struggle to make united Jerusalem the unquestioned capital of their young state. From a historic perspective, the Israeli conquest of Jerusalem may be seen as one more link in the long and ultimately failed chain of conquests. Jerusalem remains riven, a city of strife beset by violent confrontation, which has been continuing unabated for five millennia.

In my own mind, I often refer to Jerusalem as the 'City of the Dead' –

a name that encapsulates the duality of the earthly Jerusalem strewn with hundreds of thousands of graves, and heavenly Jerusalem, which in the End of Days will be witness to their resurrection. Will we have to wait until then, until the Day of Resurrection, for Jerusalem to become a city of peace?

Sometimes, at sunset, I hike up to the top of the Mount of Olives, which flanks Jerusalem to the east, to take in the magnificent view of the Old City below. For me, this place, more than any other in Jerusalem, epitomizes the contrast between the glorious vision of the Resurrection at the End of Days and the stark reality in which so many thousands of young men gave their lives for this city in the course of its long history. On my visits here, I get lost in thought, trying to divine the meaning of this dichotomy of life and death, of the great yearning for peace juxtaposed with the wars that have forever been the lot of this city.

The peak of the Mount of Olives affords a spectacular view of Jerusalem, adorned with its ramparts and towers. All the city's conquerors throughout the ages stood on this spot before giving the signal to attack. From here, five thousand years ago, commanders of armies that came from Mesopotamia in the north and from Egypt in the south gazed out upon the city. The winds of time have erased the names of most who fought here, but the myriad casualties of those battles lay buried all around here in the rocky earth. In my imagination, I try to travel back in time, to picture the hellish battles, the cries of the attackers and defenders and the moaning of the wounded and the dying. Only here, on this mountain, can one truly comprehend the meaning of the name I have given the city – the "City of the Dead."

Who today remembers the wars of the Canaanite kings of the city, Yekaram and Shesam, who tenaciously defended it against the Habiru tribes who attacked it in the 19th-century BCE? The Egyptian hieratic inscriptions and the Al-Amarna documents tell the stories of those wars, and also cite the names of the kings and heroes who now lie buried in the ground of the holy city. The Bible tells us about the Canaanite priest Malchitzedek king of Shalem, friend and ally of the patriarch Abraham. The two may have met here on this mountain in an attempt to forge a permanent peace pact between their peoples, an attempt that ultimately failed. In the mid-second millennium BCE, the city's Canaanite governor Abdi Hiba sent pleas for help to the kings of Egypt, urging them to come with military reinforcements in order to save Jerusalem from the tribes of the north, which were about to conquer it. In the Egyptian hieratic writings, we hear echoes of the time: "You are not listening to me" – Abdi Hiba writes to his Egyptian patron – "The Habiru are raiding all of the king's lands and if the archers do not come, then the king's lands, Sir, are lost and all the governors are lost and indeed the king put his name on the city Jerusalem forever and therefore I cannot abandon the land of Jerusalem . . . "

Five hundred years later, Jerusalem came under attack once again – this time by Israelite tribes under the leadership of Yehoshua Bin-Nun who led the Israelites to settle in the Land of Canaan. Five kings, led by the king of Jerusalem, Adonizedek, set out to defend the land, and not far from Jerusalem, in the Ayalon Valley, they were roundly defeated by the Israelites. Bit by bit, the land fell to the ancient Hebrews until, eventually, in the 10th century BCE, Jerusalem was conquered by King David, who made it the capital of the new kingdom of Judah. His son King Solomon built the Temple on Mount Moriah, on the holy spot where, according to Jewish tradition, stood the rock upon which Abraham prepared to sacrifice his son Isaac.

The city's thousand years of Jewish history that followed were also plagued by wars and bloodshed; Jerusalem's holiness could not prevent the violence, and perhaps had a hand in increasing it. Civil wars between the two Hebrew kingdoms – Judah and Israel – were concentrated in Jerusalem, which lay on the boundary between the two. The Bible tells us about kings who fortified the city, such as King Uziah, and about Hebrew kings who conquered it, such as Asa and Yehoash. Jew fought Jew for control of the holy city.

In the year 702 BCE, the Assyrian king Sanherib conquered the Kingdom of Israel and exiled the inhabitants. However, though he laid siege to Jerusalem for a long time, he was unable to conquer the city. The end of the rule of the Kingdom of Judah in Jerusalem came about 120 years later, in the year 587 BCE, when the Bablyonian king Nebuchadnezzar conquered the land. The fiercest battle of all, in terms of the number of casualties, took place in Jerusalem, and by the end of it the city was in ruins, its ramparts were breached and the Jewish Temple was burned to the ground. Thus began the first Exile of the Jewish people. Exiled to distant Babylonia, hundreds of thousands of Jewish slaves sang: "By the waters of Bablyon, there we sat and wept as we remembered Zion." It was there that the oath which would be repeated for 2,000 years by millions of Jews in their various Diasporas was first uttered: "If I forget thee O Jerusalem, may my right hand wither."

During the years of the Babylonian Exile, as well, when it was emptied of Jewish inhabitants, Jerusalem remained a battlefield between kingdoms from east and west: It saw the Persian king Cyrus defeat its Babylonian defenders, the Greek Alexander the Great defeat its Persian defenders, and the Greek kings Thalmi and Slavakos fight one another to succeed Alexander.

When the Jews finally returned to Jerusalem after seventy years of exile, they re-established their ancient capital as the seat of the Hasmonean kingdom. But this kingdom did not last very long. In the year 63 BCE the city was conquered by the Roman general Pompeus, and then, just over a century later, it was conquered by the Roman emperor Titus following the Jewish Revolt. Yosef Ben-Matityahu (Josephus), the famous historian who lived during that time, describes the horrors of that war in Jerusalem, in which hundreds of thousands of Jews died. The Roman legions also paid a heavy price for their conquest of the city, with thousands losing their lives. Furious, Titus decided to raze the city and burn down the Temple. But the Jews, that "stiff-necked people," as the Romans described them, returned to Jerusalem to organize another revolt. Sixty years later, the Roman emperor Hadrian re-conquered the city, and crucified and tortured to death the thousands of rebels. He brought in plows to plow under the city, and thoroughly destroyed it. Atop the ruins of the Jewish Temple he built a colossal temple to the god Jupiter.

Over the next 1,500 years, this story was repeated: Jerusalem was conquered and burned, its ramparts and temples destroyed, then rebuilt to stand until of the next enemy invader. In fact, it wasn't long before the Romans lost the city to its new conquerors: In the year 614 CE, the Persian king Khosrow II conquered the city, only to lose it a few yeas later to the Byzantine emperor Heracleus. The Byzantine empress Helena had the pagan temple of Jupiter destroyed, and built in its stead the Church of the Holy Sepulchre, at the site of Jesus' crucifixion.

Byzantine rule in Jerusalem was also short-lived. In 638, the armies of the new faith – Islam – swept out of the deserts of the Arabian Peninsula. The second Islamic caliph, Omar ibn Khattab, conquered the city – and for the first time, Jerusalem was in Muslim hands.

In the 10th century, a burgeoning religious revival in Europe gave rise to the Crusades. These campaigns, which aimed to liberate the holy tomb from the hands of the 'infidels,' wreaked more bloodshed than all of Jerusalem's earlier battles combined. In the name of the 'religion of love,' slaughter and destruction and pillaging were rampant in Jerusalem, the city of Jesus. In 1099, Duke Gottfried du Bouillon conquered the city and established the Crusader Kingdom of Jerusalem, which lasted for about a century. Kings such as Richard the Lionheart and other princes and commanders led their armies into blood-soaked battles against the Muslim infidels. Writings of the period describe rivers of Muslim blood flowing through the streets of Jerusalem, and the horses of the Christian knights wading up to their knees in the blood of the Muslim dead. Muslim infidels were not the Crusaders' only target, however. They also attacked Jews: As they made their way through Europe to the Holy Land, they slaughtered tens of thousands of Jews wherever they happened to cross paths, and the six thousand Jews who lived in Jerusalem were herded into a synagogue by the Crusaders who then set it on fire. Like all those who preceded them, the Crusaders, too, believed that from now on Jerusalem would remain a bastion of their faith. However, these hopes, like those of all their predecessors, were ultimately dashed: A hundred years later, Saladin conquered the city and restored it to Islamic rule.

Over the next eight hundred years, Jerusalem endured a further series of conquests – by the Mongols, the Tatars and the Mamluks. Ottoman rule in the city lasted the longest, about 400 years, until the city was conquered by the British General Allenby in 1917.

In 1948, Jerusalem again was a backdrop for war as the Israelis and Jordanians battled it out and ultimately split it into two cities: Jordanian Al-Quds in East Jerusalem and Israeli West Jerusalem – with the dividing line marked by a long and massive wall.

Resurrection Day: Atop the Mount of Olives

On June 6, 1967, Motta Gur, commander of my paratroop brigade, ascended the Mount of Olives. He stood in the same place where Jordan's King Abdullah, the Crusader Duke Gottfried du Bouillon, the Muslim Saladin, the Byzantine Heracleus, Jesus, the Roman Titus, the Jew King David, the Canaanite Malchizedek and many, many more commanders before him had once stood. From this place – high atop the Mount of Olives – Motta Gur gave the order to breach the Old City. This battle took the lives of my comrades Ofer Feniger, Yoram Elyashiv, Avihu Peled, Menachem Ben-Ari and Natan Shachter, along with hundreds of other Israeli and Jordanian young men, most of whom are buried in Jerusalem.

I stand at the top of the mountain, thinking about all the dead – and waiting. Waiting for the End of Days, for the day that all the great religions promise will come. The day when my dead comrades and all of Jerusalem's soldiers throughout the generations will awake from their eternal slumber and the city will become a "City of Peace."

Judaism, Christianity and Islam all say that this is the spot where the apocalyptic events of the End of Days will occur and mankind's hope for eternal life will be fulfilled. While each faith has its own holiest site – Haram al-Sharif for the Muslims, the Western Wall for the Jews and the Church of the Holy Sepulchre for the Christians – all concur as to the location where the End of Days scenario will play out: It will happen here, at the foot of the Mount of Olives, in the Valley of Jehoshaphat to the east of Mount Moriah. Not for nothing is the valley dotted with the graves of Jews, Christians and Muslims.

Judgment Day begins with a powerful wind from every corner of the land, encompassing all the winds that blow on the face of the earth. Then God exhorts his angels to go forth and bring to the Mount of Olives, to

"God's foot-rest," all the souls of the dead. Why the Mount of Olives specifically? Legend has it that when the Temple was destroyed, the Divine Presence, or *Shekhina*, rose from the flames and dwelt for three and a half years at the top of the mountain and awaited the Jewish People's repentance. Disappointed, the *Shekhina* at last rose from the mountain heavenward, never to return until the End of Days.

In the next stage, all the souls shall be conveyed to the Mount of Olives via tunnels deep inside the earth. Devout Jews and Muslims were most frightened by the prospect of the tribulations they would endure at the hands of the angels on their final journey to Jerusalem. The only ones exempt from this are the *tzaddikim* ("the righteous"), according to Jewish tradition, and the *shawahid*, Muslim martyrs who fell in the pursuit of holy war, or jihad. Another way to avoid these tribulations is simply to be buried in Jerusalem, for then it will only be a short and easy journey to the Mount of Olives. Some inhabitants of Jerusalem chose to be buried in the Valley of Jehoshaphat itself, and there we find, side by side, the graves of Jews, Muslims and Christians, who most likely did enjoy such peaceful neighborly relations during their lifetimes.

The third stage is the "Judgment Nations," as the prophet Joel says: "Let the nations rouse themselves and go up to the Valley of Jehoshaphat, for there I will sit to judge all the nations from all around . . . Multitudes upon multitudes [will fall] in the Valley of the [Final] Decision . . . The sun and moon have become blackened, and the stars have withdrawn their shine: And Hashem will roar from Zion and will emit His voice from Jerusalem; and the heavens and earth will tremble . . . " (Joel IV:12–16). The prophet Zechariah also describes the scene: "Behold, a day is coming for Hashem . . . His feet will stand on that day on the Mount of Olives, which faces Jerusalem on the east, and the Mount of Olives will split open at its middle, east to west, [forming] a wide valley . . . " (Zechariah XIV:1–4).

A Crusader-era Christian legend says that on that day, the last emperor will come to place his royal scepter and his sword on the Mount of Olives, for from then onward it shall be time for a new kingdom: a kingdom of heaven, with a new Jerusalem – "heavenly Jerusalem" – as its capital.

Muslims also identify the Valley of Jehoshaphat as the scene of Judgment Day, where, according to the Koran, "the earth will quake" and the dead shall arise from eternal sleep. The 10th-century Muslim geographer and Jerusalem native Al-Muqaddasi wrote that the place where this shall happen, *a-sahir*, is pure white, having never been defiled by blood, and that on Judgment Day "a bridge will stretch between the Golden (Mercy) Gate and the Mount of Olives and it will separate hell to the south from heaven to the north." The Muslims identify a certain pillar that protrudes from the Old City ramparts, not far from the Mercy Gate, as the spot where the prophet Mohammed will sit "and welcome his believers who march on the bridge."

I have stood there many times, on top of the Mount of Olives, imagining heavenly Jerusalem's descent to the site of earthly Jerusalem, and pictured in my mind the bridge upon which all of humanity is striding toward the Golden Gate whose double arches – the Gate of Mercy and the Gate of Repentance – are now wide open. And I wonder: How much mercy will God have to show on that day in order to convey all of his creatures to Mount Moriah and usher them into heaven, and much repentance will all of God's creatures need to perform to avoid arriving in hell?

I confess that the affairs of the dead in Jerusalem have intrigued me for many years. The Book of Deuteronomy may deem necromancy an "abomination," but I can't resist trying to conjure the dead. The city's numerous cemeteries have been the sites of some of my most interesting and stirring outings in Jerusalem. These encounters with the tombstones of the dead from every faith and every era, which inspired me to reflect upon their stories, often proved more fascinating than encounters with some of the living in this city. Once I even had the opportunity, in the context of my job in the Jerusalem municipality, to do something quite important and meaningful for them, which I am hopeful shall be to my credit when I eventually meet them in the End of Days, as we make our way together across the bridge to Mount Moriah.

But before I get to that particular tale, I would like to introduce a few of the illustrious denizens of Jerusalem's cemeteries:

Jerusalem's famous Jewish sons can be found on the Mount of Olives and Mount Zion: kings and leaders, writers and poets, Temple priests, rabbis and *tzaddikim* – from King David to Menachem Begin, Prince Absalom to the high priests, Rabbi Ovadia Bartenura to Rabbi Abraham Isaac Hacohen Kook, Rabbi Judah Halevi to Eliezer Ben-Yehuda.

The city's famous Christian sons – royalty and church leaders – can be found in the Christian cemeteries on Mount Zion and in the Church of the Holy Sepulchre. Crusader kings, bishops, foreign consuls, builders of the great churches – their graves are all here, from Gottfried du Bouillon to the Russian Grand Duchess Elizabeth Fyodorovna, from Jesus Christ to the Anglican Bishop Gobat, from Conrad Schick to Johan Ludwig Schneller.

Jerusalem's Muslim sons can be found at the Mamila cemetery in the city center and at Bab al-Rahma outside the Mercy Gate in the eastern part of the Old City walls. From Khaled ibn Walid, the brilliant 7th-century military commander who conquered Jerusalem on behalf of the Caliph Omar, to Mohammed al-Alami, Saladin's military commander who ousted the Crusaders in the 12th century.

Having participated in countless discussions with the Palestinians

about the city's political future, I have met with the descendants of some
of Jerusalem's most distinguished Arab families. Some showed me their
ancestors' graves, which have been here in the city for many hundreds of
years. A few years ago, I met in London with Wafai Dajani, a wealthy busi-
nessman whose ancestors were buried on Mount Zion over a thousand
years ago. At our first meeting, he introduced himself as Dajani Daoudi:
Daoudi is the other name of his family, which in the 12th century was
entrusted with the key to David's Tomb by Saladin himself. Dajani opened
an incredibly opulent pearl-studded gold box and lifted out an ancient,
rusty key: "This is the key," he said in a reverent hush. "Throughout all
these generations, we have guarded the honor of David, who is a king to
you and a prophet to us. The next time you're on Mount Zion, give my
regards to my ancestors who are buried there. I, however, shall be buried
in London . . . "

For many years, I had academic and political contacts with Professor
Sari Nusseibeh, the president of Al-Quds University and the son of Anwar
Nusseibeh, a Palestinian leader who served as defense minister in the
Jordanian government. Like other members of the family, his father is also
buried there next to the Golden Gate. The Nusseibeh family traces its
lineage directly to the prophet Mohammed. Sari's ancestors arrived in
Jerusalem with the Caliph Omar and remained in the holy city to guard
Jesus' tomb. In one of my meetings with him, I asked if, by chance, he had
the key to the Holy Sepulchre. His answer: "No, there's no longer any need
for it. Jesus isn't there anymore . . . "

On the Temple Mount, in one of the chambers in the graceful western
portico between the cotton-seller's gate and the iron gate, next to the place
where, according to legend, the prophet Mohammed departed on his
magical night journey, are the graves of the Husseini family. The elabo-
rate family tree, which Faisal Husseini (Hanasbi – in Arabic) once showed
me, goes all the way back to a close family relation to the Prophet himself.
Husseini's forebears were among the leaders of the Arabs of Palestine in
the past three hundred years. In the 1930s, his grandfather, Musa Qassem
Pasha, led the Palestinian national movement. Unlike his nephew, the
Mufti Hajj Amin al-Husseini, Musa Qassem was a moderate leader who
sought a path of compromise with the Zionist movement. His son, Abdel
Qader, Faisal's father, is renowned for the armed struggle he led against
the British Mandatory government. He was wounded twice by the British
in different battles, and ultimately, when he led the Palestinians in the war
against the Jews, killed in the battle for the Castel. His son Faisal sought
to lead the Palestinians to a historic compromise. In the Palestinian leadership and the PLO institutions, where he held the Jerusalem portfolio, he
was a moderate and pragmatic figure. On the day of his funeral, hundreds
of thousands of Palestinians escorted his casket. On that day, I was

honored by a request from his son Abdel Qader to be the only non-Palestinian to deliver a eulogy. The thousands who thronged around Orient House, where the casket was placed, listened with curiosity and some astonishment to the Israeli who eulogized the Palestinian leader . . . He was one of the noblest people I have ever known. He cherished Jerusalem and peace above all, and these were and remain my great loves, too, as I told the huge crowd of mourners. Since then, whenever I go up to the Temple Mount, I always visit his grave, which is next to that of his father Abdel Qader and his grandfather Musa Qassem, a former mayor of Jerusalem.

For me, visits to the military cemeteries in Jerusalem – the British one on Mount Scopus and the Israeli one on Mount Herzl – are especially poignant. As a soldier who fought and was wounded in Jerusalem, who lost many comrades during its liberation in the battles of 1967, I feel a bond with all those who ever fought in Jerusalem, a special compassion for the youths who fell for the sake of the "liberation," "defense" or "conquest" of the city throughout is long history.

It has been the practice of soldiers throughout the ages to show honor to the fallen, even if they belong to the enemy side. So I was taught in the paratroop brigade in which I served, which fought against the Palestinians, the Jordanians and the Egyptians in the course of our own brief but bloody history.

I remember how, after having built several mounds of stones in memory of the casualties from our battalion – the 71st – some of my comrades in arms set about building a memorial mound for the Jordanian soldiers who had fallen near the Rockefeller Museum. When the stones were assembled, they placed on the top a Jordanian rifle and then a Legionnaire's helmet. We saluted them, these soldiers of the Jordanian Legion who fought bravely in defense of their city and gave their lives for it.

Some 2,500 soldiers of the British Empire who fell in the 1917 campaign for Palestine and the conquest of Jerusalem are buried in the British military cemetery on Mount Scopus. "Military cemeteries have become temples in the cult of patriotism," said the sociologist George Mosse. And indeed, as I stroll among the hundreds of tombstones and read the inscriptions – the names of the fallen, their young ages and the distant places from whence they hailed – I salute them: Irishmen, Scots, Australians, New Zealanders and Indians who gave their lives so that the flag of the British Empire could fly over Jerusalem.

Buried in the British cemetery on Mount Scopus are 'liberators' of Jerusalem from all nations and faiths. The tombstones of the non-Christian fighters do not have a cross etched upon them. The twenty-four tombstones marking the graves of Jewish soldiers in the British Imperial Army are inscribed with a Star of David and the traditional Hebrew abbre-

viation *taf-nun-tzadi-bet-heh* (*tehe nishmato tzerura bitzror hehayim* –
"May his soul be bound up in the bond of eternal life"), while the tombstones of enemy fallen – Turks, Germans and a smattering of Italians – are
engraved with the symbols of their countries.

At the end of the World War I, the "Great War," King George V said:
"I have many times asked myself whether there can be more potent
advocates of peace upon earth through the years to come than this massed
multitude of silent witnesses to the desolation of war."

Of all the cemeteries I have visited, dearest to my heart is the military
cemetery on Mount Herzl. This is where some of my comrades are buried:
Some fell in the liberation of the city in 1967; others fought alongside me
in Jerusalem and fell in later battles – in Karameh in Jordan and in the
Yom Kippur War, on the other side of the Suez Canal.

I visit my comrades' graves on Mount Herzl every year – on *Yom
Hazikaron*, the Remembrance Day for the Fallen of Israel's Wars. Their
final resting place is not far from my home – they are up on the hill and
my house sits below in the nearby wadi, in Ein Kerem. Almost every day
for the past forty years, on my way to and from home, I have passed by
the cemetery where my friends, forever young and beautiful, are buried.

The peak of Mount Herzl, the highest hill in West Jerusalem at 835
meters above sea level, is covered with about four thousand tombstones,
set amid the rocky landscape and pine groves of the Jerusalem hills. The
stands of trees impart a sense of serenity to those who come to this place.
To stroll among the tombstones is to confront the contradiction between
creation and extinction. The tree roots tickle the bones of the dead, the
neatly tended flowerbeds prettily conceal what lies beneath, the towering
cypresses draw one's thoughts away from death to the beauty and vitality
of nature; the lost youth all around is a part of nature's cosmic cycle, and
perhaps the young souls are not really gone forever . . . So says the Jewish
"blessing of resurrection," recited upon visiting a cemetery: "Praised be
the Eternal, our God, the Ruler of the Universe who created you in judgment, who maintained and sustained you in judgment, and brought death
upon you in judgment; who knows the deeds of everyone of you in judgment, and who will hereafter restore you to life in judgment. Praised be
the Eternal who will restore life to the dead."

"Who will hereafter restore you to life in judgment?!" – I stand at the
grave of Itzik Penso, my buddy from Kibbutz Hulta to whom I never got
to say goodbye. He would always say to me: "Don't say goodbye, just say
– 'See you' – in this world or the next . . . " He was by my side when I was
wounded in the battle for Jerusalem, when they bandaged me and put me
on the jeep to evacuate me under fire, as the shelling in Sheikh Jarrah
continued without let-up. I barely managed to wave to him, and he smiled:
"Don't say goodbye, just say 'See you' – in this world or the next." Itzik

had been wounded twice before, and his attitude toward life was always optimistic.

A year later, when we went into battle in Karameh, just a week before our military reserve duty in the Jordan Rift Valley was due to end, and just a week and a half before his scheduled wedding to Tamar, his commander, a childhood friend from Hulta, offered to let him sit out the battalion's operation. Itzik would have none of it and insisted on taking part. As we boarded two separate trucks, he smiled and gave me his usual salutation: "See you after the war – in this world or the next!" That night, Itzik was killed by a Jordanian shell in Karameh.

Itzik always loved Jerusalem, where we met for the first time in 1964 in the guard post on the City Line on top of the Notre Dame monastery. His father, Mordechai, decided to bury him in the city which he had always cherished. Sadly, we won't meet again in this world, but perhaps, just perhaps, we will meet on that bridge there, on the Mount of Olives. On that day, Judgment Day, God is certain to restore you to life, Itzik, and to place you first on the bridge, with *tzaddikim* to your right and the ministering angels (*malakhei hasharet*) to your left, just as the tradition says.

Only in Jerusalem: A Bridge for the Dead

My numerous trips to Jerusalem's cemeteries, as well as my research about the dead whose stories helped me to picture the story of my city, led me to develop a deep respect for the dead. In my public life, I strove to work for the city's benefit and, above all, to help bring peace. Though my efforts were not as fruitful as I'd hoped, I was able to chalk up one important accomplishment – as far as Jerusalem's dead are concerned. Here is the story I promised earlier:

In the early 1990s, I was a member of the Jerusalem municipal department in charge of planning and paving roads in the capital. One of the most important roads, which took up much of my time and whose planning and building was quite involved, was Road Number 1, which leads from the Damascus Gate area up to the city's northern neighborhoods – French Hill, Pisgat Ze'ev and Neve Ya'akov. This road was crucial for the shortcut it created for drivers heading from the city center to the north of the city, and the only possible route it could take was through a former no-man's-zone between the eastern and western sections of the city, an area where there was no construction and it appeared would be fairly simple to run the road. But simple was certainly not the word for it. Such were the travails I endured in trying to get this road built that I came to refer to it as the "Via Dolorosa" – the "Way of Agony" – for in the process I managed to incur the wrath of a wide array of city residents, living and dead.

In Jerusalem, roads are political, too, and frequently a topic of for controversy, and Road Number 1 was the most controversial of all. Its construction was delayed for two years because of various public objections. First came opposition from the Likud city council members, who worried that the road "would divide Jerusalem" and determine its future borders. This line of argument did not abate until Ariel Sharon, then the Construction and Housing Minister, stepped in and offered his strong personal backing for the project. Then, when the land for the road was appropriated, its Arab owners appealed to the UN, alleging that I was "annexing East Jerusalem to Israel." My explanations that the main purpose of the road was to relieve the heavy traffic in the Arab neighborhoods were of no avail. It took me a long time to reassure the Arabs and the UN representatives who criticized the road's proposed route.

When the bulldozers finally began leveling the land in preparation for paving the road, I was asked by the Foreign Ministry to halt the work at once – because the remnants of 4th-century church had been uncovered and the Vatican itself had requested that Israel not build the road over it. Work was halted for many months until we shifted the route by a few meters to avoid damaging the remnants of the ancient church.

"Now all I need is for Jewish graves to be found," I said to myself at the time, exhausted from the public disputes concerning 'my road.' But practically all of northern Jerusalem is a "city of the dead" from the Second Temple Period, and thus it was only a matter of time until the bulldozers unearthed many dozens of graves from an ancient Jewish cemetery above which the road was supposed to run. It wasn't long before thousands of ultra-Orthodox protesters staged vocal and violent demonstrations against the construction of the road over Jewish graves.

Teddy Kollek, mayor at the time, who was aware of my great appreciation for the city's cemeteries and their inhabitants, called me in for a talk: "So, what do we do?," he asked. "It's not like with the church, where we could divert the road a bit, and it is also impossible to move the graves to another location. What do you suggest?" I suggested that he appoint a committee of two, comprising myself and his deputy mayor, Meir Porush, to find a solution that would not harm the dead while safeguarding the interests of the living in the city.

In my many meetings with Rabbi Porush, a leader of the ultra-Orthodox community, I learned another important lesson about cemeteries and the dead in Jerusalem: In terms of the *halakha* (Jewish law), a Jewish cemetery, unlike a Muslim one, is completely expropriated from the living and given over to the world of the dead, and so its land is *karka olam*, whose holiness never wanes and which the living are absolutely prohibited from using for other purposes: "In a graveyard one does not act disrespectfully. Animals shall not be grazed there and a water channel shall not be made to run through there and grasses are not picked there . . . out of respect for the dead (Babylonian Talmud, Tractate Megillah 29a)." Hence the fierce resistance to the construction of the road over the ancient graveyard. As for the deceased themselves, Rabbi Porush explained to me that the death of the body does not cancel out the existence of the spirit or soul, which are immortal. I also learned about the powers of impurity (*tum'ah* in Hebrew), which can prevent the soul from making its way on Judgment Day through the tunnels to the Mount of Olives.

"Now you understand the seriousness of paving a road over the graves," Rabbi Porush said to me, and his face lit up when I immediately affirmed his words and agreed that we had to quickly come up with a creative solution.

One evening, when we sat down with the engineers and the maps to examine the possibility of shifting the route away from the ancient graveyard, I recalled the notion of resurrected souls coming through tunnels. An image of the Judgment Day bridge suddenly came to my mind and I had an epiphany: "Why don't we build a bridge over the cemetery so that the road won't touch the ground where the graves are at all?," I proposed. Silence filled the room, and then it was broken by Rabbi Porush: "Halakhically speaking, the bridge solves the problem, of course, but practically speaking, it could significantly raise the coast of the building the road." One of the engineers did a quick calculation and found that a few tens of thousands of dollars would have to be added – a negligible sum, all concurred, if it would enable the souls of those Jews in the north of the city to reach the Judgment Day bridge.

Before long, a bridge several hundred meters long had been designed and built above the cemetery. This bridge is suspended only a few centimeters off the ground, and travelers on Road Number 1 don't even notice it. Not many people are even aware of the existence of the bridge, which serves no purpose whatsoever for the living in Jerusalem, but is priceless to the city's dead.

For me, the bridge that I built in Jerusalem remains a potent symbol of this city, 'the city of the dead' – for only in their graves do Jerusalem's inhabitants find true peace and tranquility.

That is, until the day, perhaps not so far off, when the dead will awaken in all their immense number and gather at the Mount of Olives. Then Jerusalem will turn from a city of the dead to a city of peace.

City of Peace

Israel's battle for Jerusalem, ongoing for over forty years now, is without precedent in terms of its scope and political ambition. Of all the territories it captured in 1967, Israel decided to annex only East Jerusalem. The resources poured into the policy of unifying the city exceed the country's total investment in the settlement enterprise in Judea and Samaria (the West Bank). Consider the territorial goal, one of five national objectives set by Israel's governments from 1967 to the present: Billions of dollars have been invested over the past decades for the sake of settling about 200,000 Jews in East Jerusalem. The infrastructure that was built in the East Jerusalem neighborhoods and in the surrounding settlements far outstrips the infrastructure investment in all of Israel's development towns, and has taken priority over other goals such as development of the Galilee and the Negev, or investment in transportation infrastructure and roads. More vast sums were invested in each of the other national objectives cited in this book – at the expense of other national goals. Had all this effort succeeded, then perhaps one could say that it was justified.

However, after forty years of this, Israel remains in a most difficult situation, and these goals have not been achieved. There is no peace with the Palestinians and Jerusalem, the capital, is still a 'city of strife.' I have tried, with some success I hope, to explain the reasons for this monumental failure. The commitment to a conception that became an ideology, and to territories that became sacred, gave rise to a fixed way of thinking that prevented the policy-makers from reconsidering their moves and halting the **March of Folly**. The more a policy's failure became apparent, the more the politicians stuck to it – exemplifying another key characteristic of Barbara Tuchman's definition of political folly:

> In the first stage, mental standstill fixes the principles and boundaries governing a political problem. In the second stage, when dissonances and failing function begin to appear, the initial principles rigidify. This is the period when, if wisdom were operative, re-examination and re-thinking and a change of course are possible, but they are as rare as rubies in a backyard. Rigidifying leads to increase of investment and the need to protect egos; policy founded upon error multiplies, never retreats. The greater the investment and the more involved in it the sponsor's ego, the more unacceptable is disengagement. In the third stage, pursuit of failure enlarges the damages until it causes the fall of Troy, the defection from the papacy, the loss of a trans-Atlantic empire, the classic humiliation in Vietnam . . . (Tuchman, *The March of Folly*, Knopf, 1984, p. 383)

In retrospect, it is possible to understand the circumstances that propelled the policy-makers in Jerusalem, in the early years following the city's unification, to initiate or approve hasty, overly ambitious and poorly thought-out decisions. In retrospect, it may be possible to understand, and even forgive, the mistakes that were made later on in the 1970s and 1980s when these policies were implemented over fierce opposition from experts and in disregard of Teddy Kollek's warnings. But it is not possible to understand, and certainly not to forgive, the peculiar insistence of the policy-makers and policy-implementers on persisting along the same path once the destructive consequences of their policies became undeniable.

Perhaps now, after Israel has tried in vain to achieve its goals, there will be some Israeli policy-makers who stop to undertake a serious reckoning and ask themselves: Now that we have tried almost everything, and almost everything has failed, maybe we should stop and 'rethink Jerusalem'?

This in itself would amount to a momentous change. 'To rethink Jerusalem' is more an intellectual, philosophical and Jewish challenge than it is a purely political one. How can Jerusalem, a city of strife in the previous century, become the city of peace in the 21st century?

Today, having failed to transform it into a uni-cultural, uni-religious and un-national city, the question must be asked with greater urgency: Perhaps the opposite is the right course? Perhaps with a different approach, one that defies the consensus, we shall be able to achieve what we have failed to achieve so far? Perhaps instead of trying to change the face of Jerusalem, to establish new facts in it and expand it, we simply ought to try to change ourselves – to liberate our thinking from its decades-long stagnation? Perhaps we should strive to accept Jerusalem as it is – a multicultural, multi-faith and bi-national city – and overcome our fear of these terms which so frightened us up to now? Perhaps Jerusalem is secretly laughing, scornfully observing from the depths of history the new Israelis who are trying to turn it into what it is not, and will never be? Perhaps a political outline that aspires to a 'division of Jerusalem' will achieve for us, the Israelis, more than the anachronistic political outline of the 'unification of Jerusalem' will ever achieve? And what would we really lose if the Old City – comprising less than 1 percent of the area of the capital – were to become a place where we would be partners rather than masters? And how terrible would it be if this small part, less than 1 percent of the city, were to have international status? What would happen?

This is what would happen: Jerusalem would be transformed from a problem into a solution. If we make Jerusalem the 'big key' to the conflict, in the broadest and not just the political sense, new doors will open up to us. Jerusalem can be the key to the heart of the Muslim world, to reconciliation with the Arab states, to peace with the Palestinians.

Israel's battle for Jerusalem has not ended. A resolution of the city's future seems farther off than ever. But then that has been Jerusalem's fate from time immemorial: to be fought over by different peoples, to be jolted in war after war, to ignite the imagination of millions of people throughout the world, so much so that they're willing to die for it.

In the evening, when I stand at the top of the Mount of Olives and gaze out at the city painted in reddish sunset hues, I know that this is where the great hope for peace has forever resided. And that the intensity of this hope is matched by the intensity of the disappointment in its failure to materialize.

I am still a soldier of Jerusalem and expect that I will remain so, for as long as I live.

Notes

Preface

1   The meetings in the summer of 1987 between Faisal Husseini, a PLO leader in the territories, and myself, a member of the Likud central committee and a close associate of Prime Minister Yitzhak Shamir, were described in the press at the time as "the Amirav affair." The purpose of the meetings was to bring about negotiations between Shamir and Arafat. The joint document that the two of us composed was the first of its kind, and it focused on a division of the land and of Jerusalem, and on providing extensive autonomy (almost akin to a state) to the Palestinians. Shamir, who was in on the secret, as were Dan Meridor and Ehud Olmert (the latter took part in one of the meetings), eventually refused to continue the contacts and forbade me from meeting anymore with Husseini. In wake of this, I resigned from the Likud and publicly called for peace with the PLO, the establishment of a Palestinian state and a division of Jerusalem. For more information, see Schiff, Zeev & Ya'ari, Ehud (1999) *Intifada*. Tel Aviv: Schocken, where the text of the document is cited, and also *Kol Ha'ir* (23.09.1987; 02.10.1987); *Yedioth Ahronoth* (27.09.1987; 28.09.1987; 22.12.1987); *Ma'ariv* (22.09.1987)

2   Citations of these five objectives as national goals may be found in numerous articles and books, including: Benvenisti, Meron (1973). *El Mul Hahoma Hasegura*. Tel Aviv: Weidenfeld & Nicolson; Benziman, Uzi (1973). *Yerushalayim: Ir Lelo Homa*. Jerusalem & Tel Aviv: Schocken; Berkowitz, Shmuel (2000). *Milhemet Hamekomot Hakedoshim*. Jerusalem: Jerusalem Institute for Israel Studies; Amirav, M. (1992). *Israel's Policy in Jerusalem Since 1967*. Stanford Center on Conflict and Negotiation, Working Paper Series – No. 102; Amirav, Moshe (2002). The Palestinians: From the Sidelines to Major Player in Jerusalem. In J. Ginat, E. Perkins & E. Corr (eds.), *The Middle East Peace Process: Vision Versus Reality*. Brighton & Portland: Sussex Academic Press; Amirav, Moshe (2004). *Kedusha Vepolitika Behar Habayit*. In: N. Luz (ed.), *The New East – Islam, Society and Space in Jerusalem – Past and Present*. Jerusalem: Magnes Press, The Hebrew University of Jerusalem; Klein, Menachem (1995). *Yerushalayim Bemasa Umatan Leshalom: Emdot Arviyot*. Jerusalem: Jerusalem Institute for Israel Studies; Klein, Menachem (1999). *Yonim Bishmei Yerushalayim: Tahalikh Hashalom Veha'ir Yerushalayim*. Jerusalem: Jerusalem Institute for Israel Studies; Klein, Menachem (2001) *Shovrim Tabu: Hamaga'im Lehesder Keva Be'Yerushalayim 1994–2001*. Jerusalem: Jerusalem Institute for Israel Studies; Kroyanker, David (1988). *Yerushalayim: Hama'avak 'al Mivneh Ha'ir Vehazuta*. Tel Aviv: Zmora Bitan; Romann, Michael (1984). *Yahasei*

Gomlin Bein Hamigzar Hayehudi Veha'aravi be'Yerushalayim. Jerusalem: Jerusalem Institute for Israel Studies; Romann, Michael (1989). *Shiluv Vehafrada Beyahasei Hamigzar Hayehudi Veha'aravi be'Yerushalayim – Behina Metodologit*, Yerushalyaim Yom-Yom Ir Ve'ezor, 19; Romann, Michael (1995). *Hamimsad Hayisraeli Bemizrah Yerushalayim: Hesdereim Ulekahim*. Jerusalem: Jerusalem Institute for Israel Studies; Shragai, Nadav (1995). *Har Hameriva, Hama'avak 'al Har Habayit: Yehudim Vemuslemim, Dat Upolitika Me'az 1967*. Jerusalem: Keter; Bollens, A. S. (2000). *On Narrow Ground: Urban Policy and Ethnic Conflict in Jerusalem and Belfast*. Albany: State University of New York Press; Dumper, M. (1997). *The Politics of Jerusalem*. New York: Columbia University Press; Cohen, S. E. (1993). *The Politics of Planning: Israeli–Palestinian Competition for Control of Land in Jerusalem Periphery*. Chicago and London: The University of Chicago Press; Cheshin, A., Hutman, B. & Melamed, A. (1999). *Separate and Unequal: The Inside Story of Israeli Rule in East Jerusalem*. Cambridge, MA: Harvard University Press; Kaminker, S. and Associates (1994). *Planning and Housing Issues in East Jerusalem*. High Court of Justice Petition 1091.

And also in government, municipality and public committee reports. They are explicitly cited as national goals numerous times by public committees, in public plans, in government reports and decisions, by the ministerial committee for Jerusalem affairs and the Jerusalem municipal council. They have served as binding guidelines for policymakers at all levels in formulating the urban master plans.

Chapter One   *Jerusalem Syndrome: Dreams and Failures*

1   Shragai, *Har Hameriva*, p. 18. Dayan continually opposed the occupation of the Old City, see Narkiss, Uzi (1975), *Ahat Yerushalayim*. Tel Aviv: Am Oved, p. 213. And after the occupation of the Old City, he consistently held the view that there was no need to annex it. Years later, as foreign minister in the Begin government, he was prepared to cede it and keep only the Jewish Quarter and the Western Wall (see Chapter Two).

2   Benziman, *Yerushalayim: Ir Lelo Homa*, p. 282. The team was headed by Professor Avigdor Levontin, a member of the National Academy of Sciences and an expert on international law. The team's report was submitted to the government on June 10, 1967, before the cabinet discussion (see Chapter Seven)

3   *New York Times* (July 1, 1967). Incredibly, the position of the Arab League and the Muslim states in favor of internationalization of the holy places remained the same from 1947 until 1974. At that time, they changed to supporting the Palestinians' right to Jerusalem.

4   State of Israel (2001), report of a team of experts.

5   *Haaretz* (February 2, 1999); peace index survey, Tami Steinmetz Center, Tel Aviv University.

6   Felsenstein, D. (1989). Generating the growth process: The case of the development of high technology industry in Jerusalem. *City and Region*, 19–20 (Hebrew), p. 5.

7 Shortly before the municipal elections at the end of 1993, a group of activists from the peace camp (including myself) put together a Jewish–Arab list to run for the city council under the slogan 'Two Capitals in One City.' We decided to go to Tunis to seek Arafat's consent for the Palestinians' participation in the elections, for the placement of a Palestinian candidate on our list and for votes to be cast on a separate ballot for Teddy Kollek for mayor. Foreign Ministry representatives as well as Teddy Kollek welcomed our initiative and wished us luck. Over the course of a long night in Tunis, we managed to convince Arafat to allow voting for the joint list, but not for Teddy. The opposition of the Palestinian leadership in Jerusalem took the participation of the city's Arabs in the elections off the agenda altogether, and was primarily due to their refusal to grant legitimacy to 'the united city.'

8 *Haaretz* (January 3, 2007).

Chapter Two   *How Jerusalem Became Israel's Capital*

1 Hirsch, Moshe, Housen-Couriel, Deborah & Ruth Lapidoth (1994). *Yerushalayim Le'an? Hatza'ot Bidvar Atida Shel Ha'ir.* Jerusalem: Jerusalem Institute for Israel Studies, p. 10; Lapidoth, Ruth (1997). *Yerushalayim – Hebetim Mishpatiyim: Dapei Reka Lekove'e Mediniyut. Dapei Diyun*, 3, pp. 97–103.

2 Lapidoth, *Yerhusahlayim – Hebetim Mishpatiyim*; Dinstein, Y. (1971). *Tziyon Bemishmpat Tifdeh.* Hapraklit, 27, 519–22, Hirsch, Housen-Couriel & Lapidoth, *Yerushalayim Le'an?*

3 See Golani, Motti. (1994). *Tziyonut Lelo Tziyon? Emdat Hanhagat Hayishuv u'Medinat Yisrael Beshe'elat Yerushalayim* 1947–1949. In: Avi Bareli (ed.) *Yerushalayim Hehatzuya*, Idan, 18. Jerusalem: Yad Ben-Zvi, 32–3; also, articles by Aaronsohn, Margalit Shiloh, Yossi Katz and Gideon Biger in Lavski, H. (ed.) (1989). *Yerushalayim Ba'toda'a Uba'asiya Hatziyonit.* Jerusalem: Zalman Shazar Center for Jewish History

4 Lavski, *Yerushalayim Ba'toda'a*, p. 52.

5 *Ibid.*, p. 53.

6 *Ibid.* On Herzl's attitude toward Jerusalem, see also the article by Harel, in Lavski, *Yerushalyim Ba'toda'a*, p. 77.

7 Golani, *Tziyonut Lelo Tziyon?*, p. 53; Harel, in Lavski, *Yerushalayim Batoda'a*, p. 82.

8 Ben-Gurion, David (1976), *Zikhronot* (Memoirs), Volume 4. Tel Aviv: Am Oved, p. 260. On the issue of borders and the territories, see also Galnor, Itzhak (1995). *Veshavu Banim Ligvulam: Hahakra'ot 'al Medina Ushetahim Batenu'a Hatziyonit.* Sde Boker and Jerusalem: Ben-Gurion Heritage Center, Magnes, The Hebrew University of Jerusalem.

9 State of Israel, State Archives, the Central Zionist Archive, political and diplomatic documents, December 1947–May 1948, pp. 21–4; see also Lorach, Netanel. (1978), *Al-Haram al-Sharif Basiah Hatziburi Ha'aravi Hapalestini be'Yisrael: Zehut Zikaron Kolektivi Vedarkhei Habeniya.* Jerusalem: Floersheimer Institute for Policy Studies.

10 *Ibid.*

11 *Ibid.*
12 Sharef, Ze'ev (1959), *Shelosha Yamim*. Tel Aviv: Am Oved, pp. 125–7.
13 Pa'il, in Shaltiel, Eli (ed.) (1981), *Perakim Betoldot Yerushalayim Bazman Hehadash: Sefer Zikaron le'Yitzhak Herzog.* Jerusalem: Yad Ben-Zvi, p. 357.
14 Council of the State of Israel, 6th session, 1948, June 24, 1948, pp. 9–21. See also Bialer, Uri. (1985). *Haderekh Labira: Hafikhat Yerushalayim Lemakom Moshava Harishmi shel Memshelet Yisrael Bishnat 1949.* Cathedra 35, 163–91.
15 Ben-Gurion, David (1977), *Zikhronot* (Memoirs), Volume 3, Tel Aviv: Am Oved, p. 889.
16 Government protocols, Government Archive, Record for December 11, 1949.
17 Ben-Gurion, *Zikhronot* Volume 3.
18 Brecher, in Shaltiel, *Perakim Betoldot Yerushalayim*, p. 399.
19 Sharef, *Shelosha Yamim*, p. 127; Bialer, *Haderekh Labira*, p. 163.
20 On the negotiations between Israel and Jordan on the Jerusalem issue, see Klein, *Yonim Bishmei Yerushalayim*; Morris, Benny (2006), *Haderekh le'Yerushalayim: Glubb Pasha, Eretz Yisrael Vehayehudim.* Tel Aviv: Am Oved; Benvenisti, *El Mul Hahoma Hasegura*; Al-Tal, Abdullah (1967). *Zikhronot Abdullah Al-Tal* (translated by Y. Halamish). Tel Aviv: Ma'arakhot; Ben-Gurion, David (1984), *Yoman Hamilhama: Milhemet Ha'atzmaut 1948–1949.* Tel Aviv: Hahevra Lehafatzat Mishnato Shel Ben-Gurion, Israel Defense Ministry Press; Dayan, Moshe (1977), *Avnei Derekh: Otobiyografiya.* Jerusalem: Idanim Dvir; Shlaim, Avi (1988). *Collusion Across the Jordan: King Abdullah, the Zionist Movement and the Partition of Palestine.* Oxford: Clarendon.
21 Golani, *Tziyonut Lelo Tziyon?*, pp. 291–6; Narkiss, *Ahat Yerushalayim.*
22 Adler, in Lapidoth, *Hebetim Mishpatiyim*, p. 42.
23 *Ibid.*
24 *Ibid.* See also Brecher, Michael (1972), *Dimuyim, Hahlatot Vehizun Hozer Bemediniyut Hahutz Hayisraelit.* Medina Vememshal, Aleph (3), 7–37; Barzilai, Gad. (1984), *Mediniyut Hutz Yisraelit Trom Medinatit Umedinatit 1947–1950.* Doctoral Thesis, Bar-Ilan University, Ramat Gan.
25 Narkiss, *Ahat Yerushalayim*, p. 52.
26 *Ibid.*, p. 52.
27 *Ibid.*, p. 103.
28 *Ibid.*, p. 106.
29 *Ibid.*, p. 118.
30 *Ibid.*, p. 120.
31 *Ibid.*
32 Benziman, *Yerushalayim: Ir Lelo Homa*, p. 11.
33 *Ibid.*, p. 11.
34 *Ibid.*, p. 21.
35 *Ibid.*, p. 45. On the government decisions and policies in the first year of the city's unification, see also Benvenisti, *El Mul Hahoma Hasegura*; Pedahzur, Reuven (1996), *Nitzahon Hamevukha: Mediniyut Memshelet Eshkol*

Bashetahim Le'ahar Milhemet Sheshet Hayamim. Tel Aviv: Bitan, Yad Tabenkin, Makhon Galili.

36 Berkowitz, *Milhemet Hamekomot Hakedoshim*, p. 59.

37 Blum, in Lapidoth, *Hebetim Mishpatiyim*, p. 33; Blum, Yehuda (1971), *Tziyon Bamishpat Habein-Leumi Nifdita.* Hapraklit, 27, 315–24, p. 315; Blum (1971), p. 315; Blum, Yehuda (1972), *Mizrah Yerushalayim Eino Shetah Kavush.* Hapraklit, 28, 183–90, p. 183.

38 Benziman, *Yerushalayim: Ir Lelo Homa*, p. 59.

39 Blum, in Lapidoth, *Hebetim Mishpatiyim*, p. 33; Blum, *Tziyon Bamishpat Habein-Leumi*, p. 315; Blum, *Mizrah Yerushalayim*, p. 183.

40 Benziman, *Yerushalayim: Ir Lelo Homa*, p. 59.

41 Berkowitz, *Milhemet Hamekomot Hakedoshim*, p. 58.

Chapter Three   *The Struggle for East Jerusalem*

1 On trends in planning in Jerusalem and in British, Jordanian and Israeli planning before 1967, see Efrat, Elisha (1975), *Shinuyim Bitfisat Tikhnuna Shel Yerushalayim Bahamishim Hashanim Ha'ahronot (1919–1969).* Ma'alot, Daled; Ben-Aryeh, Yehoshua (1970), *Hitpahuta Shel Yerushalayim.* Keshet, 12 (4), 29–37; Ben-Aryeh, Yehoshua (1977), *Ir Bere'i Tekufa:Yerushalayim Beme'ah Hatesha Esreh.* Jerusalem: Yad Ben-Zvi; Ben-Aryeh, Yehoshua (1979), *Ir Bere'i Tekufa: Yerushalayim Hehadasha Bereshita.* Jerusalem: Yad Ben-Zvi; Kroyanker, *Yerushalayim: Hama'avak*; Kroyanker, David (1988), *Pnei Ha'ir, Kaf-Heh Shanim Le'ihud Ha'ir: Perakim Bege'ografiya Ironit Shel Yerushalayim.* Jerusalem Institute for Israel Studies.

2 Kroyanker, *Yerushalayim: Hama'avak*; Benvenisti, *Yerushalayim: Ir Lelo Homa*; Benvenisti, Meron (1981), *Yerushalayim: Ir Ubeliba Homa.* Tel Aviv: Kav Adom, Hakibbutz Hameuhad; Amirav, *Israel's Policy in Jerusalem since 1967*; Kimhi, Israel (1980), *Yerushalayim Hahatzuya 1948–1967.* Jerusalem: Jerusalem Institute for Israel Studies.

3 Kroyanker, *Yerushalayim: Hama'avak*, p. 34.

4 Benziman, *Yerushalayim: Ir Lelo Homa*, p. 14.

5 *Ibid.*, p. 48.

6 Gazit, Shlomo (1985), *Hamakel Vehagezer: Hamimshal Hayisraeli Be'Yehuda Veshomron.* Tel Aviv: Zmora-Bitan, p. 223.

7 Benziman, *Yerushalayim: Ir Lelo Homa*, p. 48.

8 Benvenisti, Meron (1988), *Hakela Vehaela.* Tel Aviv: Kav Adom, p. 69.

9 Jerusalem master plan 1968; also Benziman, *Yerushalayim: Ir Lelo Homa* and Benvenisti, *El Mul Hahoma Hasegura.*

10 State of Israel (1970), recommendations of the inter-ministerial committee for strengthening Israel's hold on Jerusalem. On the new planning policy, see Kimhi, *Yerushalayim Hahatzuya*; Kroyanker, *Pnei Ha'ir*; State of Israel (1972), Plan for the Geographical Distribution of Israel's Population of Five Million; State of Israel (1975), the Population and Construction in Israel; Jerusalem Municipality (1971), Development Directions; and also Benziman, *Yerushalayim: Ir Lelo Homa* and Benvenisti, *El Mul Hahoma Hasegura.*

11 Jerusalem municipality (1970), Development of the Neighborhoods in

Jerusalem; State of Israel (1973), the inter-ministerial committee for examining the rate of development in Jerusalem.

12 Benvenisti, *El Mul Hahoma Hasegura*, p. 297.

13 Amos Ayalon, *Haaretz*, January 7, 1971.

14 Benvenisti, *El Mul Hahoma Hasegura*, p. 298.

15 Barzaki, Elinoar (1980), *Yerushalayim: Merkaz Ha'ir Vehashekhunot*, Jerusalem Institute for Israel Studies, p. 32.

16 Benvenisti, *El Mul Hahoma Hasegura*, p. 297.

17 *Ibid.*

18 *Ibid.*, p. 293.

19 *Ibid.*

20 Kroyanker, *Yerushalayim: Hama'avak*, p. 34.

21 *Ibid.*, p. 15.

22 Jerusalem Municipality (1978), local outline plan for Jerusalem, p. 16.

23 Kroyanker (1988A), p. 49.

24 From: *B'tselem* (1995), p. 44.

25 Jerusalem Municipality (1978), local outline plan, p. 16.

26 Jerusalem Municipality (April 13, 1975), letter from deputy mayor Y. Matza to Kollek.

27 *Haaretz*, August 6, 1993.

28 Benvenisti, *Hakela Vehaela*, p. 132.

29 Kollek, Teddy (1994). *Yerushalayim Shel Teddy*. Tel Aviv: Sifriyat Maariv, p. 106.

30 Cheshin, A., Hutman, B. & Melamed, A., *Separate and Unequal*, p. 31.

31 Jerusalem Municipality, protocols of subcommittee for planning and construction, February 22, 1993.

32 High Court of Justice (1978), 5601/78, Awda A'ida Abu Tir et al. versus the Prime Minister, Section 18 (*Taf*).

33 Jerusalem Institute for Israel Studies (1980), Barzaki, *Yerushalayim: Merkaz Ha'ir Vehashekhunot*, p. 31.

34 B'tselem (May 1995), p. 22. Hague Convention 46/B as well as Section 47 of the Fourth Geneva Convention explicitly stipulate that in the event of the annexation of territory following war, the rules of international law remain in force and apply to the inhabitants of the territory.

35 Jerusalem Municipality (2001), report on the state of construction in East Jerusalem, from the city engineer.

36 Husseini, in a conversation with me, August 7, 1990.

37 The Interior Ministry estimate is 20,000 buildings, which seems a bit excessive. The municipality estimate is 15,000 buildings. See Jerusalem Municipality (letter), July 29, 2004; *Haaretz*, March 1, 2000; B'tselem (1997); Ir Shalem (2000).

Chapter Four   *Why Israel is Losing the Jewish Majority in its Capital*

1 Ze'evi, in a conversation with me, February 12, 1989.

2 State of Israel (1972), Plan for the Geographical Distribution of Israel's

Population of Five Million, Booklet 2, p. 3; and Jerusalem Municipality (1968), population forecasts for the 1970s.

3 Jerusalem Municipality (1970), report on the activity of the department of culture, youth and sport, p. 1.

4 Jerusalem Municipality (1969), regular budget and development budget, 1968, 1969, p. 5.

5 Jerusalem Municipality (1970), report on the activity of the department of culture, youth and sport, p. 4; Kimhi, I., Hyman, B. & Claude, G. (1976), *Yerushalayim 1967–1975: Sekira Hevratit Kalkalit*. Institute for Urban and Regional Studies. The Hebrew University of Jerusalem.

6 *Ma'ariv*, June 13, 1971.

7 Barzaki, *Yerushalayim: Merkaz Ha'ir Vehashekhunot*, p. 31.

8 Council for National Planning and Economics (1970), p. 6.

9 *Ma'ariv*, June 13, 1971.

10 Council for National Planning and Economics (1972), p. 2.

11 The ratio determined by the Gafni Committee, 26.6% versus 73.4%, has changed since then, as a result of the policy's failure to achieve this goal. Within a few years it had changed to 30%–70%, and then to 31%–69%. At present, the government is trying to meet a goal of 40%–60%. The goal set by the Gafni Committee (and later on, the 30%–70% target) appears in State of Israel (1973), the inter-ministerial committee for examining the rates of development in Jerusalem, p. 3, and in many more Jerusalem municipality documents.

12 Kimhi, Hyman & Claude, *Yerushalayim 1967–1975*, p. 6.

13 *Ibid.*, p. 7.

14 City council protocols, June 17, 1984.

15 *Haaretz*, May 24, 2006.

16 *Haaretz*, January 26, 1997; *Haaretz*, March 17, 1997.

17 *Haaretz*, January 15, 1997. On the government policy concerning the denial of residency to Palestinians, see also B'tselem (April 1997).

18 *Haaretz*, November 27, 1996.

19 *Haaretz*, August 23, 1996.

20 State of Israel (1997), report of the State Comptroller, no. 96.

21 *Kol Ha'ir*, August 22, 1997.

22 *Haaretz*, February 12, 1997.

23 *Haaretz*, January 30, 2007.

Chapter Five *The Most Polarized City in the World*

1 For further details, see Amirav, Moshe (2001). *Hamilhama 'al Ofya Shel Yerushalayim: Nitzahon Shel Kevutzot Hashulayim 'al Hamerkaz Hatziyoni.* In: Avraham Brichta and Ami Pedahzur (eds). *Habehirot Lirshuyot Hamekomiyot be'Yisrael – 1988: Hemshekhiyut o Shinui?* Tel Aviv: Tel Aviv University.

2 For further details, see: Romann, *Yahasei Gomlin*; Romann, *Shiluv Vehafrada*; Gutmann, E. & Klein, C. (1980), *The Institutional Structure of Heterogeneous Cities: Brussels, Montreal, and Belfast.* In J. Kreamer (ed.).

Jerusalem: Problems and Prospects (178–207). New York: Ranger; Bollens, *On Narrow Ground*, Klein, *Yonim Bishmei Yerushalayim*; Kliot, N. & Mansfield, Y. (1997), *The Political Landscape of Partition: The Case of Cyprus*, Political Geography, 16, 495–521

3   The number of Arabs in the Jordanian city did not exceed 40,000, while the Jewish population was about 190,000. It appears that the ministers also did not know how many Arabs there were in the city, but at the same time, did not view this as a 'problem.' The first census of the city's Arab population was conducted only in September.

4   Gazit, *Hamakel Vehagezer*, p. 227.

5   'Kol Yisrael,' July 22, 1967 (Kol Yisrael film library).

6   *Lamerhav*, January 1, 1968.

7   Benvenisti, *El Mul Hahoma Hasegura*, p. 189.

8   *Ibid.*

9   Jerusalem Municipality (1968), budget proposal for the eastern region; Jerusalem Municipality (1969), regular budget and development budget.

10 Benvenisti, *El Mul Hahoma Hasegura*, p. 35.

11 Jerusalem Municipality (1974), Master Plan 1968; Jerusalem Municipality (1970), planning in the Arab sector; Jerusalem Municipality (1971); directions in the development of construction for Jerusalem.

12 *Davar*, June 23, 1967.

13 Gazit, *Hamakel Vehagezer*, p. 229.

14 *Ibid.*

15 *Ibid.*, p. 223.

16 *Ibid.*, p. 224.

17 Many testimonies regarding Kollek's vehement opposition to the appointments may be found in Benvenisti, *El Mul Hahoma Hasegura*, Benziman, *Yerushalayim: Ir Lelo Homa* and Segev, Tom (2005). *1967: Veha'aretz Shinta Et Paneha*. Jerusalem: Keter.

18 Kol Yisrael, June 20, 1969.

19 Interview on 'Kol Yisrael' (Nahman Shai) on May 25, 1969.

20 Gazit, *Hamakel Vehagezer*, p. 228.

21 *Ibid.*, p. 138.

22 Zak, Moshe (1996), *Hussein Oseh Shalom*. Ramat Gan: Bar-Ilan University, pp. 80, 161–6.

23 Romann, M. & Weingrod, A. (1991), *Living Together Separately: Arabs and Jews in Contemporary Jerusalem*. New Jersey: Princeton University Press.

24 *Ibid.*

25 *Ma'ariv*, October 10, 1990.

26 Jerusalem Municipality (1986), master plan for the development of the Arab sector, p. 12.

27 Jerusalem Municipality (July 31, 1990), collection data and development expenses; Jerusalem Municipality (July 10, 1975).

28 Kollek, *Yerushalayim Shel Teddy*, p. 106. On the poor condition of infrastructure in East Jerusalem, see Jerusalem Municipality (1975), citywide infrastructure systems.

29 Jerusalem Municipality (2000), report on comparison of services and infrastructure between the east and west of the city, the municipality director-general; Jerusalem Municipality (July 10, 1975), neighborhoods for rehabilitation in Jerusalem.

30 *Ibid.*, p. 7.

31 *Haaretz*, July 10, 1995.

32 *Haaretz*, January 27, 1997.

33 *Haaretz*, April 9, 1998.

34 Klein, *Yonim Bishmei Yerushalayim*, p. 55.

35 Rubinstein, D., Malley, R. Agha, H., Barak, E. & Morris, B. (2003), *Camp David 2000: Ma Be'emet Kara Sham?* Tel Aviv: Yedioth Ahronoth, p. 31.

36 *Ma'ariv*, October 10, 1990.

37 Conversation with Husseini, March 2, 1993.

38 Romann & Weingrod, *Living Together Separately*.

39 Klein, *Yonim Bishmei Yerushalayim*, p. 9. See also Kliot, *The Political Landscape of Partition*.

40 Romann, Michael (1995), *Hamimsad Hayisraeli Bemizrah Yerushalayim: Hesdereim Ulekahim*. Jerusalem: Jerusalem Institute for Israel Studies; Bollens, *On Narrow Ground*; Dumper, *The Politics of Jerusalem*; Kuttab, D. & Kaminker, S. (1997), *Palestinian–Israeli Contacts on the Municipal Level. Conflict Management and Conflict Resolution in Divided Cities: Brussels and Jerusalem*, 221–40. Israel–Palestine Center for Research and Information and Center for Interdisciplinary Study of Brussels.

Chapter Six   *The Failed Attempts to Bring Peace*

1 Ben-Elissar, E. (1995), *Lo Od Milhama*. Tel Aviv: Maariv, pp. 40–41.

2 *Ibid.*, p. 233. On the first Camp David summit, see also Sofer (1986).

3 *Ibid.*, p. 41.

4 *Ibid.*, pp. 219–20.

5 Klein, *Yonim Bishmei Yerushalayim*, pp. 60–1. On Jordan's role, see also Giladi, R. & Merhav, Reuven (1998), *Hamamlakha Hahashemit Hayardenit Vetafkida Behesder Keva Atidi be'Yerushalayim: Hebetim Mishpatiyim, Mediniyim Uma'asiyim*. Jerusalem: Jerusalem Institute for Israel Studies.

6 On the Palestinians' struggle for Jerusalem and their strategies, see Amirav, *The Palestinians: From the Sidelines to Major Player*; Amirav, Moshe (1991), *The Jerusalem Problem in the Twentieth Century: Positions and Solutions 1917–1992*. Stockholm: Stockholm University Press; Al-Qaq, Z. (1997), *Post 1967 Palestinian Strategies for Jerusalem. Conflict Management and Conflict Resolution in Divided Cities, Jerusalem and Brussels* (339–68). Israel-Palestine Center for Research and Information and Center for Interdisciplinary Study of Brussels.

7 One of Arafat's conditions for signing the Oslo Accords was a promise from Israel not to shut all the Palestinian institutions in Jerusalem. The promise is found in a letter from Israeli Foreign Minister Peres to the Norwegian Foreign Minister Holst, see Klein, *Yonim Bishmei Yerushalayim*, p. 109.

8 Musallam (1996), in Klein, *Yonim Bishmei Yerushalayim*, p. 60.

9 *Haaretz*, July 13, 1994; 'Mabat Lashalom' report (1995).

10 *Haaretz*, August 15, 1995.

11 *Haaretz*, December 16, 1994; *Haaretz*, December 20, 1994; 'Mabat Lashalom' (1995); Klein, *Yonim Bishmei Yerushalayim*.

12 On the conclusions of the Stanford conference, see Amirav, *The Jerusalem Problem in the Twentieth Century*; Amirav, M. & Siniora, H. (1989), *Yerushalayim – Petaron Labilti Patir*. Jerusalem: Truman Institute, The Hebrew University of Jerusalem.

13 On the Notre Dame talks and the conference that concluded three years of talks, see Amirav, *The Palestinians: From the Sidelines to Major Player*.

14 For more on their activity, see Klein, *Yonim Bishmei Yerushalayim*.

15 *Haaretz*, May 29, 1997; *Haaretz*, June 5, 1997.

16 Sher, Gilad (2001), *Bemerhak Negi'a: Ha'Mum Leshalom 1999–2000 – Edut*. Tel Aviv, Yedioth Ahronoth – Sifrei Hemed, p. 245.

17 *Ibid.*, p. 361.

18 *Ibid.*

19 The reasons for the failure of the second Camp David summit are presented in Klein, *Shovrim Tabu*; Rubinstein, Malley, Agha, Barak & Morris, *Camp David 2000*; Amirav, *The Palestinians: From the Sidelines to Major Player*; Horowitz, Uri (2001), *Ve'idat Camp David Hashniya Vehatza'ot Hagishur Shel Hanasi Clinton, Hagirsa Hapalestinit*. Tel Aviv: Strategic Assessment, Jaffe Center for Strategic Studies at Tel Aviv University.

20 See: *Haaretz*, December 9, 2002.

21 Ben-Ami, Shlomo (2004), *Hazit Lelo Oref: Masa El Gvulot Tahalikh Hashalom*. Tel Aviv: Yedioth Ahronoth, p. 195

22 Berkowitz, *Milhemet Hamekomot Hakedoshim*, p. 28.

23 *Haaretz*, January 19, 2006.

Chapter Seven   *The Struggle Over the Holy Places*

1 Ayalon, Amos (1991), *Yerushalayim, Shiga'on Ladavar*. Jerusalem: Domino, p. 109.

2 Golani, *Tziyonut Lelo Tziyon?*, pp. 32–3.

3 Berkowitz, *Milhemet Hamekomot Hakedoshim*, p. 50.

4 *Ibid.*

5 Narkiss, *Ahat Yerushalayim*, pp. 213–14; Shragai, *Har Hameriva*, p. 18; Benziman, *Yerushalayim: Ir Lelo Homa*, p. 20.

6 Benziman, *Yerushalayim: Ir Lelo Homa*, p. 20.

7 *Ibid.*, p. 282.

8 *Ibid.*

9 *Ibid.*, p. 283.

10 *Ibid.*

11 *Ibid.*, pp. 284–5; *Kol Ha'ir*, August 6, 1993.

12 Benziman, *Yerushalayim: Ir Lelo Homa*, p. 49.

13 *Ibid.*

14 *Ibid.*, p. 14.

15 *Ibid.*, p. 47.

16 *Ibid.*, p. 48.

17 *Ibid.*, p. 47.

18 *Kol Ha'ir*, December 12, 1992; Salman in a conversation with me, March 9, 1996.

19 *Ibid.*

20 On the Vatican's position, see Minerbi, Y. (1985), *Havatikan – Eretz Hakodesh Vehatziyonut.* Jerusalem: Yad Ben-Zvi; and Ferrari, Silvio (1986), *Hakes Hakadosh Ube'ayot Eretz Yisrael Aharei Milhemet Ha'olam Hashniya: Binum Yerushalayim Vehaganat Hamekomot Hakedoshim 1947–1949.* Yahadut Zemanenu, 3, 187–207.

21 Minerbi, *Havatikan*, p. 81.

22 From the *New York Times*, July 1, 1967, as cited in Berkowitz, *Milhemet Hamekomot Hakedoshim*, p. 69.

23 See Sela, Avraham (1983), *Ahdut Betokh Pirud: Ve'idot Hapisga Ha'arviyot.* Jerusalem: Magnes, The Hebrew University of Jerusalem, p. 267. For further details on the start of the Israeli–Palestinian conflict, see Porat, Yehoshua (1978). *Mimehumot Lamerida: Hatenuah Haleumit Ha'aravit Palestinit 1929–1939.* Tel Aviv: Am Oved.

24 *Ibid.*

25 Berkowitz, *Milhemet Hamekomot Hakedoshim*, p. 50.

26 *Ibid.*, p. 51.

27 Klein, *Jerusalem in the Peace Negotiations.*

28 *Ibid.*

29 *Ibid.*, p. 421.

30 Shragai, *Har Hameriva*, pp. 227–325.

31 *Ibid.*

32 Reiter, Yitzhak (1997), *Har Habayit – Al-Haram Al-Sharif; Nekudot Haskama Umahloket.* Jerusalem: Jerusalem Institute for Israel Studies, p. 161.

33 Elad, Amikam (1992), *Kedushata Shel Ir: Yerushalayim Besifrut Ha'intifada*, in Aharon Layish (ed.), *Ha'aravim Be'Yerushalayim* (pp. 151–61). Jerusalem: Jerusalem Institute for Israel Studies, p. 17.

34 For more on Jordan's struggle with the PLO via its loyalists in the religious institutions in Jerusalem in the 1980s, see Shragai, *Har Hameriva*; Klein, *Jerusalem in the Peace Negotiations*; Amirav, *The Palestinians: From the Sidelines to Major Player.*

35 Shragai, *Har Hameriva*, pp. 336–337.

36 Amirav, *The Palestinians: From the Sidelines to Major Player*, p. 5.

37 *Haaretz*, July 26, 1994.

38 *Ibid.*

39 *Haaretz*, November 2, 1994.

40 *Haaretz*, July 26, 1994; *Haaretz*, August 5, 1996.

41 *Haaretz*, July 26, 1994; *Davar*, November 2, 1994.

42 *Al-Quds*, December 16, 1994; *Haaretz*, December 22, 1994.

43 On the Israeli public's attitude toward the Temple Mount, see these important studies: Ramon, Amnon (1997), *Yahasam Shel Medinat Yisrael Vehatzibur Hayehudi Ligvanav Lehar Habayit (1967–1996).* Jerusalem:

Jerusalem Institute for Israel Studies; Reiter, *Har Habayit*; and Reiter, Yitzhak (ed.) (2001), *Ribonut Ha'el Veha'adam, Kedusha Umerkaziyut Politit Behar Habayit*. Jerusalem: Jerusalem Institute for Israel Studies.

44 Reiter, *Har Habayit*, p. 117.

45 Benvenisti, *El Mul Hahoma Hasegura*, p. 238.

46 Amirav, Moshe (ed.) (2005), *Adoni Rosh Hamemshala: Yerushalayim*. Jerusalem: Carmel, p. 130.

47 Hanoch Smith poll, *Ma'ariv*, July 5, 1981.

48 Guttman Institute poll, as cited in Ramon, *Yahasam Shel Medinat Yisrael Vehatzibur Hayehudi*, p. 135.

49 For further details on the Temple Mount issue at Camp David, see Amirav, *The Palestinians: From the Sidelines to Major Player*; Amirav, *Kedusha Vepolitika*; Amirav, *Adoni Rosh Hamemshala*; Klein, *Shovrim Tabu*; Sher, *Bemerhak Negi'a*; Ben-Ami, *Hazit Lelo Oref*.

50 Sher, *Bemerhak Negi'a*, p. 231.

51 Klein, *Shovrim Tabu*, p. 73.

Bibliography – English

Al-Qaq, Z. (1997). *Post 1967 Palestinian Strategies for Jerusalem. Conflict Management and Conflict Resolution in Divided Cities, Jerusalem and Brussels* (339–68). Israel–Palestine Center for Research and Information and Center for Interdisciplinary Study of Brussels.

Amirav, Moshe (1991). *The Jerusalem Problem in the Twentieth Century: Positions and Solutions 1917–1992.* Stockholm: Stockholm University Press.

Amirav, Moshe (1992). *Israel's Policy in Jerusalem Since 1967.* Stanford Center on Conflict and Negotiation, Working Paper Series – No. 102.

Amirav, Moshe (1993). *Visions for the City of Peace. Jerusalem: Vision and Reconciliation.* United Nations Information Department.

Amirav, Moshe (2002). *The Palestinians: From the Sidelines to Major Player in Jerusalem.* In J. Ginat, E. Perkins & E. Corr (eds.), *The Middle East Peace Process: Vision Versus Reality.* Brighton & Portland: Sussex Academic press.

Bollens, A. S. (2000). *On Narrow Ground: Urban Policy and Ethnic Conflict in Jerusalem and Belfast.* Albany: State University of New York Press.

Cheshin, A., Hutman, B. & Melamed, A. (1999). *Separate and Unequal: The Inside Story of Israeli Rule in East Jerusalem.* Cambridge, MA: Harvard University Press.

Cohen, S. E. (1993). *The Politics of Planning: Israeli–Palestinian Competition for Control of Land in Jerusalem Periphery.* Chicago and London: The University of Chicago Press.

Dumper, M. (1997). *The Politics of Jerusalem.* New York: Columbia University Press.

Gutmann, E. & Klein, C. (1980). The Institutional Structure of Heterogeneous Cities: Brussels, Montreal, and Belfast, in J. Kreamer (ed.), *Jerusalem: Problems and Prospects* (178–207). New York: Ranger.

Kaminker, S. and Associates (1994). *Planning and Housing Issues in East Jerusalem.* High Court of Justice Petition 1091.

Kliot, N. & Mansfield, Y. (1997). *The Political Landscape of Partition: The Case of Cyprus,* Political Geography, 16, 495–521.

Kuttab, D. & Kaminker, S. (1997). *Palestinian–Israeli Contacts on the Municipal Level. Conflict Management and Conflict Resolution in Divided Cities: Brussels and Jerusalem,* 221–40. Israel–Palestine Center for Research and Information and Center for Interdisciplinary Study of Brussels.

Romann, M. & Weingrod, A. (1991). *Living Together Separately: Arabs and Jews in Contemporary Jerusalem.* New Jersey: Princeton University Press.

Shlaim, Avi (1988). *Collusion Across the Jordan: King Abdullah, the Zionist Movement and the Partition of Palestine.* Oxford: Clarendon.

Bibliography – Hebrew

Al-Tal, Aobdullah (1967). *Zikhronot Abdullah Al-Tal* (translated by Y. Halamish). Tel Aviv: Ma'arakhot.

Amirav, M. & Siniora, H. (1989). *Yerushalayim – Petaron Labilti Patir*. Jerusalem: Truman Institute, The Hebrew University of Jerusalem.

Amirav, Moshe (1992). *Mediniyuta Shel Yisrael Biyerushalayim Me'az 1967*. Jerusalem: Jerusalem Municipality.

Amirav, Moshe (2001). *Hamilhama 'al Ofya Shel Yerushalayim: Nitzahon Shel Kevutzot Hashulayim 'al Hamerkaz Hatziyoni*. In: Avraham Brichta and Ami Pedahzur (eds). *Habehirot Lirshuyot Hamekomiyot be'Yisrael – 1988: Hemshekhiyut o Shinui?* Tel Aviv: Tel Aviv University.

Amirav, Moshe (2004). *Kedusha Vepolitika Behar Habayit*. In: N. Luz (ed.), *The New East – Islam, Society and Space in Jerusalem – Past and Present*. Jerusalem: Magnes Press, The Hebrew University of Jerusalem.

Amirav, Moshe (ed.) (2005). *Adoni Rosh Hamemshala: Yerushalayim*. Jerusalem: Carmel.

Ayalon, Amos (1991). *Yerushalayim, Shiga'on Ladavar*. Jerusalem: Domino.

Barzaki, Elinoar (1980). *Yerushalayim: Merkaz Ha'ir Vehashekhunot*, Jerusalem: Jerusalem Institute for Israel Studies.

Barzilai, Gad. (1984). *Mediniyut Hutz Yisraelit Trom Medinatit Umedinatit 1947–1950*. Doctoral Thesis, Bar-Ilan University, Ramat Gan.

Ben-Ami, Shlomo (2004). *Hazit Lelo Oref: Masa El Gvulot Tahalikh Hashalom*. Tel Aviv: Yedioth Ahronoth.

Ben-Aryeh, Yehoshua (1970). *Hitpahuta Shel Yerushalayim*. Keshet, 12 (4), 29–37.

Ben-Aryeh, Yehoshua (1977). *Ir Bere'i Tekufa:Yerushalayim Beme'ah Hatesha Esreh*. Jerusalem: Yad Ben-Zvi.

Ben-Aryeh, Yehoshua (1979). *Ir Bere'i Tekufa: Yerushalayim Hehadasha Bereshita*. Jerusalem: Yad Ben-Zvi.

Ben-Elissar, E. (1995). *Lo Od Milhama*. Tel Aviv: Maariv.

Ben-Gurion, David (1976). *Zikhronot* (Memoirs), Volume 4. Tel Aviv: Am Oved.

Ben-Gurion, David (1977). *Zikhronot* (Memoirs), Volume 3, Tel Aviv: Am Oved.

Ben-Gurion, David (1984). *Yoman Hamilhama: Milhemet Ha'atzmaut 1948–1949*. Tel Aviv: Hahevra Lehafatzat Mishnato Shel Ben-Gurion, Israel Defense Ministry Press.

Benvenisti, Meron (1973). *El Mul Hahoma Hasegura*. Tel Aviv: Weidenfeld & Nicolson.

Benvenisti, Meron (1981). *Yerushalayim: Ir Ubeliba Homa*. Tel Aviv: Kav Adom, Hakibbutz Hameuhad.

Benvenisti, Meron (1988). *Hakela Vehaela*. Tel Aviv: Kav Adom.

Benziman, Uzi (1973). *Yerushalayim: Ir Lelo Homa.* Jerusalem & Tel Aviv: Schocken

Berkowitz, Shmuel (2000). *Milhemet Hamekomot Hakedoshim.* Jerusalem: Jerusalem Institute for Israel Studies.

Berkowitz, Shmuel (2006). *Ma Nora Hamakom Hazeh: Kedusha, Politika Umishpat Be'Yerushalayim Ubamekomot Hakedoshim Be'Yisrael.* Jerusalem: Carta.

Bialer, Uri. (1985). *Haderekh Labira: Hafikhat Yerushalayim Lemakom Moshava Harishmi shel Memshelet Yisrael Bishnat 1949.* Cathedra 35, 163–91.

Blum, Yehuda (1971). *Tziyon Bamishpat Habein-Leumi Nifdita.* Hapraklit, 27, 315–24.

Blum, Yehuda (1972). *Mizrah Yerushalayim Eino Shetah Kavush.* Hapraklit, 28, 183–90.

Brecher, Michael (1972). *Dimuyim, Hahlatot Vehizun Hozer Bemediniyut Hahutz Hayisraelit.* Medina Vememshal, Aleph (3), 7–37.

Dayan, Moshe (1977). *Avnei Derekh: Otobiyografiya.* Jerusalem: Idanim Dvir.

Dinstein, Y. (1971). *Tziyon Bemishmpat Tifdeh.* Hapraklit, 27, 519–22.

Efrat, Elisha (1975). *Shinuyim Bitfisat Tikhnuna Shel Yerushalayim Bahamishim Hashanim Ha'ahronot (1919–1969).* Ma'alot, Daled.

Elad, Amikam (1992). *Kedushata Shel Ir: Yerushalayim Besifrut Ha'intifada.* In: Aharon Layish (ed.), *Ha'aravim Be'Yerushalayim* (pp. 151–61). Jerusalem: Jerusalem Institute for Israel Studies.

Felsenstein, D. (1989). Generating the growth process: The case of the development of high technology industry in Jerusalem. *City and Region,* 19–20 (Hebrew).

Ferrari, Silvio (1986). *Hakes Hakadosh Ube'ayot Eretz Yisrael Aharei Milhemet Ha'olam Hashniya: Binum Yerushalayim Vehaganat Hamekomot Hakedoshim 1947–1949.* Yahadut Zemanenu, 3, 187–207.

Galnor, Itzhak (1995). *Veshavu Banim Ligvulam: Hahakra'ot 'al Medina Ushetahim Batenu'a Hatziyonit.* Sde Boker and Jerusalem: Ben-Gurion Heritage Center, Magnes, The Hebrew University of Jerusalem.

Gazit, Shlomo (1985). *Hamakel Vehagezer: Hamimshal Hayisraeli Be'Yehuda Veshomron.* Tel Aviv: Zmora-Bitan.

Giladi, R. & Merhav, Reuven (1998). *Hamamlakha Hahashemit Hayardenit Vetafkida Behesder Keva Atidi be'Yerushalayim: Hebetim Mishpatiyim, Mediniyim Uma'asiyim.* Jerusalem: Jerusalem Institute for Israel Studies.

Golani, Motti. (1994). *Tziyonut Lelo Tziyon? Emdat Hanhagat Hayishuv u'Medinat Yisrael Beshe'elat Yerushalayim 1947–1949.* In: Avi Bareli (ed.), *Yerushalayim Hehatzuya,* Idan, 18. Jerusalem: Yad Ben-Zvi (32–3).

Hirsch, Moshe, Housen-Couriel, Deborah & Ruth Lapidoth (1994). *Yerushalayim Le'an? Hatza'ot Bedvar Atida Shel Ha'ir.* Jerusalem: Jerusalem Institute for Israel Studies.

Horowitz, Uri (2001). *Ve'idat Camp David Hashniya Vehatza'ot Hagishur Shel Hanasi Clinton, Hagirsa Hapalestinit.* Tel Aviv: Strategic Assessment, Jaffe Center for Strategic Studies at Tel Aviv University.

Kimhi, I., Hyman, B. & Claude, G. (1976). *Yerushalayim 1967–1975: Sekira*

Hevratit Kalkalit. Institute for Urban and Regional Studies. The Hebrew University of Jerusalem.

Kimhi, Israel (1980). *Yerushalayim Hahatzuya 1948–1967*. Jerusalem: Jerusalem Institute for Israel Studies.

Klein, Menachem (1990). *Emdot Arviyot Beshe'elat Yerushalayim*. Jerusalem: Jerusalem Institute for Israel Studies.

Klein, Menachem (1995). *Yerushalayim Bemasa Umatan Leshalom: Emdot Arviyot*. Jerusalem: Jerusalem Institute for Israel Studies.

Klein, Menachem (1999). *Yonim Bishmei Yerushalayim: Tahalikh Hashalom Veha'ir Yerushalayim*. Jerusalem: Jerusalem Institute for Israel Studies.

Klein, Menachem (2001). *Shovrim Tabu: Hamaga'im Lehesder Keva Be'Yerushalayim 1994–2001*. Jerusalem: Jerusalem Institute for Israel Studies.

Kollek, Teddy (1994). *Yerushalayim Shel Teddy*. Tel Aviv: Sifriyat Maariv.

Kroyanker, David (1988). *Yerushalayim: Hama'avak 'al Mivneh Ha'ir Vehazuta*. Tel Aviv: Zmora Bitan.

Kroyanker, David (1988). *Pnei Ha'ir, Kaf-Heh Shanim Le'ihud Ha'ir: Perakim Bege'ografiya Ironit Shel Yerushalayim*. Jerusalem Institute for Israel Studies.

Lapidoth, Ruth (1997). *Yerushalayim – Hebetim Mishpatiyim: Dapei Reka Lekov'e Mediniyut*. Dapei Diyun, 3.

Lavski, H. (ed.) (1989). *Yerushalayim Ba'toda'a Uba'asiya Hatziyonit*. Jerusalem: Zalman Shazar Center for Jewish History.

Lorach, Netanel. (1978), *Al-Haram al-Sharif Basiah Hatziburi Ha'aravi Hapalestini be'Yisrael: Zehut Zikaron Kolektivi Vedarkhei Habeniya*. Jerusalem: Floersheimer Institute for Policy Studies.

Minerbi, Y. (1985). *Havatikan – Eretz Hakodesh Vehatziyonut*. Jerusalem: Yad Ben-Zvi.

Morris, Benny (2006). *Haderekh le'Yerushalayim: Glubb Pasha, Eretz Yisrael Vehayehudim*. Tel Aviv: Am Oved.

Narkiss, Uzi (1975). *Ahat Yerushalayim*. Tel Aviv: Am Oved.

Pedahzur, Reuven (1996). *Nitzahon Hamevukha: Mediniyut Memshelet Eshkol Bashetahim Le'ahar Milhemet Sheshet Hayamim*. Tel Aviv: Bitan, Yad Tabenkin, Makhon Galili.

Porat, Yehoshua (1978). *Mimehumot Lamerida: Hatenu'ah Haleumit Ha'aravit Palestinit 1929–1939*. Tel Aviv: Am Oved.

Ramon, Amnon (1997). *Yahasam Shel Medinat Yisrael Vehatzibur Hayehudi Ligvanav Lehar Habayit (1967–1996)*. Jerusalem: Jerusalem Institute for Israel Studies.

Reiter, Yitzhak (1997). *Har Habayit – Al-Haram Al-Sharif; Nekudot Haskama Umahloket*. Jerusalem: Jerusalem Institute for Israel Studies.

Reiter, Yitzhak (ed.) (2001). *Ribonut Ha'el Veha'adam, Kedusha Umerkaziyut Politit Behar Habayit*. Jerusalem: Jerusalem Institute for Israel Studies.

Romann, Michael (1984). *Yahasei Gomlin Bein Hamigzar Hayehudi Veha'aravi be'Yerushalayim*. Jerusalem: Jerusalem Institute for Israel Studies.

Romann, Michael (1989). *Shiluv Vehafrada Beyahasei Hamigzar Hayehudi Veha'aravi be'Yerushalayim – Behina Metodologit*, Yerushalyaim Yom-Yom Ir Ve'ezor, 19.

Romann, Michael (1995). *Hamimsad Hayisraeli Bemizrah Yerushalayim: Hesdereim Ulekahim.* Jerusalem: Jerusalem Institute for Israel Studies.

Rubinstein, D., Malley, R. Agha, H., Barak, E. and Morris, B. (2003). *Camp David 2000: Ma Be'emet Kara Sham?* Tel Aviv: Yedioth Ahronoth.

Schiff, Zeev & Ya'ari, Ehud (1999). *Intifada.* Tel Aviv: Schocken.

Segev, Tom (2005). *1967: Veha'aretz Shinta Et Paneha.* Jerusalem: Keter.

Sela, Avraham (1983). *Ahdut Betokh Pirud: Ve'idot Hapisga Ha'arviyot.* Jerusalem: Magnes, The Hebrew University of Jerusalem.

Sharef, Ze'ev (1959). *Shelosha Yamim.* Tel Aviv: Am Oved.

Sher, Gilad (2001). *Bemerhak Negi'a: Ha'Mum Leshalom 1999–2000 – Edut.* Tel Aviv, Yedioth Ahronoth – Sifrei Hemed.

Shragai, Nadav (1995). *Har Hameriva, Hama'avak 'al Har Habayit: Yehudim Vemuslemim, Dat Upolitika Me'az 1967.* Jerusalem: Keter.

Shaltiel, Eli (ed.) (1981). *Perakim Betoldot Yerushalayim Bazman Hehadash: Sefer Zikaron le'Yitzhak Herzog.* Jerusalem: Yad Ben-Zvi.

Shragai, Nadav (1995), *Har Ha'meriva*: The Struggle for the Temple Mount: Jews and Muslims, Religion and Politics since 1967. Jerusalem: Keter.

Zak, Moshe (1996). *Hussein Oseh Shalom.* Ramat Gan: Bar-Ilan University.

Also:
Government Protocols – Dohot Medinat Yisrael
Municipality Reports – Dohot Iriyat Yerushalayim

Index

1929 Riots, 175
1959 Jerusalem Master Plan, 70, 78
1968 Jerusalem Master Plan, 60, 64–5, 68, 83, 106
1978 Jerusalem Master Plan, 59, 70, 72

A
Abdel Malik, 158–60, 162, 165
Abdullah (King of Jordan), 6–7, 37, 45–7, 175–6, 197
Abed Rabbo, Yasser, 150
Abraham (Jewish patriarch), 15, 160, 165, 194–5
Abu Dis, 146
Abu Tor, 46, 50, 148
Agliardi (Vatican Nuncio), 39
Al Aqsa Mosque, 119–20, 149, 162, 164–6
Al Quds, 21–2, 98, 190, 197, 200
Al-Alami, Mohammed, 199
Albin, Cecilia, 144
Alexandria, Egypt, 60
Al-Husseini, Hajj Amin, 40, 133, 174, 200
Al-Khatib, Ruhi, 108–9
American Colony Hotel, 141
Amir, Raphael, 14
Amirav, Iri (the author's son), 17
Amman, 8, 51, 109, 112–13, 175, 177
Analogical approach, 104, 155, 189
Annexation, 18–19, 20–1, 23, 26, 44, 47–8, 53–4, 56, 63–4, 82–3, 103–4, 125, 155, 169–70
Antiquities Law, 179
Arab League, 37, 139, 175–7, 183–4, 187, 191
Arab states, 19, 26–7, 56, 113, 125, 128, 130, 157, 172, 176–9, 183–4, 186–7, 191, 207
Arabs/Palestinians in the territories, 25, 104, 107, 112, 118, 132, 135
Arafat, Yasser, 33, 120, 130–2, 134–6, 138, 141, 143–5, 149–50, 152–4, 161–3, 173, 178–9, 182–3, 188, 190–1
Aran, Zalman, 19, 170
Architects' revolt, 23, 68
Armon Hanatziv, 10, 51–2
A-Tur, 148
Autonomy talks, 118, 129
Autonomy, Cultural, 110
Autonomy, Economic, 110

Autonomy, Educational, 110–11
Autonomy, Functional, 148
Autonomy, Municipal, 124
Autonomy, Palestinian, 126, 128, 130
Autonomy, Religious, 19, 189
Avnery, Uri, 55
Ayalon, Amos, 66

B
Barak government, 145–6
Barak, Ehud, 28–9, 33, 145–6, 148, 150–4, 156, 161, 64, 181–2, 184, 186, 188
Barzaki, Elinoar, 29, 74–5
Barzilai, Yisrael, 170
Begin, Menachem, 27, 52, 88, 107–8, 112, 125–30, 153, 155, 168, 170, 180, 184, 199
Beirut, 101
Beit Hanina, 106
Belfast, 101–2, 121–2
Ben-Ami, Shlomo, 20, 150, 152–3, 188
Ben-Elissar, Eliahu, 125–7
Ben-Gurion, David, 3–4, 19, 26, 35, 40–4, 47–50, 57, 110, 126, 153–4, 156, 170–2, 175, 190
Ben-Haim, Shaul, 104
Bentov, Mordechai, 107, 170–1
Benvenisti, Meron, 63, 68
Ben-Yehuda, Eliezer, 38, 199
Benziman, Uzi, 52, 170
Berkowitz, Shmuel, 29
Betar Illit, 24, 146
Betar movement, 3–5, 175
Bethlehem, 39–40, 46, 64, 173
Big decisions, 18, 20, 62
Blum, Yehuda Zvi, 54
Britain, 122, 141, 187
Brussels, 101

C
Cairo, 51
Caliph Omar, 21, 158, 160–4, 196, 199–200
Camp David, 11, 20, 28, 118, 120, 124, 126, 129, 142–3, 145–50, 152–6, 164, 176, 179, 181–3, 186, 188–9, 191
Carter, Jimmy, 127, 129, 150
Cheshin, Amir, 29, 74
Christians, 11–12, 37–8, 159–60, 163–4, 166, 168, 173, 197–8

Church of the Holy Sepulchre, 160, 166,
    196–7, 199–200
City Line, 6–7, 9, 46–7, 203
Clinton, Bill, 129, 139, 149–50, 156, 182
Construction and Housing Ministry, 68, 74
Costa Rica, 27, 157
Crown Prince Hassan, 178

D
Damascus Gate, 59, 203
Dayan, Moshe, 19–20, 46, 52–3, 107,
    110–12, 125–6, 152, 168, 170–1, 180
De facto, 48–9, 138, 143, 189
De jure, 48–9, 143, 189
Della Pergola, Sergio, 99
Demographic problem, 20, 86–7, 98
Dome of the Rock, 113, 158–65

E
East Jerusalem, 22–3, 25, 29–31, 37, 50,
    52–7, 59, 61–8, 71–7, 79–83, 97–9,
    104–5, 107–10, 112–18, 120, 126,
    129–30, 132, 134, 137, 140–1, 143,
    147–8, 151, 153, 155–6, 166–71, 174,
    178–9, 182, 197, 204, 206
Eban, Abba, 24, 45, 49, 51, 53–4, 57, 171,
    173
Efrat, 24, 88, 146
Egypt, 35, 51, 60, 65, 124–7, 130, 150, 152,
    154, 176, 178–9, 184, 187–9, 191, 194,
    201
Ein Kerem, 14, 133–4, 147, 202
El Salvador, 27, 157
Eldad, Yisrael (Scheib), 3–4
Elyashiv, Yoram, 210
Eshkol, Levi, 19, 22, 27, 52–3, 57, 62, 64,
    71, 79, 82, 104–7, 110–12, 126, 167–8,
    170–1, 173, 184, 189

F
Facts in the field, 68, 179, 103, 110, 121,
    154
Finance Ministry, 87
First Intifada, 11, 25, 29, 103, 114–15,
    117–19, 137, 140, 173, 177, 180
Foreign Ministry, 10, 19, 104, 141, 169, 172,
    178, 204
Foundation Stone, 15, 158–9, 162, 164
France, 3, 5–7, 36, 122, 141, 172
Functional Internationalization, 18–19, 27–8,
    46, 49, 57, 170, 172–3, 176, 185,
    188

G
Gafni Committee, 87
Gafni, Arnon, 87
Gazit, Shlomo, 112–13
Givat Hamivtar, 105
Givat Shapira, 78, 105

Givat Ze'ev, 24, 88, 144, 146
Golden (Mercy) Gate, 3, 198–200
Goren, Rabbi Shlomo, 180
Gottfried du Bouillon, 13, 196–7, 199
Greenberg, Uri Zvi, 2–4, 15, 17
Guardian of the (Islamic) Holy Places, 130,
    175–6, 178–9, 187–8
Gur, Motta, 12, 16, 28, 197

H
Hadassah Hospital, 14, 40, 47
Hadrian, 21, 196
Haifa, 42, 64, 165
Haram al-Sharif, 19, 11, 126, 130, 148, 150,
    165–6, 168–9, 174–7, 179–80, 183–4,
    190–2, 197
Heavenly and Earthly Jerusalem, 38, 194,
    198, 199
Hebrew University, 28–9, 39–40, 47, 77–8,
    125, 143
Hebron, 111, 175
Herzl, Theodore, 39, 42, 153, 186, 190
Herzog, Yaakov, 158, 172
Husseini, Abdel Qader, 133, 200–1
Husseini, Faisal, 79, 97, 118–20, 131–8,
    140–5, 147–9, 161–4, 186–8, 200

I
IDF, 6, 9, 10, 12, 21, 42, 45, 47, 50, 52–3,
    167, 169, 171, 179
Indonesia, 127, 192
Interior Ministry, 63, 80, 89, 97
International Community, 27–8, 36–7, 47–8,
    56, 138, 147, 154, 167–8, 170, 179,
    185–6, 189, 191
International legitimacy, 19, 26, 37,
    46, 48, 56, 147, 153, 155–6,
    168, 184, 186
Internationalization, 26–8, 36–7, 41, 44–9,
    57, 169–70, 172–4, 176, 184
Iran , 127
Islam, 30, 35, 39, 11, 128, 158, 161–5, 167,
    178–9, 187, 189, 192, 196–7
Islamic Holy Places, 18–9, 21, 37, 47, 52, 57,
    119, 128, 130, 138–40, 150, 167, 170,
    174–6, 178–9, 184, 188–9
Israel Police, 84, 105
Israelization, 24–5, 103–10, 112–14, 117,
    140
Italy, 122–3, 128, 160

J
Jaffa, 38, 134, 165
Jerusalem and Homeland Building
    Committee, 148
Jerusalem Institute for Israel Studies (JIIS),
    145, 157
Jerusalem municipal elections, 24, 99, 100,
    104, 106–7, 122

Jerusalem municipality, 22, 24–5, 29–31, 33, 39, 62–3, 66–8, 71, 75–6, 78, 80, 83–4, 87–9, 97–9, 104–6, 108–9, 116–7, 143, 177, 199
Jerusalem Syndrome, 34, 69, 131, 134, 156
Jesus, 12, 163, 166, 193, 196–7, 199–200
Jewish Quarter, 28, 43, 46–7, 50, 125–6, 148–9, 151, 160, 164, 169
Jordan, 6, 9, 26–7, 37, 44–51, 53–4, 56, 60, 65, 77, 97, 107, 112–14, 118, 127–30, 138–40, 154, 172–3, 175–9, 184, 187, 189, 191, 197, 202–3
Jordanian City, 20–2, 63, 104, 108–9
Jordanian Option, 28, 11, 118, 124, 127, 129–32, 139, 155
Jordanization, 103, 110, 112
Judaism, 35, 160–2, 164, 180, 187, 197
Judea and Samaria, 24, 54, 85, 88–9, 103, 126, 206

K
Katamon, 46, 143, 147
Kaufman, Yehezkel, 1
King David, 43, 156, 165, 195, 197, 199
King Hussein, 28, 51, 64, 112–13, 118, 129–31, 134, 154–55, 178–9
Klein, Menachem, 29, 128, 176
Kollek, Teddy, 20, 23, 25, 29–34, 64, 66–7, 69, 72–3, 84–86, 87, 101, 104–12, 114–16, 119, 204, 207
Kroyanker, David, 61, 69–70

L
Lapidoth, Ruth, 28, 188
Levontin, Avigdor, 168–9
Lilienblum, M. L, 39, 41
London, 159, 200
London Agreement, 118, 130, 155
Lupolianski, Uri, 82, 89, 98, 99

M
Ma'aleh Adumim, 24, 88–9, 144, 146
Madrid conference, 129, 138–9, 141, 173
Mandelbaum Gate, 9, 55
Ma'oz, Moshe, 29, 143–4
Mapai, 3–4, 40, 43, 110
March of Folly, 33, 100, 206
Mecca, 8, 165, 175, 178
Meir, Golda, 22–3, 42, 60–1, 65, 67–9, 71, 73, 84–7, 99, 110, 113–14, 173
Menachem-Mendel, 2–5, 13, 15, 17
Mendelsohn, Moses, 4
Meridor, Dan, 131–2, 134, 136
Metropolitan Jerusalem, 144, 146
Michael, B., 73
Ministerial Committee for Jerusalem Affairs, 65, 86
Mohammed (Prophet), 160, 162, 165, 177, 192, 199–200

Montreal, 101
Morocco, 125–7, 176, 178–9, 187, 191
Mosque of Omar, 8, 13, 16, 38, 158, 169
Mosse, George, 201
Mount Herzl, 11, 201–2
Mount of Olives, 3, 12–13, 46–7, 50, 53, 59, 125–6, 159, 165–6, 194, 197–9, 203, 205, 208
Mount Scopus, 7–9, 39–40, 46–7, 50, 52, 59, 77, 126, 159, 168, 170, 201
Mount Zion, 4, 17, 59, 159, 166, 199–200
Mourners of Zion, 2–3, 5, 16
Municipal Committee to Equalize Services and Infrastructure in East Jerusalem, 115
Municipal Cooperation Ordinance, 53
Muslim Waqf, 11, 141, 176–7, 179, 184–5
Muslims, 11–13, 16, 28, 38, 111, 119, 125, 159–60, 162, 164–6, 168–9, 174, 184–5, 191–2, 197–8
Musrara, 143

N
Narkiss, Uzi, 14, 50–2, 168
National Insurance Institute, 24, 83, 97
National objectives, 22, 24, 206
National unity government, 55, 118
Nazareth, 39, 156
Netanya, 2–3, 5, 8, 17, 42, 151
Netanyahu, Benjamin, 117, 119, 180
Neve Ya'akov, 203
New York, 30–1, 171, 191–2
Nicosia, 101–2, 121–2
No-man's land, 8, 10
Notre Dame monastery, 5–9, 11–12, 144–5, 203
Notre Dame talks, 144–5

O
Objectives in Jerusalem:
  demographic objective, 23, 85, 87–9
  diplomatic objective, 25–6
  inter-religious objective, 27, 188
  political objective, 24–5
  territorial objective, 22–3, 39, 61, 69–71, 73, 206
Odysseus, 2, 17
Old City, 2, 4–15, 17–19, 21–3, 26–8, 38–41, 43–53, 56, 59–64, 71, 77, 103, 116, 125–6, 128, 138, 144–6, 148–51, 153–4, 156, 159, 164, 168–71, 173–6, 179, 182, 184, 189, 194, 197, 199, 207
Organization of the Islamic Conference (OIC), 177, 184, 187
Orient House, 134, 140–3, 148, 201
Oslo Accords, 129, 140–1, 145, 191
Outer ring neighborhoods, 23–4, 30, 68, 71–2

P

Pa'il, Meir, 43
Pakistan, 127, 175
Palestine, 36–42, 48–9, 54, 133–4, 137–8, 143–4, 150, 165–6, 171–2, 175–6, 179, 183, 187, 189–91, 200–1
Palestinian National Council, 142, 148
Palestinian Option, 127, 139, 155
Palestinization, 25, 103, 117
Paratroops, 2,7, 10–12, 15–17, 21, 53, 151, 168, 197, 201
Peel Commission, 40
Penso, Itzik, 7, 11–12, 202
Peres, Shimon, 85, 118, 130–1
Planning and Construction Law, 67, 75, 78–9
PLO (Palestinian Liberation Organization), 33, 35, 118, 129–35, 137–9, 141, 143–4, 173, 184, 200
Pope Paul VI, 173
Protection of Holy Places Law, 179, 185

R

Rabin, Yitzhak, 146, 178–9
Ramon, Amnon, 180
Raymond de Aguiliers (knight), 13
Reagan, Ronald, 129–30
Rockefeller Museum, 12–13, 52, 201
Rogers Plan, 65–6, 155
Romann, Michael, 114, 120
Rome, 122–3, 128, 166
Rome Convention, 185
Ross, Lee, 144
Russia, 36, 141, 187
Russian Compound, 43, 59

S

Saladin, 197, 199–200
Salman, Ya'akov, 109, 171
Samuel, Herbert, 172
Sapir, Pinhas, 112
Sasson, Eliahu, 63, 170–1
Sasson, Moshe, 104
Saudi Arabia, 126–7, 165, 176, 178–9, 187
Second Intifada (Al Aqsa Intifada), 120, 149, 154, 157, 164
Settlements, 24, 68, 88–9, 100, 143, 146, 206
Sha'ath, Nabil, 143–4
Shamir, Yitzhak, 88, 118, 129–38, 141, 155, 180
Shapira, Moshe Haim, 63, 170
Shapira, Yaakov Shimshon, 55, 63, 170
Sharef, Ze'ev, 42, 45, 66–7
Sharett, Moshe, 43, 49
Sharon, Ariel, 119, 120, 141, 149, 192, 204
Sher, Gilad, 146, 150, 152–3
Shuafat, 64, 106
Silwan, 148
Sinai Campaign, 170–1
Sinai Peninsula, 19

Siniora, Hanna, 11, 137, 143–4, 173
Six-Day War, 7, 28, 34, 41, 51, 103, 157, 167, 184, 189
Smilansky Street (Netanya), 17
Sovereignty, 18–19, 21, 26–9, 37, 40, 45, 47–9, 53–6, 61, 65, 82, 107, 112, 114, 123–4, 126, 128–9, 138–9, 145–6, 148–51, 153–6, 167–70, 176, 178–89, 191
Stanford University, 143–4
Strategic Master Plan for Jerusalem 2020, 98–9
Sultan Suleiman, 6, 21, 59, 148
Supreme Muslim Council, 141, 176–7
Syria, 27, 50–1

T

Taba talks, 149–50, 182–3, 186
Talbiyeh, 46
Tancred, 5–6, 13
Tel Aviv, 3, 29, 42–3, 51, 53, 4, 66, 85–6, 157, 181
Temple Mount, 3, 13–16, 19–20, 28–9, 40, 46, 50, 59, 111, 115, 119–20, 126–8, 130, 148–53, 155, 158, 161–5, 167, 169, 174, 176–7, 179–92, 200–1
Temple Mount Faithful, 119, 181
Titus, 196–7
Toledano, Shmuel, 104
Tower and Stockade, 68
Treblinka, 3, 15
Troy, 2, 206
Truman Institute, 29, 143–4
Tuchman, Barbara, 206
Tuhami, Hassan, 125–6, 152

U

Ultra-Orthodox, 33, 38–9, 99–100, 204
United Nations (UN), 24, 36, 45, 49, 51, 68, 171, 185, 187
United Nations—Australian internationalization proposal, 44
United Nations—Committee on Palestine (UNSCOP), 36, 49
United Nations—General Assembly, 48, 53, 56–7, 171
United Nations—Resolution 181, 26, 46–7, 41, 46, 49, 55, 147, 175–6
United Nations – Resolution 242, 56, 147
United Nations – Sanctions, 26, 57, 80
United Nations – Security Council, 26, 56, 187
United States, 26–7, 30, 46, 56–7, 65, 69, 129, 135, 139, 141, 146, 155–6, 182, 185, 187

V

Via Dolorosa, 166, 203

W
Wadi Joz, 148
Wahid, Abdurrahman, 192
War of Independence, 3, 18, 43, 50, 171
Weingrod, Alex, 114, 120
West Bank, 20–1, 23–5, 47, 50, 52, 60–1,
    63–4, 73, 86, 88, 97, 103–4, 107,
    112–13, 118–20, 126, 127, 129–31,
    137, 139, 151, 169, 182, 206
West Jerusalem, 12, 26, 40, 43, 45–9, 56, 71,
    114, 120, 147–8, 156, 189, 197, 202
Western Wall, 2–4, 12–17, 28, 46–7, 50, 53,
    11, 119–20, 125–6, 148–51, 164–5,

    167, 169, 174–5, 180, 185–6, 197
Western Wall tunnel, 119
Wild West, 23, 76, 79–80
Wilner, Meir, 55

Y
Yeshurun, Meir'ke, 4
Yishai, Eli, 89, 98

Z
Ze'evi, Rehavam, 82
Zionist movement, 19, 27, 34, 37–9, 41, 46,
    171, 175, 184, 188–90, 200